Getting Started with V Programming

D1546781

An end-to-end guide to adopting the V language from
basic variables and modules to advanced concurrency

Navule Pavan Kumar Rao

BIRMINGHAM—MUMBAI

Getting Started with V Programming

Copyright © 2021 Packt Publishing

Group Product Manager: Richa Tripathi

Publishing Product Manager: Richa Tripathi

Senior Editor: Ruvika Rao

Content Development Editor: Vaishali Ramkumar

Technical Editor: Pradeep Sahu

Copy Editor: Safis Editing

Project Coordinator: Deeksha Thakkar

Proofreader: Safis Editing

Indexer: Manju Arasan

Production Designer: Vijay Kamble

First published: November 2021

Production reference: 3071221

Published by Packt Publishing Ltd.
Livery Place
35 Livery Street
Birmingham
B3 2PB, UK.

ISBN 978-1-83921-343-4

www.packt.com

Contributors

About the author

Navule Pavan Kumar Rao is a full-stack software consultant with product development experience in the banking, finance, corporate tax, and automobile domains. He pursued an Executive M.Tech in Data Science from the **Indian Institute of Technology (IIT)**, Hyderabad. He also pursued an Executive MBA in IT specialization from the Indian School of Business Management and Administration, and also holds a B.Tech in Electronics and Communication Engineering from Vaagdevi Institute of Technology and Science.

He is a **Microsoft Certified Professional (MCP)** and **Microsoft Certified Technology Specialist (MCTS)**. He has played key roles in identifying business requirements and converting them into viable products with the help of his vast software development skills at various companies. He also played a key role in the architecting, development, and deployment of software applications that become a part of the CI/CD pipeline to cloud platforms such as Azure, GCP, and also to on-premise infrastructures.

Kudos to the creator of V, Alexander Medvednikov for such a promising programming language, and thanks to the entire V community for actively maintaining it.

There are many weekends and restless nights that were sacrificed to write this book and I would like to thank my parents, and my wife who understood and supported me during this journey.

A lot of thanks to Packt, my team at Packt, and a special mention to the editors Vaishali Ramkumar and Ruvika Rao for their valuable efforts, which helped this book take a proper shape.

Finally, I would like to convey my sincere gratitude to all the people who actively or passively helped me to succeed in writing this book.

About the reviewer

Daniel Däschle started his career as a software developer. Since then, his focus has been mainly on developing web applications with React.js and Angular. Besides his professional activities, he is very enthusiastic about developing compilers. That's why he has followed the V project from the beginning and has been working on the implementation and improvement of the V programming language for 2 years as part of the vlang organization.

Ivo Balbaert was a Lecturer in (Web) Programming and Databases at CVO Antwerpen, a community college in Belgium. He received a Ph.D. in Applied Physics from the University of Antwerp in 1986. He has worked for 20 years in the software industry as a Developer and Consultant in several companies, and for 10 years as a Project Manager at the University Hospital of Antwerp. From 2000 onwards, he switched to partly teaching, developing software, and writing technical books.

Duarte Roso is a Game Developer currently working at Socialpoint. He graduated from the University of Joseph Fourier with a degree in Computer Science and later completed a degree in Game Development at the school of Creajeux, both in France. Duarte has now been working in the games industry for 10 years, working on innovative games and in-house engines. Throughout his career, he worked on successfully-released titles for both consoles and mobile devices, some of which belong to famous franchises such as Angry Birds, F1 Racing, or Lemmings. Duarte enjoys learning about new technologies, experimenting with them, and trying new programming languages that would make game development more accessible.

Table of Contents

Section 2: Basics of V Programming

3

Variables, Constants, and Code Comments

4

Primitive Data Types

7
Functions

8
Structs

Section 3: Advanced Concepts in V Programming

10
Concurrency

11

Channels – An Advanced Concurrency Pattern

12

Testing

13

Introduction to JSON and ORM

14

Building a Microservice

Other Books You May Enjoy

Index

Preface

Learn a new statically typed compiled programming language to build maintainable and fast software with the help of this comprehensive guide to V programming. V programming comes with high performance and simplicity, which allows software programmers to do rapid prototyping of applications at scale.

Who this book is for

This book is for you if you are any of the following:

- A beginner who is interested in learning a programming language that comes with a quick and short learning curve

- An experienced programmer who is looking to switch to a new and better statically typed and compiled programming language

- Willing to write quick and rapid prototyping of applications at scale using a new language with powerful concurrency features

What this book covers

Chapter 1, Introduction to V Programming, introduces the V programming language and its features. It also looks at the past, present, and future of V. Learn about the cross-compatibility of V and the list of operating systems V runs on.

Chapter 2, Installing V Programming, offers step-by-step details that will help you learn how to install the V programming language on the Windows and *nix OSes. You'll also learn how to ensure V is added to environment variables on Windows and symlinking on *nix OS, which will facilitate you accessing V from any directory.

Chapter 3, Variables, Constants, and Code Comments, introduces you to basic programming concepts such as how to define and work with variables and constants in V. This chapter also covers how to add single- and multi-line comments in V.

Chapter 4, Primitive Data Types, acquaints you with the world of primitive data types. You'll come to understand various primitive data types in V such as `string`, `bool`, `rune`, and other numeric types. You'll also learn how to work with these types. This chapter also introduces you to the various operators you can use on these data types such as relational, logical, arithmetic, bitwise, and shift operators. If you are an absolute beginner to the world of software programming, this chapter is highly recommended to get you hands-on with the concepts related to the primitive data types that are similar in all other programming languages.

Chapter 5, Arrays and Maps, covers different ways to declare arrays and how to initialize them using various properties available to define an array. You'll also see how to use `in` and `<<` operators on arrays. We then walk through the details about working with fixed-size arrays and multi-dimensional arrays. You will also understand arrays by performing the most frequently performed operations on arrays, such as cloning, sorting, and filtering techniques.

You will also learn about maps that hold data in the form of key-value pairs. Maps in the V language are often referred to as dictionaries in other programming languages, such as C# and Python. You will learn how to work with maps, and understand various ways we can declare and initialize maps. You will also learn how to perform various operations on a map, such as retrieving the key-value pair given a key, and handling the retrieval of non-existent keys using an `or` block. Then you will see how to add, update, and delete key-value pairs from a map.

Chapter 6, Conditionals and Iterative Statements, looks in detail at conditionals and iterative statements in the V programming language. You'll learn about working with conditional blocks such as `if`, `if-else`, and chaining `else-if` along with the usage of `goto` statements supported by labels. You will also learn in depth about `match` block, which is used for use cases that involve pattern matching or conditional code branching. In the later parts of this chapter, we will look at the various types of operations performed on maps, arrays using `for` loops, and then you will see the different ways to write iterative statements using a `for` loop.

Chapter 7, Functions, introduces the various types of functions V lang offers. You will then be able to write basic functions, anonymous functions, and higher-order functions. This chapter will also guide you through the vast features that functions come equipped with, along with code examples for each feature.

Chapter 8, *Structs*, looks at how to write structs that involve struct fields having different access modifiers and also defining struct fields with default values. You will then learn the skill of defining and initializing structs. You will then have a fair understanding of how to add methods that belong to a struct and create and work with functions with structs as input arguments.

Chapter 9, *Modules*, first introduces the basic syntax to define and import modules. In the later sections, you will see how to create a simple project in V, and then learn how to create and import modules defined in our simple project. You will then learn how to create multiple files and work with those in a module and understand the access scope.

You will also learn about best practices that include the benefits of the initializer function and conditions to define the initializer function for a module. This chapter also covers problems that arise in V when we have cyclic imports while creating modules. In addition, you will understand member scopes and the accessibility of members, including constants, structs, and embedded structs across modules. By the end of this chapter, you will be well-versed in the concept of modules and how to leverage them while writing programs in V.

Chapter 10, *Concurrency*, looks at concurrency, which is a crucial topic when it comes to V. The main essence of V lies in the concurrency capabilities that it offers programmers. In this chapter, you will learn in depth about the concept of concurrency, along with detailed code examples. This chapter begins with an explanation of a simple real-life scenario, which is about performing daily morning routines. The chapter also looks at a comparison of the results of the tasks when they were performed sequentially, and the benefits when similar tasks are performed concurrently.

In addition to the more intuitive explanation on concurrency in this chapter, the chapter sets foundational knowledge on concepts such as time modules and thread types to get started with concurrent programming in V.

By the end of this chapter, you will be confident enough to write concurrent code in V using the go keyword and handling concurrent functions using thread types. You will be able to understand the benefit of writing concurrent code in contrast to sequential code. This chapter will also help you understand how to concurrently spawn void functions, functions that return values as well as anonymous functions. You will also learn how to share data between the main thread and the tasks that are spawned to run concurrently using locks.

Chapter 11, Channels – An Advanced Concurrency Pattern, covers channels, which is the advanced concurrency pattern in V. They solve the problem of explicitly handling data synchronization techniques among coroutines. In the context of concurrency, channels facilitate us to share data by establishing a communication channel between concurrent tasks. These concurrent tasks are often termed coroutines, which share the data by communicating through channels.

We can communicate between coroutines with the help of shared objects. But the problem with this approach is you need to take explicit care of concurrency synchronization techniques such as protecting the shared objects using locks such as the read-only `rlock` or the read/write lock to prevent data races. This is where channels in V come into the picture. Channels implicitly take care of all the aforementioned data synchronization techniques among coroutines, which otherwise are cumbersome to manage manually.

In this chapter, we begin by looking at the syntax to declare channels and then understand different types of channels, such as buffered and unbuffered channels. We then learn about the properties of channels. Later, we learn about various methods available on a channel.

Chapter 12, Testing, covers how to write test cases for functions in V. This chapter also covers what the minimum prerequisites are for your code and file structure in order for V to identify and run them as tests.

Chapter 13, Introduction to JSON and ORM, explains how to work with the built-in libraries in V, namely `json` and `orm`. When building web services such as RESTful APIs, it is essential to understand the content type that you are exchanging with the clients or other RESTful APIs. The **JavaScript Object Notation (JSON)** format has become the new normal for modern applications to exchange data. This chapter will touch upon a brief introduction to JSON and how to work with JSON in V.

When building data-driven applications, **Object Relational Mappers (ORMs)** become a crucial part to establish communication between the world of objects and the world of relational databases. This chapter also introduces the built-in library `orm`, which ships along with the V installer.

Chapter 14, Building a Microservice, looks at how to build a simple microservice in V using a RESTful approach. To achieve the implementation, you will be using the built-in libraries `vweb` and `orm`. You will also leverage the power of SQLite, by installing it as a third-party library. With the help of the SQLite library, you will learn how to establish a database connection and interact with it. You will use the JSON data format as a form of communication.

To get the most out of this book

Software/hardware covered in the book	Operating system requirements
V (version 0.2.4)	Windows, macOS, or Linux
Command-line terminal	Windows, macOS, or Linux
Notepad	Windows, macOS, or Linux
Postman	Windows, macOS, or Linux

If you are using the digital version of this book, we advise you to type the code yourself or access the code from the book's GitHub repository (a link is available in the next section). Doing so will help you avoid any potential errors related to the copying and pasting of code.

Download the example code files

You can download the example code files for this book from GitHub at `https://github.com/PacktPublishing/Getting-Started-with-V-Programming`. If there's an update to the code, it will be updated in the GitHub repository.

We also have other code bundles from our rich catalog of books and videos available at `https://github.com/PacktPublishing/`. Check them out!

Download the color images

We also provide a PDF file that has color images of the screenshots and diagrams used in this book. You can download it here: `https://static.packt-cdn.com/downloads/9781839213434_ColorImages.pdf`.

Conventions used

There are a number of text conventions used throughout this book.

`Code in text`: Indicates code words in text, database table names, folder names, filenames, file extensions, pathnames, dummy URLs, user input, and Twitter handles. Here is an example: "The x variable is declared with a value of `100` using the `:=` symbol."

A block of code is set as follows:

```
const (
    app_name = 'V on Wheels'
    max_connections = 1000
    decimal_places = 2
    pi = 3.14
)
```

When we wish to draw your attention to a particular part of a code block, the relevant lines or items are set in bold:

```
import json

fn main() {
    m := Note{
        id: 2
        message: 'Get groceries'
        status: false
    }

    j := json.encode(m)
    println(j)
}
```

Any command-line input or output is written as follows:

```
sudo apt -y update
sudo apt install -y build-essential
```

Bold: Indicates a new term, an important word, or words that you see onscreen. For instance, words in menus or dialog boxes appear in **bold**. Here is an example: "Now select the **Body** tab, and check the **raw** radio button."

Tips or important notes
Appear like this.

Get in touch

Feedback from our readers is always welcome.

General feedback: If you have questions about any aspect of this book, email us at customercare@packtpub.com and mention the book title in the subject of your message.

Errata: Although we have taken every care to ensure the accuracy of our content, mistakes do happen. If you have found a mistake in this book, we would be grateful if you would report this to us. Please visit www.packtpub.com/support/errata and fill in the form.

Piracy: If you come across any illegal copies of our works in any form on the internet, we would be grateful if you would provide us with the location address or website name. Please contact us at copyright@packt.com with a link to the material.

If you are interested in becoming an author: If there is a topic that you have expertise in and you are interested in either writing or contributing to a book, please visit authors.packtpub.com.

Share Your Thoughts

Once you've read *Getting Started with V Programming*, we'd love to hear your thoughts! Scan the QR code below to go straight to the Amazon review page for this book and share your feedback.

https://packt.link/r/1-839-21343-4

Your review is important to us and the tech community and will help us make sure we're delivering excellent quality content.

Section 1: Introduction to the V Programming Language

This section provides a detailed introduction to the V programming language. You will also gain an understanding of various features of V and the suite of modules and libraries available within the V ecosystem.

This section also introduces you to approaches to install the V programming language on the various operating systems, which will help readers get started with hands-on examples that will be covered in this book.

This section has the following chapters:

- *Chapter 1, Introduction to V Programming*
- *Chapter 2, Installing V Programming*

1
Introduction to V Programming

The V programming language is a statically typed compiled programming language that's used to build maintainable and robust software applications. It comes with high performance and simplicity, which allows software programmers to do rapid prototyping of applications at scale. You can write simple and clean code with minimal abstraction using V. V comes with performance as fast as C. V is not derived from any other programming language and is written in V itself and compiles itself in under 1 second.

The design of V has been influenced by programming languages such as Go, Rust, Oberon, Swift, Kotlin, and Python. The V language has similar syntax compared to the popular Go programming language. It is a simple, fast, safe, and compiled programming language. V offers all safety features by default, such as immutable variables, immutable structs, and pure functions. V offers great support for concurrency that is on par with Go programming.

In this chapter, we will cover the following topics:

- The past, present, and future of V
- V is a statically typed and compiled programming language
- Simple and maintainable syntax
- Backward compatibility, stability, and easy to upgrade to future versions

- Features of V programming
- V as a framework
- Operating systems V supports

By the end of this chapter, you will have learned about the V language and its features. You will also understand **Vinix**, an operating system (OS) written completely in V.

Let's begin our journey by understanding how V came into existence, who created it, and what its future is.

The past, present, and future of V

V is a new programming language created in early 2019 by *Alexander Medvednikov*. The creator has come up with an extensive vision for the V language and the features it offers. Therefore, the V language and its various features are undergoing heavy development. The official website is `https://vlang.io/`. The V programming language is open sourced and licensed under MIT. You can refer to the entire source code of V on its official GitHub repository at `https://github.com/vlang/v`.

V has an active community of developers and contributors. The community is highly active and responsive to issues raised on GitHub. You can participate in discussions at `https://github.com/vlang/v/discussions` and the team is also available on Discord: `https://discord.gg/vlang`.

V comes with a lot of performance optimizations that are on par with C compared to any other programming language, such as Go, Java, or Python to mention a few.

From version 0.3, V is expected to have the ability to translate C code to human readable V code. Also, you will be able to generate V wrappers on the top of C libraries.

V is a statically typed and compiled programming language

A programming language is designed to have certain typing and execution phenomena. Typing could refer to either statically typed or dynamically typed, while the execution phenomena could be referred to as compiled or interpreted. Let's look at these terms in more detail.

Statically typed versus dynamically typed

A programming language is referred to as **statically typed** when the type checking of the variables happens during compile time instead of runtime.

In a **dynamically typed** programming language, the types are determined during runtime based on the values assigned to the variables. The advantage of dynamically typed programming languages is that the programmers do not have to explicitly mention the type of variables while they code. This capability eases and speeds up development times.

Compiled versus interpreted languages

A programming language is said to be **compiled** when the code is directly translated into machine code or byte code. This phenomenon makes the resulting program run significantly faster in contrast to interpreted languages. V compiles ~1 million **lines of code (LOCs)** per CPU per second.

On the other hand, the term **interpreted** refers to programming languages where the interpreter runs the program by executing the commands line by line. And this phenomenon makes interpreted languages significantly slower than compiled languages.

The V programming language is a statically typed compiled programming language. So, the type checking in V happens during compile time itself. Also, when you build a V program, it generates an executable file as output that contains all the instructions written in the program translated into machine code.

Simple and maintainable syntax

As we've already learned, V is inspired by the Go programming language, and its design has also been influenced by Oberon, Rust, Swift, Kotlin, and Python. V comes with the simplest form of coding style when it comes to syntax and semantics. If you are a Go programmer, writing a program in V gives you an adrenaline rush because of the simplicity of the syntax. The syntactic simplicity offered by V lets beginners of this programming language learn quickly and understand the basics instead of trying to learn about the semantics.

V takes a similar or even fewer number of LOCs to mimic functionality written in Go. It has only one standard format for writing code, and this is managed by vfmt, a built-in library that helps format the code. vfmt strictly formats your code according to a globally unique coding standard across all V projects.

All it takes to write a simple program in V is just the following three LOCs:

```
fn main() {
    println('Hello, from V lang!')
}
```

You don't even need `fn main()` { and the closing bracket, }. Just place the following line in a file named `hello.v` and run it using the `v run hello.v` command:

```
println('Hello, from V lang!')
```

In contrast to V, where we can write a simple program in just a line, a similar program written in Go, after formatting, takes at least seven LOCs, which appear as follows:

```
package main

import "fmt"

func main() {
    fmt.Println("Hello from Go lang!")
}
```

As you can see, compared to the preceding code, the V program shown earlier looks concise and minimal while at the same time offering readability and avoiding a lot of unnecessary imports.

Backward compatibility, stability, and easy to upgrade to future versions

The V programming language, at the time of writing this book, is still in development. But it has evolved a lot since its inception and has received a lot of appreciation from software engineering communities across the world. This book attempts to introduce various programming features that V has already got in detail throughout this book.

Although it is noteworthy that V is still in development at the time of writing this book, beginning with version 1, it will be highly stable and also offers a backward compatibility guarantee. V's formatter, `vfmt`, automatically takes care of upgrading your code for you. So, you don't have to manually identify the incompatible syntax when you upgrade your version of V.

Features of V programming

Despite being a very new and constantly evolving programming language, V has got all the most sought-after features that satisfy the needs of modern-day programmers. In this section, we will explore various features of V.

Performance

V has Clang, GCC, or MSVC as its primary backend, depending on the OS, which allows it to compile to human-readable C. Having these compilers as the main backend allows V to have easy interoperability with C. V, with its innovative memory management, performs a minimal amount of memory allocation by using value types and string buffers. A program written in V gets compiled to native binaries without any dependencies. Also, V compiles the whole application into a single binary, which makes it easy to deploy.

Speed

At the time of writing this book, according to the official website, `https://vlang.io/`, with a Clang backend, V compiles ~110k LOCs per second, per CPU core. With x64 and a TCC backend, V compiles ~1 million LOCs per CPU core.

No null values

A null value indicates nothing. A null value neither represents an empty nor a default value. Having null values in a programming language enforces you to handle the null scenarios using multiple checks. These checks, when missed, might lead to errors.

V does not have null or nil values, unlike other programming languages such as Java, C#, Python, or Go. This is because all the types in V are *zeroed in* by default. Zeroed in means that they are assigned with default values, such as an empty string for string types, 0 for integers, and false for Boolean types. Thus, V does not rely on the compiler to check whether the type is null or not, thereby preventing the program from creating several errors.

No global variables

Global variables allow you to maintain the state at the application level. Though this sounds comforting, global variables slowly lead to reliability problems that arise due to the growing number of actors on such variables.

In V, global variables are disabled by default. These global variables can be declared using the __global keyword and running the V program with the -enable-globals argument. The reason why V facilitates working with global variables is to allow the implementation of low-level applications such as programming OS kernels or system drivers. In such cases, you may need to have variables that can be accessed globally.

No undefined values

In V, when you declare a variable of any type, you must initialize it. Otherwise, it leads to compilation errors. Also, in the case of structs, which are detailed in *Chapter 8, Structs*, the fields of a struct are zeroed into their default values.

Error handling

V has a very simple approach to dealing with errors. You have the flexibility to deal with these errors using an or {} block or let the errors propagate using the optional operator, ?. You can also build custom errors using the built-in error method, which accepts a string as an input argument. The different ways to deal with errors will be demonstrated in the *Functions can have optional return types* section of *Chapter 7, Functions*.

Powerful concurrency

V has a very powerful concurrency framework. It is essential for an application running on a high-end computing device to be able to utilize its resources, such as its CPU cores, efficiently. Through V's built-in concurrency model, using the go keyword, you can spawn functions to run concurrently on other threads, different from the thread where the main program runs. The functions that run concurrently are called **coroutines**.

You can have shared variables to synchronize the data between coroutines by enforcing read-only locks using the rlocks keyword or read/write/modify locks using the lock keyword. This approach is demonstrated in the *Sharing data between the main thread and concurrent tasks* section of *Chapter 10, Concurrency*. With this traditional concurrency synchronization technique, the coroutines communicate by sharing data or memory.

As creating shared variables and manually enforcing locks is often cumbersome, V has a built-in library called `sync` that implements advanced concurrency patterns known as **channels**. A channel allows you to share data by establishing a communication channel among coroutines. A channel acts as a medium where a coroutine pushes data into it and other channels pop the data out of it. We will learn about channels, along with their features and how to work with buffered and unbuffered channels, in *Chapter 11, Channels – An Advanced Concurrency Pattern*.

Easy cross-compilation

V allows you to generate cross-platform binaries with its cross-platform compilation capabilities. With this feature, from a *nix OS, you can generate your application's executable that targets *nix OS variants, as well as Windows or macOS. From a *nix OS, let's say Ubuntu, create a file named `hello.v` and add the following code to it:

```
module main

fn main() {
    os := $if windows { 'Windows' } $else { 'Unix' }

    println('Hello, $os user!')
}
```

The $ symbol in the preceding code tells the compiler to evaluate the following `if` condition right away during compile time. Also, `windows` is a built-in term that's used to identify the OS type.

Run the preceding code using the `v run hello.v` command. You will see `Hello, Unix user!` as the output.

From the *nix OS, you can run the following command to create a cross-compiled executable targeting the Windows OS.

Before you start generating a cross-compiled binary for the `hello.v` program, you need to install `mingw-64`, which is required to generate an executable targeting the Windows OS. To install `mingw-64`, run the following command:

```
sudo apt install -y mingw-w64
```

Alternatively, you can try `sudo apt install -y mingw-w64` on Debian-based distributions or `sudo pacman -S mingw-w64-gcc` on Arch.

Once `mingw-64` has been installed, run the following command from the Ubuntu OS to generate the executables that can run on the Windows OS, as follows:

```
v -os windows hello.v
```

The preceding command will generate an executable named `hello.exe`. Now, transfer the `.exe` file to the Windows OS. Running the executable from Command Prompt will output `Hello, Windows user!`.

You can also cross-compile to generate *nix binaries from a Windows OS. All you need to do is install Clang for Windows, as described at `https://clang.llvm.org/get_started.html`, and run the following command, which generates the *nix binary:

```
v -os linux hello.v
```

Similarly, to generate an executable for macOS, run the following command:

```
v -os macos hello.v
```

V to JavaScript conversion

In addition to C as a primary backend, V also has JavaScript and WASM backends. V programs can be translated into JavaScript. To translate the `hello.v` into JavaScript, you can run the following command:

```
v -o hello.js hello.v
```

It is as simple as the preceding command. The outcome will produce a JavaScript file named `hello.js` that reflects the functionality written in the `hello.v` program.

Profiling

V has a built-in profiling tool that you can use to analyze how your program is behaving or how many times a function gets called on average by a function per call. You might need this information to debug and optimize the application code. To run the profiler against the V program, let's say `hello.v`, run the following command:

```
v -profile profile.txt hello.v
```

Notice the usage of the `-profile` argument, followed by the text file. Running the preceding command generates a binary for the `hello.v` program. Running the binary generates `profile.txt` with a detailed list of all the function calls with three columns. Each of the columns in the text file represents the number of calls, average time per call, and total time per call.

V as a framework

With the suite of packages V comes with, it can be considered equivalent to a framework. A framework generally comprises all the features of full-blown programming, along with the ability to smoothly plug and play the external packages. Using V, you can write enterprise-grade software, even though it is still in development. In the following sections of this chapter, we will look at the various suites of libraries and features that are written and implemented using V, which will help us build robust software applications.

Memory management using the autofree engine

V offers robust memory management with automatic garbage collection capabilities. Most of the objects are freed by V's **autofree** engine. Starting with V version 0.3, the autofree engine is enabled by default. You can also forcefully enable the autofree engine using the `-autofree` flag.

With the help of the autofree engine, the V compiler invokes the necessary calls to automatically free up objects during compilation. A small fraction of the objects is released from memory via reference counting. V also offers the ability to turn off the automatic garbage collection capability with the help of the `-noautofree` flag.

Built-in ORM

It is unlikely that a programming language will be available with a built-in **Object Relational Mapper** (**ORM**), but V is. Though the `orm` library is in an alpha state at the time of writing this book, it has all the basic features, which are enough to implement data-driven applications that have relational databases as backends.

Currently, the `orm` library supports SQLite, MySQL, and Postgres and has planned support for popular relational databases such as MS SQL and Oracle.

The built-in `orm` eases the development time by offering you the standard V-based queries to interact with all the aforementioned relational databases. You will learn more about ORM in *Chapter 13, Introduction to JSON and ORM.*

Built-in web server

The vweb web server is a built-in library. Though it is in an alpha state at the time of writing this book, it offers various features in its current state, including the following:

- Built-in routing.
- Handling parameters.
- Templating engine.
- Very fast performance, like C on the web.
- Building the project using vweb generates a single binary, thus simplifying deployments.

You will learn how to implement a microservice with RESTful endpoints using vweb, along with other libraries such as orm and json, in *Chapter 14, Building a Microservice*.

Native cross-platform GUI library

V has a cross-platform ui library. Using this library, you can leverage the power of building cross-platform GUI applications. The ui library can be found at the official GitHub repository at https://github.com/vlang/ui, which is licensed under GPL 3.0.

V has a ui module that uses native GUI toolkits: WinAPI/GDI+ on Windows and Cocoa on macOS. On Linux, custom drawing is used.

Vinix – an OS kernel written in V

Vinix is an effort to write a modern, fast, and useful OS using V. Vinix is purposefully built to facilitate writing low-level software.

The Vinix OS is licensed under GPL 2.0, and you can find its entire source code on its official GitHub repository at https://github.com/vlang/vinix. You can always download the latest version of the Vinix OS in the form of ISO from the official link: https://builds.vinix-os.org/repos/files/vinix/latest/vinix.iso.

Vinix aims to have the following features:

- Make a usable OS that can run on emulators, virtual machines, and physical hardware
- Target modern 64-bit architectures, CPU features, and multi-core computing

- Maintain good source-level compatibility with Linux, which helps with porting programs between Vinix and Linux

- Explore V's capabilities in bare-metal programming

- Improve the compiler in response to the uncommon needs of bare-metal programming

Operating systems V supports

The V programming language is cross-platform compliant. The V language runs on almost all the major operating systems. V runs on all versions of Windows, on all *nix variants such as CentOS, Fedora, and Ubuntu, and also on macOS. V also runs on the popular mobile OS known as Android. V runs on all the Windows OS variants where **Windows Subsystem for Linux (WSL)** is supported. V can also be used in the **Internet of Things (IoT)** as it supports running on IoT platforms such as Raspberry Pi.

Summary

In this chapter, we started with a brief introduction to V programming. We looked at the past, present, and future of V. We then explored the V language, since it is a statically typed and compiled programming language, and learned about the simplicity it has to offer when it comes to writing code. We also learned how, even though V is still in development and constantly evolving, it provides guaranteed backward compatibility, stability, and easy upgrades to future versions.

Later, we learned about the various features of V programming, Vinix, an OS kernel written using V, and considered V as a framework. Finally, we learned about what operating systems V supports.

In the next chapter, we will learn how to install V on the Windows and Ubuntu operating systems. We will also learn how to add a V executable to an environment variable so that it can be accessed from any directory in the OS.

2
Installing V Programming

The V programming language supports various **operating systems (OSes)** such as Windows, Linux (including **Window Subsystem for Linux (WSL)**), macOS, BSD, Solaris, Android, and Raspbian. In this chapter, we will focus on how to install V on the most popularly used OSes (such as **Windows** and **Ubuntu**) for development activities. Additionally, we will gain an understanding of how to add V to the environment variables on Windows. For Ubuntu OS, we will examine how to make V globally accessible by creating a symbolic link. This will enable us to access V from any directory within the OS using the **Command-Line Interpreter (CLI)**.

In this chapter, we will cover the following topics:

- Installing V on the Windows OS
- Adding V to environment variables in the Windows OS
- Installing V on the Linux OS (Ubuntu)
- Symlink V to make V globally accessible in Ubuntu

Technical requirements

The following requirements are needed for this chapter:

- Access to the command-line terminal on the OS that is being installed

- Admin rights (optional)

- Optionally, the GCC Compiler, which is mentioned in the OS-specific installation steps.

Installing V on the Windows OS

Windows is the most popular OS used by the majority of developers and V supports it. We will proceed with the installation of the V programming language on the Windows 10 OS. There are two ways to install V on the Windows 10 OS:

- Install V from portable binaries (these can be downloaded from the official V website at `https://vlang.io/`).

- Install V from the latest source code (this can be cloned from V's official GitHub repository at `https://github.com/vlang/v`).

Let's take a look at both of those installation methods in more detail. You can skip the alternate approach if you follow any one of the two installation methods on the Windows OS.

Approach 1 – installing V from portable binaries on the Windows OS

In general, portable installations give you the flexibility to simply extract the software packaged as an archive to the location of your choice without actually modifying any system behavior or registry settings. In this approach, we will be downloading the portable binaries of V directly and dropping them into a location of our choice:

1. Download and install the GCC Compiler from `https://github.com/vlang/v/releases/download/v0.1.10/mingw-w64-install.exe`.

2. Download the portable binaries from the official V website at `https://vlang.io/`. The URL to download the portable binaries is `https://github.com/vlang/v/releases/latest/download/v_windows.zip`.

3. Once the download is complete, locate the archive named `v_windows.zip` in your default downloads directory. Right-click on the archive and click on **Properties**. Find and select the **Unblock** checkbox and then click on **OK**, as follows:

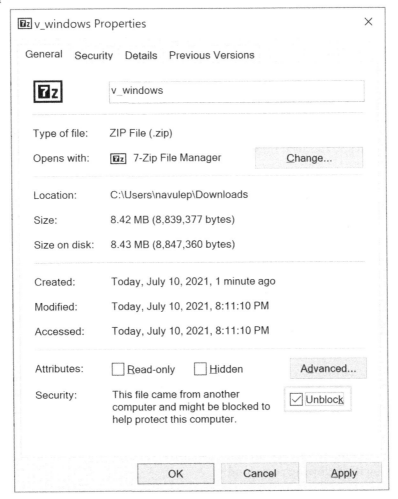

Figure 2.1 – v_windows Properties displaying the Unblock archive

Note

You might or might not see the **Unblock** option for the `v_windows` archive depending on the Windows setting. The **Unblock** option appears if Windows has blocked access to a file downloaded from the internet. Another possible reason could be that the archive that you downloaded was created on an OS other than Windows.

4. Extract `v_windows.zip` to the C drive. If you wish to install it on any other directory, you can do so by extracting it to the directory of your choice. Let's say you have extracted it to `C:`; you will find the v directory that holds all of the binaries and executables at the `C:\v` location.

5. Open Command Prompt and run the following commands to check that v is installed correctly:

```
cd c:\v
v version
```

6. You should be able to view the output that displays the version of V that has been downloaded and installed on your PC. It will appear as follows:

```
V 0.2.4 d373eba
```

From the output of the `v version` command, the `V 0.2.4` part indicates the version of V in the *major.minor.patch* format. In addition to the version information, you will also optionally see the commit ID from the official V GitHub repository, which, in this case, is `d373eba`. You might observe a different commit ID as V is constantly being updated.

Approach 2 – installing V from source on the Windows OS

As long as V is in development, the recommended approach is to always work on the latest available source of V from the official V GitHub repository at `https://github.com/vlang/v`. Ensure that you download and install the open source software Git for Windows from `https://git-scm.com/download/win`. Perform the following steps to install V from the source:

1. Open the command-line terminal in Windows and clone the latest source by running the following command:

```
cd C:\
git clone https://github.com/vlang/v
```

2. Wait for `git` to clone the official V repository onto your PC. Once downloaded, let's move to the V directory by running the following command:

```
cd v
```

3. Now, it's time for us to compile the source code to produce an executable for V, named v.exe. To generate v.exe, we need to run the batch script, named make. bat and located in the v directory, from the command-line terminal:

```
make.bat
```

Notice that the output of the make.bat command generates the following log on the command-line console:

```
Bootstraping TCC...
 > TCC not found
 > Downloading TCC from https://github.com/vlang/tccbin


Cloning vc...
 > Cloning from remote https://github.com/vlang/vc


Building V...
 > Clang not found
 > GCC not found
 > Attempting to build v_win.c with TCC
 > Compiling with .\v.exe self
 > V built successfully
 > To add V to your PATH, run '.\v.exe symlink'.


V version: V 0.2.4 d373eba
```

Notice how, this time, the V version indicates the same version but with a different git commit ID. You can match it with the latest commit ID on the official GitHub repository of V. You might view a different commit ID as V is in constant development.

A new executable file named v.exe is generated in the V directory as a result of running the make.bat command. From the terminal, you can run .\v.exe symlink. This will add V to the environment variables. In this scenario, you can skip the following section and continue reading from the *Accessing V programming using REPL* section. In the next section, I will explain, in detail, the manual process of adding V to the environment variables.

Adding V to the environment variables in the Windows OS

To access V from any directory from within the OS, we need to add V directory's path, where v.exe is located, to the system environment variables. In both of the installation methods on the Windows OS, as mentioned in the previous sections, we have installed V in the C:\v location. This indicates that we have installed V in a directory named v, that is located in C drive. If we examine the contents of the directory, we will find the V executable with the name of v.exe. So, we will be adding the C:\v path to the environment variables.

Open the **Environment Variables** window by running the following command from the command-line terminal:

```
rundll32 sysdm.cpl,EditEnvironmentVariables
```

You will notice the window has two sections, as follows:

- **User variables** for the active user
- **System variables**

If you want V programming to be available for all users of your system, edit the variable named Path underneath the **System variables** section. Click on the **New** button. Then, in the empty row, provide the path where v.exe is located. In our case, this will be C:\v.

If you want V programming to be only available for the logged-in user, then edit the variable named Path underneath **User variables** for the logged-in user and click on **New**. Then, in the empty row, provide the path where v.exe is located. In our case, this will be C:\v.

For these changes to take effect, close all of the command-line terminals and reopen them to access V from any directory within the PC.

Accessing V programming using a REPL

REPL stands for **read-eval-print loop**. Many popular programming languages in addition to V, such as Python, PHP, Rust, and R, to name a few, have a REPL.

As we have installed V and added V to the **Environment Variables** window, we can access V's REPL by running the following command from the command-line Terminal:

```
v
```

You should see the following result when you successfully enter the command
into V's REPL:

```
Welcome to the V REPL (for help with V itself, type 'exit',
then run 'v help').
V 0.2.4 d373eba
Use Ctrl-C or 'exit' to exit, or 'help' to see other available
commands
>>>
```

Alternatively, you can type v repl into Command Prompt and hit *Enter*. Pay attention
to the three forward arrows, >>>, which indicate the terminal that takes V commands.
To begin, let's print a string in a new line by running the following V code, as follows:

```
>>> println('Hello World!')
Hello World!
```

Pay attention to the output printed right underneath the command. Notice that it does not
have three arrows before the Hello World! output string.

As the V program has compiled for the first time and you run the println statement,
a directory named .vmodules will be created in the %USERPROFILE%/.vmodules
location. This folder contains cached build artifacts from the V build system.

When you land in the REPL mode of V, running the help command will display
a list of all of the commands, such as list, reset, clear, and more, as shown here:

```
C:\>v repl
V 0.2.4 d373eba
Use Ctrl-C or 'exit' to exit, or 'help' to see other available
commands
>>> help
V 0.2.4 d373eba

help                      Displays this information.
list                      Show the program so far.
reset                     Clears the accumulated program,
so you can start a fresh.
Ctrl-C, Ctrl-D, exit    Exits the REPL.
clear                     Clears the screen.
```

Now that you have learned how to access V programming via a REPL, let's learn how to install V on the Linux OS.

Installing V on the Linux OS (Ubuntu)

The majority of the development community loves open source Unix-like OSes such as Ubuntu. Ubuntu is a distribution based on the Debian infrastructure and architecture. V supports running on Ubuntu. When we install V on a fresh instance of Ubuntu, it will download and install the TCC compiler as a default C backend. It's a very lightweight compiler and the installation is quick.

TCC, or **Tiny C Compiler**, is a lightweight C compiler. TCC is fast when it comes to compilation times in comparison to **GNU Compiler Collection (GCC)**. However, TCC comes with limitations such as the limited optimization of the resulting binaries, and the executable that is built with the TCC compiler will be slower. For production builds, it is recommended that you have GCC installed.

As a prerequisite to installing V, we would like to have GCC as a C compiler. Please note that, in addition to GCC and TCC, Clang is also a supported compiler on *nix-based OSes. However, let's proceed with the installation of GCC.

Open the command-line Terminal and navigate to the user directory. Run the following command from the command-line Terminal to install the C compiler on Debian/Ubuntu:

```
sudo apt -y update
sudo apt install -y build-essential
```

Once we have GCC installed as a part of the build-essential package, we can go ahead with downloading the source from the official GitHub repository of V. You can do this by running the following command:

```
git clone https://github.com/vlang/v
```

Once you have download the source code, you will find a directory named v. Navigate to the directory by running the following command from the command-line Terminal:

```
cd v
```

Now you are in the directory where the official v source code is located. Now, we will compile the source code by running the make command, as follows:

```
make
```

Once you have run the `make` command successfully, verify the installation by running the command to check the version of `v`, as follows:

```
v version
```

The output should appear as follows:

```
V 0.2.4 d373eba
```

From the output of the `v version` command, the `V 0.2.4` part indicates the version of V in the *major.minor.patch* format. In addition to the version information, you can also, optionally, view the commit ID from the official V GitHub repository (`https://github.com/vlang/v/`), which, in this case, is `d373eba`. You might see a different commit ID as V is constantly being updated.

Next, let's take a look at how we can access V globally using Symlink V.

Using Symlink V to make V accessible globally in Ubuntu

To access the `V` executable from any directory within the OS, it is a good practice to create `symlink`. A `symlink` is a symbolic link that will allow you access to programs from anywhere within the system. To create a `symlink`, run the following command from the command-line Terminal:

```
sudo ./v symlink
```

Once you have run the preceding command, you will find a reference to the `V` executable in the `/usr/local/bin/v` location. Navigate to the directory of your choice and type in the `v` command. The CLI will print the following message on V's REPL:

```
Welcome to the V REPL (for help with V itself, type 'exit',
then run 'v help').
V 0.2.4 d373eba
Use Ctrl-C or 'exit' to exit, or 'help' to see other available
commands
>>>
```

Pay attention to the three arrows that indicate the Terminal takes v commands. To get started, let's print a string in a new line by running the following V code, as follows:

```
>>> println('Hello World!')
Hello World!
```

Congratulations! You have successfully installed V on your Ubuntu OS. We have also created a symlink so that you can access it from anywhere within the system.

Summary

In this chapter, we learned that V, being cross-platform compliant, supports various OSes. We also learned how to successfully install V on Windows and Ubuntu-based OSes. After the successful installation on each of these OSes, we also learned how to configure V to be accessible from any location within the OS by adding the location of the V executable to the environment variables.

In the next chapter, we will learn about the basics of V programming, such as variables, constants and how to add code comments in V.

Section 2:
Basics of V Programming

This section focuses on the basics of V programming. You will gain an understanding of the basic programming principles, such as primitive data types, declaring variables, constants, and adding code comments. You will also get an in-depth understanding of primitive data types in V and learn how to use various operators, such as arithmetic, logical, bitwise, shift, and relational operators. In addition, this section also covers basic data structures in V such as arrays and maps.

You will also learn about writing conditional statements using `if` and `match`, and then you will learn different ways of writing iterative statements using `for` loops. In addition to basic programming, you will gain additional knowledge of the building blocks of programming, such as functions, structs, and modules in the V programming language.

This section has the following chapters:

- *Chapter 3, Variables, Constants, and Code Comments*
- *Chapter 4, Primitive Data Types*
- *Chapter 5, Arrays and Maps*
- *Chapter 6, Conditionals and Iterative Statements*
- *Chapter 7, Functions*
- *Chapter 8, Structs*
- *Chapter 9, Modules*

3
Variables, Constants, and Code Comments

In the previous chapter, we learned how to install V on various operating systems. Now, it's time for us to learn about the basic concepts in V. This chapter will cover the absolute basics to get started in V, including defining and working with variables, constants, and code comments.

Variables are the foundational concepts of any programming language, and programmers will encounter them almost all the time when they code. Therefore, it is essential to know about the details of variables. Similarly, we will also learn about constants that offer reusability and consistency during programming software applications. Constants hold a value that never changes for the entire lifetime of the application.

Finally, we will gain an understanding of how to make comments in the code. Code comments are an essential part of software development, and they help fellow programmers to read and understand the functionality of the logic where the comment has been made. In this chapter, we are going to learn about the following topics:

- Understanding variables in V
- Working with constants

- Variables versus constants
- Adding code comments in V

By the end of this chapter, you will have a working knowledge of how to define and work with variables, constants, and code comments.

Technical requirements

Most of the code in this chapter can be run by accessing V's REPL, as detailed in the *Accessing V programming using REPL* section of *Chapter 2, Installing V Programming*. It is recommended that you restart REPL for every section in this chapter as you might encounter the usage of the same variable names.

You will find all of the code snippets for this chapter at `https://github.com/PacktPublishing/Getting-Started-with-V-Programming/tree/main/Chapter03`.

Additionally, you can save the code snippets to a filename of your choice with the `.v` extension and then access the command-line Terminal to run the code, as follows:

```
v run filename.v
```

Understanding variables in V

A **variable**, by definition, holds a value or reference to another variable. Generally, a variable is identified by a name. In fact, when a variable is declared, it is given a meaningful name that generally reflects the value held by it. A variable declaration is a typical V statement in which you assign a variable with an initial value. This is often termed as **defining a variable** or **declaring a variable**. A variable in V can be assigned with any value, including values in the form of primitive data types, complex data types such as a struct, or they can be assigned with anonymous functions. We will cover anonymous functions in *Chapter 7, Functions*, and structs in *Chapter 8, Structs*.

A variable, when declared, is *immutable* by default. An immutable variable indicates that the value can be assigned only once during its declaration and cannot be updated after it has been declared. V facilitates the declaration of mutable variables with the help of the mut keyword. Mutable variables allow you to reassign the values of the variables. We will gain a better understanding of mutable variables as we go through the phases of this chapter. However, for now, let's take a look at a simple variable declaration in V, as follows:

```
x := 100
```

Though the preceding statement looks short enough, there are various things you need to know. They are mentioned here:

- The statement indicates that a variable has been declared.

- The variable is named x.

- The x variable is declared with a value of 100 using the := symbol.

- The x variable is immutable since no mut keyword has been specified.

- The data type of the variable is identified by the value it holds, which, in this case, is an integer.

The value held by the variable is allocated on the stack. For those of you who are not aware of the stack, it is a simple structure that allows elements to be inserted into it and taken out of it in **Last In, First Out** (**LIFO**) order.

This is a very basic example of variable declaration and V, being sophisticated, has various features in regard to variables. Before jumping into the various features of variables in V, let's take a look at the different ways of how to assign variables in V.

The variable naming convention

V allows the presence of alphanumeric characters for naming variables. In addition to alphanumeric characters, an underscore symbol is also allowed in the variable names. To ensure variables names have consistent style across projects, V enforces the following rules for naming variables:

- A variable name can only start with the lowercase alphabet.

- A variable name cannot contain the uppercase alphabet.

- Special characters are not allowed except for underscores.

- Variable names can end with numbers and underscores.

- Lengthy variable names can have words separated with _ to enhance readability and consistency across the code. This type of variable naming convention is often referred to as **snake_case**.

The following table will help you to understand naming conventions for variables in V:

Example code	Is valid	Reason
`1x := 'hi'`	Invalid	A variable name cannot start with a digit and shows the following error message: `error: this number has unsuitable digit 'x'`
`x := 'hi'`	Valid	A variable name can start with the lowercase alphabet.
`firstName := 'Navule'`	Invalid	The `firstName` variable name cannot contain uppercase letters; use `snake_case` instead.
`first_Name := 'Navule'`	Invalid	The `first_Name` variable name cannot contain uppercase letters; use `snake_case` instead.
`first_name := 'Navule'`	Valid	A lengthy variable name using `snake_case` provides better readability.
`counter_ := 10`	Valid	A variable name can end with an underscore, but it is unlikely that a variable can be named that ends with `_`. Generally, such a style is used for reserved keywords such as `struct_`.
`_counter := 10`	Invalid	The `_counter` variable name cannot start with `_`.
`counter1 := 10`	Valid	A variable name can end with a digit.
`lengthy_variable_name_1 := 'hi'`	Valid	A variable name can have multiple underscores in between.

Table 3.1 – Naming conventions in V

Variable assignment

Two basic symbols are used when dealing with variable assignments in V. They are as follows:

- `:=` is a colon followed by an equals sign and is used to declare a variable in V.

- `=` is an equals sign used to reassign a value to the already declared mutable variables only.

With the help of these two symbols, V supports various styles of variable assignment that include *parallel variable declaration and assignment* and *augmented assignment.*

Parallel variable declaration and assignment

A parallel assignment in V allows multiple variables to be declared at once in a single line, as follows:

```
a, b, c := 3, 4, 5
```

This statement indicates that the simultaneous declaration of the immutable variables named a, b, and c is assigned the values of 3, 4, and 5, respectively.

Similarly, you can simultaneously declare all mutable variables as follows:

```
mut i, mut j := 'Hi', 'Hello'
```

The preceding statement indicates that the i and j mutable variables are simultaneously declared and initialized with the Hi and Hello strings, respectively.

As the i and j variables are mutable, we can perform a parallel reassignment of values such as the following:

```
i, j = 'Hi there', 'Hello, Good Day!'
```

Here, the = symbol is being used to reassign the values to the i and j mutable variables. The values of the i and j mutable variables are being updated with Hi there and Hello, Good Day!, respectively, using the parallel variable assignment approach.

You can declare variables that are both mutable and immutable in a parallel form of declaration. Consider the following code:

```
mut msg, i := 'Hello', 32
println(msg) // Hello
msg = 'Hi'
println(msg) // Hi
println(i) // 32
i = 2 // error: 'i' is immutable, declare it with 'mut' to
      // make it mutable
```

In the preceding code, msg is a mutable variable that holds a string value and i is an immutable variable that holds an integer value.

Augmented variable assignment

An **augmented assignment** is the method of in-place updating mutable variables instead of explicitly mentioning them as a part of an update statement. V allows an augmented variable assignment for mutable variables only. Let's consider a mutable variable that has been declared as follows:

```
mut greet := 'Hi'
```

Let's suppose the greet variable needs to be concatenated with additional text. Then, normally, the statement looks like this:

```
greet = greet + ' there, How are you?'
```

Using an augmented assignment, the greet variable can be concatenated in place, as follows:

```
greet += ' Hope you have a great day!'
```

Alternatively, let's consider the following example:

```
mut cnt := 10
```

Let's say that you wish to increment the cnt variable by 5; typically, you will write the statement that adds the value of cnt with 5 and then write a statement again that updates the cnt variable, as follows:

```
cnt = cnt + 5
```

Alternatively, you can perform an in-place augmented assignment to the cnt variable, as follows:

```
cnt += 5
```

In this case, the cnt mutable variable of the integer type is being incremented by 5 in place using the augmented assignment approach.

Features of variables in V

Variables in V adhere to the following features:

- Variables can be declared mutable or immutable.
- A variable, once declared, must be assigned to a value.
- All of the variables must be consumed once declared.

Let's take a look at each of the properties of V, as mentioned in detail here, and gain a better understanding of them using code examples.

Variables can be declared mutable or immutable

A variable can be declared as either mutable or immutable. We will explore, in detail, how to work with mutable and immutable variables in V.

Mutable variables

The term **mutable** indicates that a value can be altered. In V programming, it is highly important to define such behavior for variables during their declaration, allowing them to be modified later. A mutable variable is declared using the mut keyword and initialized using the : = symbol. The subsequent updates for the mutable variable can be done using the = symbol or using the augmented variable assignment, as detailed earlier.

The following is the syntax for a mutable variable:

```
mut <variable_name> := <initializing_value>
```

The syntax to update the mutable variable is as follows:

```
<variable_name> = <updated_value>
```

Let's consider an example of declaring a mutable variable and updating it with a different value:

```
mut i := 10
i = 100
```

This example demonstrates that the i mutable variable is declared and initialized with a value of 10 using the : = symbol. In the next statement, it is updated using = with the new value of 100.

> **Note**
> The mutable variables during the reassignment require the new value to be of the same data type as the value held by the variable before modification.

Let's try to update the i mutable variable of the int type with a string, as follows:

```
i = 'Apple'
```

This assignment leads to an error despite the i variable being mutable. This is because the variable is of the int type but is being updated with a different data type string, so it will show an error as follows:

```
error: cannot assign to 'i': expected 'int', not 'string'
```

Immutable variables

The term **immutable** refers to a value that remains unaltered once it has been defined. In V, the variables, unless declared with the mut keyword, are immutable by default. The following is the syntax for declaring an immutable variable:

```
<variable_name> := <initializing_value>
```

Let's consider the following example:

```
msg := 'Hello'
```

The statement indicates the declaration of the variable named msg and initializes it with the Hello value using the := symbol. As the variable is not specified with the mut keyword in its statement, the msg variable is immutable by default. So, the msg variable cannot be updated further.

Let's forcibly update the msg immutable variable with the similar syntax that we used to update the mutable variable:

```
msg = 'Good Day!'
```

Updating an immutable variable leads to error, as shown here:

```
error: 'msg' is immutable, declare it with 'mut' to make it
mutable
```

A variable once declared must be assigned with a value

V requires you to define a variable with an initial value. Unlike other programming languages, such as C# or Java, which allow you to declare a variable without having to initialize a value, you must assign a specific value to the variable during the declaration. This is because V tries to avoid having null values as they often result in application crashes.

So, it is recommended that you declare variables as mutable if you are not sure of what to initialize the values with. Therefore, you have the flexibility to update the mutable variables as and when required during the computation.

Let's consider the following example:

```
mut i := 0
```

As per the syntax, it is necessary to initialize variables with some values. Let's discover what happens if you just declare a variable and leave the value unassigned, as follows:

```
mut a
```

The compiler will throw an error, as follows:

```
error: expecting ':=' (e.g. 'mut x :=')
```

All the variables must be consumed once declared

Any variable that is declared but unused will lead to a warning or error depending on the mode in which you run the program. V doesn't recommend leaving the declared variables unused, and such instances are treated as warnings during development mode and as errors when in production mode.

To demonstrate, let's take a look at the following code:

```
i := 'hello' // i is not used anywhere, so warns when run
// in dev mode and throws error when run in prod mode
x := 3
y := 2
println(x + y)
```

The preceding code declares the i, x, and y variables and, finally, prints the sum of the x and y variables to the console. However, the i variable is simply declared and not utilized anywhere during the scope of execution of the main function.

Now, save this code to a file named unused-variable.v. From Command Prompt, navigate to the location where the file is saved and run the command to execute the file using v, as follows:

```
v run unused-variable.v
```

The console logs the warnings and then prints the sum of the x and y variables, as follows:

```
unused-variable.v:1:2: warning: unused variable: 'i'
    1 | i := 'hello' // i is not used anywhere, so warns when
run in dev mode and throws error when run in prod mode
      |   ^
```

```
2 | x := 3
3 | y := 2
5
```

Now, we will observe the output when this program is run in production mode using the `-prod` flag with the following command:

```
v -prod unused-variable.v
```

The console will output an error and stop executing the code further. This is because, in production mode, unused variables are treated as errors:

```
unused-variable.v:4:9: error: unused variable: 'i'
2 |
3 |     fn main() {
4 |             i := 'hello'
  |             ^
5 |             x := 3
6 |             y := 2
```

The limitations of variables in V

There are certain limitations when it comes to working with variables in V:

- Global variables are not allowed in V.

- The redeclaration or redefinition of variables is not allowed in V.

- Variable shadowing is not allowed in V.

Let's take a look at these limitations and try to understand them in more detail.

Global variables are not allowed in V

Global variables allow you to interact and modify the code outside the scope of the program they are defined in. They facilitate coupling between the components of the software and might lead to the introduction of defects into the system.

By default, V does not allow a global state, and hence, global variables are not allowed. When it comes to variable declaration, V limits the variables to be declared inside the functions. So, the scope of the variable is limited to the function where it is declared.

V facilitates the enabling of global variables using an -enable-globals compiler flag when you typically want to run the program. However, the intention of this compiler flag is to make the variables available for low-level applications such as drivers and kernels. There is a dedicated *Functions do not allow access to module variables or global variables* section, in *Chapter 7, Functions*, where I demonstrate how to work with global variables along with code examples and how to run the code using the -enable-globals compiler flag.

Let's consider the following code, which demonstrates that the scope of the variable is limited to the function it is declared within:

```
module main

fn method1() {
        msg := 'Hello from Method1'
        println(msg)
}

fn main() {
        method1()
        println(msg) // Will throw error as msg declared
                     // and accessible only in method1
}
```

In the preceding code snippet, method1 and main are functions. We will learn about functions, in more detail, in *Chapter 7, Functions*. The msg variable is declared inside method1, but we are trying to access it from main. This code will fail to run with the error message of error: undefined ident: msg.

The variable declared in the conditionals and iterators is only scoped to the respective conditionals or iterators. Let's consider the following code:

```
module main

fn method1() {
        if true {
                mut b := 10
                b++
        }
        println(b)
```

```
        }
```

```
fn main() {
        method1()
}
```

Here, `method1` has defined a `b` variable inside the `if` condition and assigned it with the value of `10`, and then it is incremented by 1. When we try to access the `b` variable outside the `if` condition and print it, it will fail to execute with the `error: undefined ident: b` message.

The redeclaration or redefinition of variables is not allowed in V

A variable, once declared, cannot be redeclared within the scope where the variable is accessible. For example, let's consider the following code:

```
module main
```

```
fn main() {
        x := 3
        y := 2
        println(x + y)
        x := 5 // re-definition of variable x is not
                // allowed
}
```

The preceding code will fail to run and show an error message that says `error: redefinition of x`.

V only allows you to define variables within functions and scripts; the names of the variables are only reserved for the scope of the function. Let's consider the following code snippet where the `msg` variable is declared in two methods:

```
module main
```

```
fn method1() {
        msg := 'Hello from Method1'
        println(msg)
}
```

```
fn method2() {
```

```
        msg := 'Hello from Method2'
        println(msg)
}

fn main() {
        method1()
        method2()
}
```

In the preceding code, the two functions, namely, `method1` and `method2`, declare the variable with the same name of `msg`. This code will compile properly because the scope of the variable is limited to the method in which it is declared.

Variable shadowing is not allowed in V

In some programming languages such as Python, Java **variable shadowing** is allowed, where the definition of a variable in the inner scope with the same name as the variable in the outer scope contains a different value from the variable defined in the outer scope. The variable declared in the outer scope will be the same throughout its scope of execution, except in the inner scope where the variable is shadowed. V does not allow you to shadow variables. As we learned, declaring the variables with the same name will lead to an error. Consider the following code:

```
module main

fn scope_demo() {
        x := 10
        println(x)
        if true {
                x := 20 // throws error as shadowing is
                        // not allowed
                println(x)
        }
        println(x)
}

fn main() {
        scope_demo()
}
```

The x variable defined in the scope_demo method with a value of 10 is scoped at the method level and its nested blocks. In the inner scope of the if condition, we are trying to redefine the variable with the same name of x, which is a kind of shadowing or masking of the variable declared in the outer scope pertaining to the if block. If we try to run the preceding code, it will fail, saying error: redefinition of x.

Now that we have learned all about variables in V, let's take a look at how constants work in V.

Working with constants in V

Sometimes, your program must have certain values that never change throughout the application's lifetime. V facilitates the declaration of such values as constants using the const keyword. A constant, once assigned to a value, can never be changed. Unlike variables that can only be declared inside the functions, V allows constants to be declared outside of the functions, and they can be scoped at the module level.

In V, you can define constants that are having values of primitive types such as int, string, bool. In addition to it, you can also define constants of complex values such as structs. We will learn how to define complex constants in the following sections of this chapter.

Naming conventions for constants

Similar to variables, constants have the following naming conventions:

- The name of a constant can only start with the lowercase alphabet.
- The name of a constant cannot contain the uppercase alphabet.
- Special characters are not allowed except underscores.
- The name of a constant can end with numbers and underscores.
- Lengthy constant names can have words separated with _ to enhance readability and consistency across code. This type of naming convention is often referred to as snake_case.

Defining constants

The following is the syntax for defining a constant using the const keyword:

```
const <constant_name> = <constant_value>
```

In the preceding syntax, a constant is declared using the const keyword that is specified before the name of the constant. The value of the constant is assigned to the = symbol.

Defining a single constant

The following example shows how to define a single constant named `app_name` with a value of a string data type:

```
const app_name = 'V on Wheels'
```

Here, you can see that the single constant is defined using the `const` keyword followed by the name of `app_name` and then =, followed by the value we want to assign to the constant.

Defining multiple constants

Sometimes, you need to define multiple constants. Having understood the syntax of how to define a constant, as demonstrated earlier, you might tend to define multiple constants, as follows:

```
const app_name = 'V on Wheels'
const max_connections = 1000
const decimal_places = 2
const pi = 3.14
```

The preceding code for declaring multiple constants is valid, but you can also define multiple constants of different data types, as shown here:

```
const (
    app_name = 'V on Wheels'
    max_connections = 1000
    decimal_places = 2
    pi = 3.14
)
```

The multiple constants can be declared by grouping them inside rounded brackets and defining each constant in a separate line. This approach looks clean and prevents you from specifying the `const` keyword for multiple constant declarations in each line.

Defining complex constants

V facilitates the declaration of complex constants, including structs and functions. The constants with values set as a result of a function are evaluated at compile time. So, let's take a look at how to define complex constants in V.

Defining a constant of the struct type

V allows you to create complex constants that have a value set as a `struct` data type. Let's consider the following code, which demonstrates declaring a constant as a `struct` data type:

```
module main

struct Space3D {
mut:
        x int
        y int
        z int
}

const origin = Space3D{
                x: 0
                y: 0
                z: 0
        }

fn main() {
        println(origin)
}
```

The output is as follows:

```
Space3D{
    x: 0
    y: 0
    z: 0
}
```

In the preceding example, the `Space3D` struct has three fields, x, y, and z, that represent the coordinates of a three-dimensional coordinate system. It is beneficial to define the origin as a constant so that it can be reused across multiple places. So, we defined a constant named `origin` with a value of the `Space3D` struct type with its x, y, and z fields initialized with an integer value of 0.

Defining a constant as a result of function

V allows the result of functions to be assigned to constants. In the process of assigning functions to a constant, the values are evaluated at compile time.

To demonstrate how to define constants as a result of the evaluation of a function, consider the following code:

```
module main

struct Space3D {
mut:
        x int
        y int
        z int
}

fn get_point(x int, y int, z int) Space3D {
        return Space3D{
                x: x
                y: y
                z: z
        }
}

const origin = get_point(0, 0, 0)

fn main() {
        println(origin)
}
```

The output is as follows:

```
Space3D{
    x: 0
    y: 0
    z: 0
}
```

As the origin of a 3D space has all the coordinates set to zero, we are defining it as a constant named `origin`.

In the preceding code, the `get_point` function returns the `Space3D` struct type with its fields initialized with the values received as x, y, and z input arguments.

Then, we define a constant named `origin`; however, this time, a value is returned as a result of the evaluation of a function named `get_point` that accepts the three arguments of x, y, and z. As this is a constant built from the return value of the function, the assignment of the constant, in this case, happens during the compile time of the program.

Best practices when working with constants

There are certain things to bear in mind when working with constants in V. These are often the best practices that will help you to write clean and effective code. They are specified as follows:

- Constants must be defined at the module level.
- Constants must be accessed with their module prefix.

You will learn about modules in *Chapter 9, Modules*. However, for now, we will learn about the aforementioned practices, in detail, along with code examples.

Constants must be defined at a module level

Constants should only be declared at the module level. They cannot be declared inside the functions. Let's consider the following example that defines constants:

```
module main

const app_name = 'V on Wheels'

fn main() {
        println(app_name)
}
```

The output is as follows:

```
V on Wheels
```

From the preceding code snippet, we declared a string constant named `app_name`. And inside a function, we are printing its value. Additionally, notice that we are directly accessing the constant with its variable name as it is defined in the main module. For the constants that are declared in other modules, you need to specify the module prefix to access the constant. We will learn how to do this in the next section.

Now, let's consider how to define a constant inside a function, as shown in the following code snippet:

```
module main

const app_name = 'V on Wheels'

fn main() {
        const greet = 'hi'
        println(app_name)
}
```

Notice that we have defined a constant named `greet` inside the function that doesn't compile. Therefore, the preceding code will fail with a message that says `error: const can only be defined at the top level (outside of functions)`.

Constants must be identified with their module prefix

The constants, unless otherwise defined in the main module, need to be identified with their modules even if they are consumed within the same module they are defined in. We will learn more about modules in the upcoming chapter. However, for brevity, let's assume we are defining constants in a module named `mod1`, as follows:

```
module mod1

const greet_count = 5

pub fn do_work() {
        println(mod1.greet_count)
}
```

In the preceding code snippet, we declared a constant named `greet_count` in a file that belongs to the `mod1` module. Although it is being used in the same module in the public `do_work` function, which simply does the printing of the `greet_count` constant, we need to specify the module to which it belongs, which, in this case, is `mod1`.

We will further explore how to deal with constants in modules in *Chapter 9, Modules*, where we will learn about *accessing the constants of a module*. However, from the preceding code, it is evident that in order to consume the constant defined inside or outside the module, it is necessary to specify the module name and then the constant name with a dot in between.

As the constants (except for the ones that are defined in the main modules) must be identified with their module prefix, this approach provides us with a leeway in which to define constants with the same names across different modules. Next, we will examine the key distinguishing factors between a variable and a constant in V.

Variables versus constants

The following table lists the key differences between a variable and a constant in V:

Variable	Constant
Variables are declared using : =	Constants are declared using =
A value can be altered in the case of mutable variables	The value remains constant
Variables can only be declared at the function level	Constants can only be declared at the module level

Table 3.2 – Variables versus constants

Now, let's move on to learn how to add code comments in V.

Adding code comments in V

Imagine a situation where you have started looking at a new repository that has a lot of code and you want to quickly understand what any particular function or piece of logic does. You can spend some time looking at the logic and you might come up with an assumption of what the piece of code actually does. Often, it is a tedious task for other programmers to spend time reading the code to understand what the code is doing. Most of the time, even the programmer who wrote the code tends to forget what the logic actually does and only recollects after spending time on what they wrote.

Most of the programming languages allow you to add comments to the code. These comments can be single-line comments or multiline comments.

Single-line comments

Single-line comments are used to write short details about the code being commented on that generally fit in a line. A single-line comment starts with a double forward slash, //, followed by the comment that you want to describe the code:

```
// greet function prints greetings to the console
pub fn greet() {
        println('Hello, Welcome to the Jungle!')
}
```

Anything that is written after // becomes part of the comment. Occasionally, programmers comment out the code during the development of a program to try out various approaches to solve a problem.

Multiline comments

Sometimes, the description becomes too detailed and overflows onto multiple lines, or you need to include comments in between the list items, such as food := ['apple', 'orange', 'lays' /* not fruit */, 'mango']. V allows multiline comments that start with the /* tag and end with the */ tag, and whatever is written in between these two tags is treated as a comment.

Ensure that when you start a multiline comment with /*, it has a proper and corresponding closing */ tag, as follows:

```
module main


/*
multiply accepts two integer arguments
namely x and y.
It then performs multiplication of input arguments and returns
the product which is again a type of integer as specified in
the function signature.
x is an input argument accepts values of type of int
y is an input argument accepts values of type of int
multiply function returns the result of type int which is a
multiplication of input arguments x and y
*/
fn multiply(x int, y int) int {
        return x * y
```

```
        }

fn main() {
        println(multiply(4, 5))
}
```

The comments can fit anywhere inside the module, function, or struct. Single-line comments can also start in the code where the statements end, as follows:

```
module main


// Space3D A struct indicating the 3 dimensional
// coordinate system
struct Space3D {
mut:
        x int // x is an integer field that represents
// coordinate
        y int // y is an integer field that represents
// coordinate
        z int // z is an integer field that represents
// coordinate
}


/*
get_point is a function that returns a struct of Type Space3D
with points x,y,z passed as input arguments to it
x is an input argument accepts values of type of int
y is an input argument accepts values of type of int
z is an input argument accepts values of type of int
get_point function returns a Struct result of type Space3D with
its coordinate set as value passed as input arguments x, y and
z
*/
fn get_point(x int, y int, z int) Space3D {
        return Space3D{
                x: x
                y: y
                z: z
```

```
        }
}

const origin = get_point(0, 0, 0) // Defining origin as a
// constant

fn main() {
        // origin := Space3D {x: 0, y: 0, z:0}
        println(origin)
}
```

The preceding code snippet shows a heavily commented V program that demonstrates the usage of single-line and multiline comments in the code.

Summary

In this chapter, we learned about various basic concepts in V such as variables, naming conventions associated when defining variables, and mutable and immutable variables. We also learned about the limitations of variables such as global scopes, redeclaration, and variable shadowing. Additionally, we learned how to define and work with constants and understood how to define constants of complex types such as structs and functions.

In the later parts of this chapter, we also explored various ways in which we can add descriptive and short-form code comments such as multiline and single-line comments.

Having gained knowledge on how to define and work with variables, constants, and code comments in V, we will move on to the next chapter where we will learn about primitive data types in V.

4

Primitive Data Types

In the previous chapter, we learned about working with variables and constants in detail. We also learned how to make single- and multi-line comments in the code that offer readability. In this chapter, we will learn about primitive data types.

As we learned when defining variables in the previous chapter, the variables we define hold data that belongs to certain types, such as string, Boolean, or rune, or it could be one of the numeric types, such as the family of integer types or floating-point types. This chapter will cover in detail the nature of these types and how to work with them.

In this chapter, we will learn various types and concepts related to primitive types as follows:

- Primitive data types
- The Boolean data type
- Numeric data types
- Operations on numeric data types
- The string data type
- The rune data type
- Operations on the string data type

By the end of this chapter, you will understand various primitive data types, such as strings, runes, and numeric types that include the family of integers and float types. You will also study string manipulation techniques and learn about what signed and unsigned integers are, and gain knowledge of the minimum and maximum values that these numeric ranges hold.

Technical requirements

Most of the code in this chapter can be run by accessing V's REPL as detailed in *Chapter 2, Installing V Programming*, under the *Accessing V Programming REPL* section. Due to the usage of same variable names across the code examples in this chapter, it is recommended to clear variables in REPL using the `reset` command.

You will find all the code snippets for this chapter here: https://github.com/ PacktPublishing/Getting-Started-with-V-Programming/tree/main/ Chapter04.

You can also save the code snippets to a filename of your choice with the .v extension and then access the command-line terminal to run the code as follows:

```
v run filename.v
```

Introducing primitive data types

Primitive data types are data types in their purest form and cannot be represented as a reference or derivation from other forms of data. V has a variety of primitive data types, such as Boolean, rune, and string, and numeric data types, such as integers, unsigned integers, and float types.

Before we delve into understanding data types, we will see how to determine the type of any variable using the built-in typeof() function as follows:

```
typeof(variable).name
```

With this very brief introduction to primitive data types, let's begin our journey to study these types in depth. We will begin with learning about the Boolean data type along with various operators that yield a Boolean result, with code examples.

The Boolean data type

A Boolean is a data type that is used to represent one of the two possible values, `true` or `false`. The following code demonstrates the declaration of a Boolean variable:

```
completed := true
```

From the preceding statement, we notice that the Boolean variable named `completed` is assigned with a value `true`. Notice that there are no quotes on the right-hand side of the statement. Declaring Boolean variables just needs either of the two values `true` or `false` to be assigned to the variable.

A Boolean data type is represented with the `bool` keyword. The usage of the `bool` keyword will be seen while defining arguments or return types for functions, or fields of a struct or interfaces.

Logical operators

Logical operators generally evaluate two operands and yield a Boolean result. The logical operator requires its operands to be of type `bool`.

Operator	Name	Description
&&	Logical AND	Evaluates to `true` when both the operands are `true`.
||	Logical OR	Evaluates to `true` if at least one of the operands is `true`.
!	Logical NOT	This is a unary operator and evaluates to `true` when the operand is `false` and vice versa.

Table 4.1 – Logical operators

The following code shows that performing various logical operations on Boolean variables will yield a Boolean result:

```
module main

fn main() {
        t := true
        f := false


        // Logical And using && operator
        and_tt := t && t
```

```
    and_tf := t && f
    and_ft := f && t
    and_ff := f && f

    println('Logical And using && operator')
    println('$t && $t = $and_tt')
    println('$t && $f = $and_tf')
    println('$f && $t = $and_ft')
    println('$f && $f = $and_ff')
    println('')

    // Logical OR using || operator

    or_tt := t || t
    or_tf := t || f
    or_ft := f || t
    or_ff := f || f

    println('Logical OR using || Operator')
    println('$t || $t = $or_tt')
    println('$t || $f = $or_tf')
    println('$f || $t = $or_ft')
    println('$f || $f = $or_ff')
    println('')

    // Logical not using ! Operator

    not_t := !t
    not_f := !f

    println('Logical not using ! Operator')
    println('!$t = $not_t')
    println('!$f = $not_f')
}
```

Here is the output:

```
Logical And using && operator
true && true = true
true && false = false
false && true = false
false && false = false

Logical OR using || Operator
true || true = true
true || false = true
false || true = true
false || false = false

Logical not using ! Operator
!true = false
!false = true
```

Relational operators

We learned that logical operations are performed when the operands are of the Boolean type only and the result of the Boolean operation is also of type `bool`. We can also perform operations that evaluate to a relation indicating a Boolean value on operands of a different data type. We can achieve that using relational operators.

Comparing two variables of the same data type using relational operators results in a Boolean data type `true` or `false`. The default value held by a Boolean field is `false`.

The following table shows the list of relational operators available in V:

Operator	Name	Description
<	Less than	Evaluates to true when the operand or left-hand side is of smaller value than the operand on the right-hand side of the statement; otherwise evaluates to false.
>	Greater than	Evaluates to true when operand on the left-hand side is a larger value than the operand on the right-hand side of the statement; otherwise evaluates to false.
==	Equals to	Evaluates to true if both the operands are equal; otherwise false.
!=	Not equals to	Evaluates to true if the operands are not equal to each other; otherwise false.
<=	Less than or equals to	Evaluates to true if the left-hand operand is less than or equal to the operand on the right-hand side of the statement.
>=	Greater than or equals to	Evaluates to true if the left-hand operand is greater than or equals to the operand on the right-hand side of the statement.

Table 4.2 – Relational operators

The following code demonstrates the use of various relational operators in V:

```
module main

struct Note {
        id          int
        detail      string
        completed bool
}

fn main() {
        mut n := Note{
                id: 1001
                detail: 'get groceries'
        }
        println(n.completed) // un-assigned bool field
```

```
// will be false by default

            // Comparing using Relational operator >
            if n.id > 1000 { // comparison of note id of
// integer type to another integer evaluates to a boolean
                    println('The note id is greater than
                    1000')
            } else {
                    println('The note id is less than
                    1000')
            }


            // Comparing using Relational operator ==
            if n.detail == 'get groceries' {
                    println('The note details about
                    groceries')
            }


            // Comparing using Relational operator !=
            if n.detail != 'get dairy products' {
                    println('The note does not details
                    about dairy products')
            }
}
```

Here is the output:

```
false
The note id is greater than 1000
The note details about groceries
The note does not details about dairy products
```

In the preceding code, the Note struct is initialized without assigning a completed value, which is a Boolean field, whereas the value for id is assigned. Now if we run the code, we see the default value for the completed Boolean field is false.

Also, the comparison of two values of the same data type as demonstrated in the preceding code evaluates to a Boolean result. Here, the id field of the Note struct is of data type int and is compared with the integer value 1000. Since id is initialized with a value of 1001, which is greater than 1000, the result of the comparison with the greater than > operator is evaluated to true and hence the code prints the text The note id is indeed greater than 1000 to the console. Next, we will examine numeric data types.

Numeric data types

The number types or numeric types in V constitute a family of primitive numeric types, such as integers and floating-point types. Integer and floating-point types are further classified based on the ranges they support. Let's learn about the numeric types in detail.

A variable assigned with a whole number will be of the default data type int, which represents a 32-bit integer:

```
x := 1
typeof(x).name // int
```

V supports assigning numbers with _ as a separator. The _ is just for readability and doesn't affect the value of the number being defined.

Consider the following declarations here:

```
i := 1_000
j := 1000


println(i == j) // true
```

V allows you to declare integer variables with hexadecimal notation beginning with 0x, binary notation beginning with 0b, and octal notation beginning with 0o, as shown here:

```
module main


fn demo() {
        h1 := 0x64          // hexadecimal starts with 0x
        b1 := 0b1100100     // binary starts with 0b
        o1 := 0o144         // Octal starts with 0o


        println('Value of var h1 with hexadecimal value
            : $h1')
```

```
        println('Data type of var h1 with hexadecimal
                value : ${typeof(h1).name}')
        println('Value of var b1 with binary value :
                $b1')
        println('Data type of var b1 with binary value :
                ${typeof(b1).name}')
        println('Value of var o1 with octal value :
                $o1')
        println('Data type of var o1 with octal value :
                ${typeof(o1).name}')
}

fn main() {
        demo()
}
```

Here is the output:

```
Value of var h1 with hexadecimal value : 100
Data type of var h1 with hexadecimal value : int
Value of var b1 with binary value : 100
Data type of var b1 with binary value : int
Value of var o1 with octal value : 100
Data type of var o1 with octal value : int
```

As demonstrated, notice that the values, regardless of their notation, hexadecimal, binary, or octal, are assigned as integer values, which is evident from the output shown.

Signed and unsigned integers

To start with, we have integer types `i8`, `i16`, `int` (32-bit integer), and `i64`, and unsigned integer types `byte` (which is referred to as `u8`), `u16`, `u32`, and `u64`.

Signed integers support both positive and negative ranges of values, typically to represent whole numbers. Unsigned integers don't represent any sign and are non-negative numbers. The following table indicates the range of all the integer types:

Type	Min	Max
i8	-128	127
i16	-32768	32767
i32	-2147483648	2147483647
i64	i64(-9223372036854775807 – 1)	9223372036854775807
byte (u8)	0	255
u16	0	65535
u32	0	4294967295
u64	0	18446744073709551615

Table 4.3 – Min and max values for signed and unsigned integers

In the preceding table, notice that the minimum value for `i64` is represented as `i64(-9223372036854775807 – 1)` because the C compilers parse literal values without sign and 9223372036854775808 overflows the maximum value possible for `i64`, which is 9223372036854775807. Ideally, there is no bigger type beyond `i64` that holds a value greater than 9223372036854775807. Hence, we represent the minimum value as the result of an evaluation of subtracting 1 from -9223372036854775807.

Floating-point types

Floating-point types are used to represent numeric values along with fractional parts. In V, we have two variants to support floating-point data types. They are `f32` and `f64`.

When it comes to floating-point types, we measure the ranges in terms of the largest and smallest non-zero fractions held by these types, which are tabulated here:

Type	Smallest non-zero fraction	Largest fraction
f32	1.40129846432481707092372 9583289916131280e-45	3.40282346638528859811704183484 516925440e+38
f64	4.94065645841246544176568 7 928682213723651e-324	1.79769313486231570814527423731 7043567981e+308

Table 4.4 – Floating-point type ranges

Mathematically, we can represent the largest and smallest ranges supported by the floating-point types, as tabulated here:

Type	Smallest non-zero fraction	Largest fraction
f32	$\dfrac{1}{2^{(127-1+23)}}$	$\dfrac{2^{127} \times 2^{24} - 1}{2^{23}}$
f64	$\dfrac{1}{2^{(1023-1+52)}}$	$\dfrac{2^{1023} \times 2^{53} - 1}{2^{52}}$

Table 4.5 – A mathematical representation of floating-point type ranges

Promoting numeric types

As the numeric types constitute a family of distinguished data types depending on the range and limits with regards to the numeric data it supports, the smaller types can easily be promoted or typecast to the bigger types. The hierarchy is shown as follows:

```
i8 → i16 → int → i64
                  ↘      ↘
                      f32 → f64
                  ↗      ↗
byte → u16 → u32 → u64 ↴
       ↘      ↘      ↘        ptr
       i8 → i16 → int → i64 ↲
```

Figure 4.1 – Promoting numeric types by hierarchy

The graphical representation taken from the official V documentation represents the possible promotion of data types, starting from the left to larger types on the right, denoted by arrows if they fit the data range.

To demonstrate the flow indicating the promotion of types, let's consider the following code:

```
module main

fn demo() {
        ia := i8(2)
        ib := i16(2)
        ic := int(2)

        println('----type definitions----')
        println('variable ia is of type:
            ${typeof(ia).name}')
        println('variable ib is of type:
            ${typeof(ib).name}')
        println('variable ic is of type:
            ${typeof(ic).name}')
        println('')
        iaa := ia + ia // i8 with i8 results i8
        ibb := ib + ib // i16 with i16 results i16
        icc := ic + ic // int with int results int

        println('----mixing types----')
        println('variable iaa is of type:
            ${typeof(iaa).name}, after adding type
            ${typeof(ia).name} with itself')
        println('variable ibb is of type:
            ${typeof(ibb).name}, after adding type
            ${typeof(ib).name} with itself')
        println('variable icc is of type:
            ${typeof(icc).name}, after adding type
            ${typeof(ic).name} with itself')
        println('')
        iab := ia + ib // i8 with i16 results in i16
```

```
        ibc := ib - ic // i16 with i32 results in i32


        println('----type promotion----')
        println('variable iab is promoted to type:
            ${typeof(iab).name}, after adding type
            ${typeof(ia).name} with ${typeof(ib).name}')
        println('variable ibc is promoted to type:
            ${typeof(ibc).name}, after subtracting type
            ${typeof(ib).name} with ${typeof(ic).name}')


        iba := ib / ia // the division of i16 and i8
                       // types


        println('Variable iba is promoted to the higher
                data type ${typeof(iba).name} which is
                carried from ib of type
                ${typeof(ib).name} divided from variable
                ia of type ${typeof(ia).name}')


        fa := f32(2)


        fa_iba := fa + iba // fa is type of f32 and iba
                           // is of type i32


        println('Variable fa_iba is promoted to the
                higher data type ${typeof(fa_iba).name}
                which is carried from fa of type
                ${typeof(fa).name} when added with
                variable iba of type ${typeof(iba).name}')
}


fn main() {
        demo()
}
```

```
----type definitions----
variable ia is of type: i8
variable ib is of type: i16
variable ic is of type: int

----mixing types----
variable iaa is of type: i8, after adding type i8 with itself
variable ibb is of type: i16, after adding type i16 with itself
variable icc is of type: int, after adding type int with itself

----type promotion----
variable iab is promoted to type: i16, after adding type i8
with i16
variable ibc is promoted to type: int, after subtracting type
i16 with int
Variable iba is promoted to the higher data type i16 which is
carried from ib of type i16 divided from variable ia of type i8
Variable fa_iba is promoted to the higher data type f32 which
is carried from fa of type f32 when added with variable iba of
type i16
```

We observe that the variable of type i8 when interacting with i16 is promoted to i16. Also, when you perform mathematical operations among numeric data types int and f64, the resulting value will be floating-point type f64. Now that we have understood the numeric data types, let's have a look at the operators available in V.

Operations on numeric data types

During the development of any software program, it is crucial to crunch numbers at some point. It might involve performing basic math or comparing numbers. V allows you to do so by providing various operators that can be applied to primitive types.

The operators that can be applied on numeric data types are categorized as follows:

- Arithmetic operators
- Bitwise operators
- Shift operators
- Relational operators

As we already learned about relational operators while learning about Boolean data types earlier in this chapter, we will take a look at the remaining arithmetic, bitwise, and shift operators and also understand how to work with these operators, with the example code using V.

Arithmetic operators

You can perform basic arithmetic operations on numeric types in V, such as addition, subtraction, multiplication, division, and modulo. The following table indicates the basic arithmetic operators and describes what the operator does when dealing with numeric data types:

Operator	Name	Applicable data types	Description
+	sum	integer, float, string	Adds two numeric types and returns the sum
-	difference	integer, float	Subtracts two numeric types and returns the value along with a sign-in case of a result less than zero
*	product	integer, float	Multiplies two numeric types and returns the product
/	quotient	integer, float	Divides two numeric types and returns the quotient
%	remainder	integer	Divides two numeric types and returns the remainder

Table 4.6 – Arithmetic operators

The following code demonstrates the usage of arithmetic operators:

```
module main

fn main() {
        a := 10
        b := 2

        // add using +
        sum := a + b
```

```
        // subtract using -
        diff := b - a


        // product using *
        prod := a * b


        // / results in quotient
        quotient := a / b


        // % modulo results in remainder


        remainder := a % b


        println('Sum of $a and $b is $sum')
        println('Subtracting $a from $b is $diff')
        println('Product of $a and $b is $prod')
        println('Quotient when $a divided by $b is
            $quotient')
        println('Remainder when $a divided by $b is
            $remainder')
}
```

Here is the output:

```
Sum of 10 and 2 is 12
Subtracting 10 from 2 is -8
Product of 10 and 2 is 20
Quotient when 10 divided by 2 is 5
Remainder when 10 divided by 2 is 0
```

Bitwise operators

Before we look at bitwise operators, let's look at some terminology related to binary, bits, and bytes.

The name binary indicates the possibility of two values. In a binary number system, these two values are often termed bits. A bit is either represented as 0 or 1. 8 bits form a byte.

As we saw, the integer types in V available are `i8`, `i16`, `int` (32-bit), and `i64` represent bits of information these data types can accommodate. The default `int` is 32 bits or 4 bytes in V. The max size of an integer type is `i64`, which is 8 bytes. To verify this, V offers an in-built `sizeof` function that takes one input argument as a variable you want to check the size for. The `sizeof` function returns the integer value that represents the number of bytes occupied by the variable whose size is being checked.

The following code shows usage of the `sizeof` function:

```
z := 345 //int is of 32-bit so size of variable z is 4 bytes.
println(sizeof(z)) // 4
```

Bitwise operations can only be performed on integer data types. The following are the bitwise operations tabulated that we can perform on integer types in V:

Operator	Name	Description
&	Bitwise AND	Performs bitwise AND operation of two integers and returns an integer value type
|	Bitwise OR	Performs bitwise OR operation of two integers and returns an integer value type
^	Bitwise XOR	Performs bitwise XOR operation of two integers and returns an integer value type
~	Bitwise NOT	Performs bitwise NOT operation on an integer and returns an integer value type

Table 4.7 – Bitwise operators

The following code demonstrates the usage of various bitwise operators:

```
module main

fn main() {
    a := 0b00000110 // 6
    b := 0b00000010 // 2

    // bitwise AND operation of two binary nums using & operator
    b_and := a & b

    // bitwise OR operation of two binary nums using | operator
```

```
    b_or := a | b


    // bitwise XOR operation of two binary nums using ^
operator
    b_xor := a ^ b


    // bitwise NOT operation of an binary nums using ~ operator
    not_a := ~a // Not operation yields value which is equal to
-(a+1) in its integer form
    println('Bitwise AND: ${a:08b} & ${b:08b} = ${b_and:08b}')
    println('Bitwise OR: ${a:08b} | ${b:08b} = ${b_or:08b}')
    println('Bitwise XOR: ${a:08b} ^ ${b:08b} = ${b_xor:08b}')
    println('Bitwise NOT: ~${a:b} = ${not_a:b}')
}
```

In the preceding code, we initialized variables a and b with a binary representation of 6 and 2, respectively. We then performed bitwise operations on these numbers. The result of these operations is printed to the console in binary format. We notice that to print variable a, for example, in binary format, we are specifying it as ${a:08b}. This will print the binary value of a in 8-bit format.

Here is the output:

```
Bitwise AND: 00000110 & 00000010 = 00000010
Bitwise OR: 00000110 | 00000010 = 00000110
Bitwise XOR: 00000110 ^ 00000010 = 00000100
Bitwise NOT: ~110 = -111
```

Shift operators

Shift operations performed on integer data types in V are logical in nature. The shift operator acts on the bit allocations of the integer and thereby moves the bits left or right based on the << and >> operators, respectively, filling the shifted positions with 0.

Here the symbols << and >> denote the left-shift operator and right-shift operator respectively.

The syntax for performing shift on integers is as follows:

```
INTEGER << POSITIONS_TO_SHIFT
```

The left-hand side of the preceding statement needs to be a value of the integer type followed by << or >>, followed by the number of positions to shift in the direction of the shift operator mentioned in between. << indicates to shift the bits to the left and >> indicates to shift the bits to the right. The right-hand side of the shift statement needs to be a non-negative integer. So, while programming, it is recommended to specify unsigned integers on the right-hand side of the shift operation.

Let's consider the following code, which demonstrates the shift operation on an integer of 8 bits:

```
module main

fn main() {

        // declare 8 bit integer with value 3
        a := i8(3)

        // 8 bits equals to 1 byte
        println('a is ${sizeof(a)} byte(s)') // a is 1
                                             // byte(s)

    // declare 8-bit unsigned integer to shift by 1 position
        pos := byte(1)

        // Shift left the value 3 by 1 position
        a_left_shift := a << pos
        println('${a} << ${pos} = ${a_left_shift}')
}
```

Here is the output:

```
a is 1 byte(s)
3 << 1 = 6
```

In the preceding code, the a variable with an assigned value of 3 is of type i8, which represents an 8-bit integer. In 8-bit format, the values of 3 are represented as follows:

2^7	2^6	2^5	2^4	2^3	2^2	2^1	2^0
0	0	0	0	0	0	1	1

Figure 4.2 – Representing the digit 3 in 8-bit format

Adding the value of powers of 2 where the bit value 1 is represented in the 8-bit block will evaluate to 3, as shown here:

```
0 * 2⁷ +  0 * 2⁶ + 0 * 2⁵ + 0 * 2⁴ + 0 * 2³ + 0 * 2² + 1 * 2¹ + 1
* 2⁰
```

```
1 * 2¹ + 1 * 2⁰
```

```
1 * 2 + 1 * 1
```

```
2 + 1
```

```
3
```

We defined the pos variable of type byte and assigned it with the value 1 to indicate the number of positions to shift. We then performed the left-shift operation on the a variable that holds the value 3 using the << operator. The bits shifted left by 1 position will now appear as follows:

2^7	2^6	2^5	2^4	2^3	2^2	2^1	2^0
0	0	0	0	0	1	1	0

Figure 4.3 – Digit 3 after left shift by 1 position becomes 6 as represented in 8-bit format

After the shifting operation, adding the value of powers of 2 where the bit value 1 is represented in the 8-bit block will evaluate to 6, as shown here:

```
0 * 2⁷ +  0 * 2⁶ + 0 * 2⁵ + 0 * 2⁴ + 0 * 2³ + 1 * 2² + 1 * 2¹ + 0
* 2⁰
```

```
1 * 2² + 1 * 2¹
```

```
1 * 4 + 1 * 2
```

```
4 + 2
```

```
6
```

As we understand how the shift operator works, let's look at the following example, which demonstrates the left shift of an initial integer of type i8 with value 1 and evaluates its value over the different positions it is operated by shifting positions that start from 0 to 7:

```
module main

fn main() {
        val := i8(1)

        bits := sizeof(val) * 8

        println('Performing left shift using <<
                Operator')

        for i in 0 .. bits {
                after_shift := val << i
                println('$val << $i = $after_shift
                        \/\/ type after shift operation:
                        ${typeof(after_shift).name}')
        }
}
```

Here is the output:

```
Performing left shift using << Operator
1 << 0 = 1 // type after shift operation: i8
1 << 1 = 2 // type after shift operation: i8
1 << 2 = 4 // type after shift operation: i8
1 << 3 = 8 // type after shift operation: i8
1 << 4 = 16 // type after shift operation: i8
1 << 5 = 32 // type after shift operation: i8
1 << 6 = 64 // type after shift operation: i8
1 << 7 = -128 // type after shift operation: i8
```

Note that for the last iteration, the `i8` variable with value 1 when shifted by 7 positions to the left the value becomes -128. This is because the range of values `i8` holds is from -128 to 127. With `i8` being a signed integer data type that holds both positive and negative numbers, the shift operation resulted in -128. If you perform `1 << 8`, the result will be 0, which is eventually pushing the most significant bit present in the extreme left out of the 8 bit bucket, resulting in all the bits becoming 0. Hence, the value will evaluate to 0. Now that we have learned about the numeric operators, let's look at the string data type.

The string data type

A string is used to represent words, phrases, or paragraphs of text. It can hold all the alphanumeric characters, special characters, and symbols.

The syntax to declare a variable of string data type is shown here:

```
<VARIABLE_NAME> := '<TEXT>'
```

From the preceding syntax, we notice that the variable name to the left of the `:=` symbol and value held by the variable is placed to the right. We also notice that the value held by the variable is enclosed in single quotes ('). V also allows you to declare variables with values enclosed in double quotes (").

For example, consider the following code snippet:

```
h := 'hello'
println(h) // hello
println(h.len) // 5
typeof(h).name // string
```

The preceding code demonstrates how to declare a string variable and the usage of the default field named `len`, which indicates the length of the string.

Working with the string data type

There are certain properties related to the string data type that you need to know when working with it. The string data type has the following properties:

- A string is a read-only array of bytes.
- Strings are immutable by default.
- You can declare a mutable string by using the `mut` keyword.
- The elements of a string cannot be mutated.

Let's look at each of these properties of the string data type in detail.

A string is a read-only array of bytes

A string in V is implemented using a struct type that has two fields, str and len, marked as public using the pub keyword. The str field is a byte pointer with a default value of 0 assigned to it. The len field is of the int type, representing the length of a string. So, a string in V is a read-only array of bytes. We will learn more about structs and struct fields in *Chapter 8, Structs* briefly, a string in V is often represented as a read-only array of bytes. Consider the following code:

```
fruit := 'Orange'
```

Here, the fruit variable is assigned the Orange string, which is six characters in length. Consider the following code:

```
println(typeof(fruit[0]).name) // byte
println(fruit[0]) // 79
```

The indexing of array elements in V starts from 0. As a string is a read-only array of bytes in V, if we index each character at a position and check for its data type, it will result in byte. The value held at each position returns the code point representation of the character. In this case, the decimal code point of the uppercase glyph *O* is 79. This shows that the string data in V is UTF-8 encoded.

Strings are immutable by default

Strings, when declared, are immutable by default. This means that you cannot modify or update a string once it is declared. Let's look at the following example:

```
s := 'hello' // variable s is immutable
s = 'Hello!' // this results in error
```

In the preceding code snippet, we declared a variable named s and assigned it the string value hello. Then, when we try to update the s variable with Hello!, this operation will result in an error that says s is immutable, declare it with mut to make it mutable.

So, the error is descriptive and suggests that we declare the variable as mutable with the mut keyword. Let's look at how to declare mutable strings and work with them.

Declaring mutable strings

You can declare a mutable string by using the mut keyword, and the value can be assigned to the variable using : = , as shown:

```
mut msg := 'Hello Friend!'
```

To alter the value of mutable variables, use = instead of : =. Now that we have defined a mutable string, let's try to replace the value of msg with something else, as shown:

```
msg = 'Hope you are doing good.'
println(msg) // Hope you are doing good.
```

With a mutable msg variable, you can also perform various other operations on strings, such as updating the msg variable by concatenating it with some other string using +, as shown:

```
msg +=  ' There is a surprise for you.'
println(msg) // Hope you are doing good. There is a surprise
for you.
```

We can see that we have updated msg as a result of the concatenation of msg and an extra string, using the concatenation operator +.

The elements of a string cannot be mutated

As we saw, the elements of a string can be indexed, which starts from position 0; however, programmers sometimes tend to update the value of a character in a string at a certain position. This is not allowed for strings even if they are declared as mutable because strings are read-only arrays of bytes:

```
mut greet := 'good Day'
greet[0] = 'G' // this results in error
```

If we try to update the element at position 0, which is the lowercase g for the variable named greet, with an uppercase G, it will throw an error that says cannot assign to s[i] since V strings are immutable (note, that variables may be mutable but string values are always immutable, like in Go and Java).

Before we understand how to perform various operations on the string data type, we will look at a new primitive type know as the rune, which is available in V.

The rune data type

Before we study working with runes in V, we will see why you might need to use the rune type. In UTF-16 encoding, code points lower than 2^{16} are encoded using a 16-bit code unit, which is equal to the numerical value of code point. The newer code points greater than or equal to 2^{16} are encoded by compound values of two 16-bit code units. For example, the Cyrillic lowercase á is a combination of U+0430 and U+0301. Such values are not used as characters in UTF-16 and there is no way to code them as individual code points. To overcome this limitation, we have the rune type in V. Using the rune type, we can represent compound code points as a single integer value that can range between 0 and 4294967295, as specified in *Table 4.3* for u32. So, with rune, it can be any u32 value, including surrogate code points and values that are not legal in Unicode code points.

Briefly put, character literals have a specific data type called a rune. A rune represents a Unicode code point. The rune type is an alias for the unsigned integer u32 in V.

Variables of the rune data type are declared with the value enclosed between backticks (`), as shown:

```
l := `a`
typeof(l).name // rune
```

By typecasting a rune to a string, you can perform string operations such as concatenating rune types with strings, checking whether a string contains a rune, and so on. Consider the following code:

```
beverage := 'café'
s := `é` //declare rune

beverage.count(s.str()) // 1
```

In the preceding code snippet, we declared a rune with the s variable, and we are typecasting it to the string type to count the occurrences of the value held by the s variable. Here, we are counting the occurrence of é in the variable named beverage with the value café. Now, let's understand the various operations that can be performed on the string data type.

Operations on the string data type

As we code, there are many occasions where we need to manipulate the representation of a string, be it writing a customized result to output or manipulating the string to use it for further evaluation.

String interpolation

String interpolation is the way to represent a string, along with a mix of different types of variables that get evaluated to their value and converted to the string data type during runtime.

String interpolation of primitive data types

String interpolation is achieved by the following syntax:

```
println('SAMPLE TEXT $primitive-data-type')
```

The preceding syntax shows how to perform string interpolation on primitive data types using the $ symbol as a prefix to the variable name. Consider the following code:

```
a := 'coding'
b := 'fun'
println('$a is $b')
```

Here is the output:

```
coding is fun
```

When accessing struct fields, it is recommended to wrap them with { and } double curly braces along with a prefix $ sign, as shown:

```
println('${STRUCT1.FIELD1} is ${STRUCT1.FIELD_2}')
```

The preceding code shows how to access struct fields using the approach of string interpolation. We will learn more about structs and accessing struct fields in *Chapter 8*, *Structs*.

String manipulation techniques

We will study the commonly used string manipulation and interpolation techniques in V.

Escaping special characters

Although it is recommended to enclose the value assigned to a string variable in single quotes ('), this becomes challenging when the value itself contains a single quote. For example, consider this sentence: It's my daughter's birthday. In this sentence, the single quote (') is present as a part of two words, It's and Daughter's. To declare such strings, we need to escape the quotes using \, a backward slash symbol, as shown:

```
sen := 'It\'s my daughter\'s birthday!'
println(sen)
```

Here is the output:

```
It's my daughter's birthday!
```

We notice that the string that has the content with the single quote (') is escaped using \, and it is made available as a part of the value.

Declaring raw strings

Occasionally, strings contain a backward slash symbol (\) as a part of the text being assigned to a variable. If not escaped, the \ will not appear and sometimes lead to special behavior when certain characters such as n and t occur right next to the backward slash. This means \n and \t have special meanings, indicating a new line and tab space respectively. In such situations, you can either add an extra backslash like \\ or declare the string as raw text by indicating it with the lowercase letter r before starting the single quotes.

The following code shows how the output appears when we do not have raw string declaration:

```
i :='hi \how are you/?'
println(i)
```

Here is the output:

```
hi how are you/?
```

Notice that the output is missing \, and to prevent it, we can declare it as a raw string, as follows:

```
i := r'hi \how are you/'
println(i)
```

Note the declaration of the i variable with the value that starts with ' ', which indicates assigning the raw text to the variable.

Here is the output:

```
hi \how are you/?
```

Concatenating strings

Concatenation is the process of combining two strings together. Using V allows you to concatenate strings using the + operator:

```
a := 'con'
b := 'cat'
println(a + b) // concat
```

Using + for string concatenation requires you to have both the literals being concatenated by the string data type. The following type of concatenation leads to an error:

```
i := 1
j := 'man army'
println(i + j) // i is int and j is string, throws error
```

The preceding concatenation will fail to execute as the i and j variables are not of the same data type. i is of type int and j is of the string data type. i + j will throw an error that says infix expr: cannot use string (right expression) as int.

But you can achieve the concatenation of variables of different data types that results in a string literal by using the string interpolation technique. The code will effectively be written as follows:

```
i := 1
j :='man army'
println('$i $j')
```

Here is the output:

```
1 man army
```

The preceding code snippet demonstrates the concatenation of variables of different data types, which is achieved using string interpolation, resulting in a string type.

Extracting a substring from a string literal

A string can be manipulated to extract only a part of it using the `substr` function. The `substr` function accepts two input arguments. The first one is an `int` type, which indicates the starting position in the string. The second argument is also an `int`, which indicates the ending position excluding itself.

Consider the following code snippet:

```
a :='Camel'
b := a.substr(0,3)
println(b) // Cam
```

The preceding code demonstrates the usage of a substring, where we are taking the substring out of the word `Camel` from the starting index `0` to the index that ends at position `3`, as assigned to the b variable. Now, the b variable will hold the value `Cam`.

Splitting a string

To split a string, we use the `split` function, which takes a single input argument of a string type that represents the delimiter value you want to split. The result of the split will return an array of strings that are a result of a split operation based on the delimiter provided:

```
sp :='The tiny tiger tied the tie tighter to its tail'
res := sp.split(' ')   // split by space as delimiter

println(typeof(res).name) // []string
println(res) // // ['The', 'tiny', 'tiger', 'tied', 'the',
//'tie', 'tighter', 'to', 'its', 'tail']
```

From the preceding code, we see that the sp string variable, when split using the delimiter as a space represented by `'   '`, resulted in an array of strings where each element represents a word of the sentence.

Converting a string to an array of runes

We learned that a string is implemented using a **struct** in V, and it has a `runes` method. This method returns an array where each element is of type `rune`. You will learn more about the struct methods in the *Defining methods for a struct* section of *Chapter 8, Structs*.

Consider the following code:

```
doge_moon :=  '🐕+ 🚀= 🌑'
doge_moon_runes := doge_moon.runes()
println(doge_moon_runes)
```

In the preceding code, we declared `doge_moon` as a variable of the string type and called the `.runes()` function. We are capturing the result of `.runes()` on `doge_moon` in a variable, `doge_moon_runes`, and then we print its output to the console. The preceding code gives the following output:

```
[`🐕`, `+`, `🚀`, `=`, `🌑`]
```

As you will note from the output, each element of the array is surrounded by backticks (`'`), and thus it indicates the resultant array is of the type `[]rune`. We can also check the type of `doge_moon_runes` using the following code:

```
println(typeof(doge_moon_runes).name)  //  []rune
```

Counting the occurrences of a substring in a string

The `count` function is used to identify the presence of a particular character or sequence of characters in a given string. `count` takes one argument of the string data type and returns the number of occurrences as the `int` data type. `count`, when no match is found, will return `0` as a result.

Consider the following example:

```
sp := 'The tiny tiger tied the tie tighter to its tail'
println(sp.count('t'))          // 10
println(sp.count('T'))          // 1
println(sp.count('tie'))        // 2
println(sp.count('-'))          // 0
```

The preceding code demonstrates the usage of `count` on the `sp` string variable. Then, we count the occurrences of lowercase t, uppercase T, a literal `tie`, and the symbol -, which resulted in occurrence counts of 10, 1, 2, and 0 respectively.

It is worth observing that the `count` method is case-sensitive and provided different counts for `t` and `T`.

Checking for the existence of a string using contains

We can check for the existence of a substring in a given string using `contains`. The `contains` function accepts one input argument of type string, and it evaluates for the presence of the input provided and returns `true` or `false` of the `bool` type. If the substring provided is found in the given string, `contains` will evaluate to `true`, failing which it evaluates to `false`.

The following code demonstrates the usage of `contains`:

```
module main

fn main() {
        hs := 'monday'

        if hs.contains('mon') {
                println('$hs contains mon')
        } else {
                println('$hs does not contains mon')
        }
}
```

Here is the output:

```
monday contains mon
```

From the preceding code, we are checking for the presence of the `mon` substring in the word `monday`, which evaluates to `true`, and hence it prints the output `monday contains mon`.

Now, let's change the code a bit and update the value for the variable to `Monday`, which has an uppercase letter `M`, instead of `monday`, and try to run the following code:

```
module main

fn main() {
        hs := 'Monday'
```

```
        if hs.contains('mon') {
                println('$hs contains mon')
        } else {
                println('$hs does not contains mon')
        }
}
```

Here is the output:

```
Monday does not contains mon
```

It is evident that `contains` is a case-sensitive operation and, in this case, it has evaluated to the `else` part of the `if` condition, printing the resultant literal `Monday does not contains mon`.

Summary

In this chapter, we have looked at various primitive data types, such as Boolean, numeric types such as integer and float, and string and rune. We also saw various operations, such as logical and relational operations on Boolean types. We then covered numeric types and learned about performing operations on numeric types, which included arithmetic, bitwise, and shift operations, along with detailed examples.

In the later parts of this chapter, we learned about string data types and understood various concepts of strings related to the mutability and immutability of a string. We also covered rune data types along with examples. In the final section of this chapter, we saw how to perform various operations such as string interpolation and different techniques to manipulate string types.

Having understood the primitive types in V, we will learn about working with complex types such as **arrays** and **maps** in V in the next chapter.

5
Arrays and Maps

Now that we have understood basic concepts in V, including variables, constants, and primitive types, in this chapter, we will focus on arrays and maps. We will learn about the different ways in which to declare arrays and how to initialize them during their declaration using the various properties available to define an array. Additionally, we will explore how to use the `in` and `<<` operators in arrays. Then, we will walk through the process of working with fixed-size arrays and multidimensional arrays. We will also gain a better understanding of arrays by implementing the most frequently performed operations on them, including cloning, sorting, and filtering techniques.

In this chapter, we will also learn about maps that hold data in the form of key-value pairs. Maps in V are often referred to as dictionaries just like other programming languages, such as C# and Python. We will examine how to work with maps and understand various ways in which we can declare and initialize maps. We will also learn how to perform various operations on a map such as retrieving the key-value pair given a key and handling the retrieval of non-existent keys using an `or` block. Then, we will learn how to add, update, and delete key-value pairs from a map.

In this chapter, we will cover the following topics:

- Arrays
- Maps

Technical references

The full source code for this chapter is available at `https://github.com/PacktPublishing/Getting-Started-with-V-Programming/tree/main/Chapter05`.

Arrays

An **array** is used to represent the collection of items. These items should be of same data types such as a list of marks obtained by a student or the names of members of a family. The items of an array must belong to a same data type.

In V, arrays can hold elements of similar data types that comprise primitive types or advanced types such as **structs**. By default, when an array is created, the memory allocation happens on the heap. You can create an array of a fixed size whose memory is allocated within the stack. Arrays can have more than one dimension. By default, arrays in V are immutable. Mutable arrays can be declared using the `mut` keyword.

The following is the syntax to declare an array:

```
arr := [VAL_1, VAL_2, .. VAL_N]
```

The preceding syntax demonstrates the declaration of a one-dimensional immutable array. The variable name is `arr` followed by the `:=` symbol. To the right of the statement, we have a list of values that must be of a similar data type. The values of `VAL_1`, `VAL_2`, and so on must be separated by a comma and all of these values should be enclosed between the `[` and `]` square brackets.

Different methods to declare arrays

Arrays can be declared in multiple ways. We will examine each of those approaches in further detail. Note that the arrays are immutable by default, and if we want to alter the elements or append elements to the array, we must declare them as mutable using the `mut` keyword.

Declaring and initializing arrays

An array can be declared and initialized with multiple values at a time. The following is a general way in which most programming languages allow you to declare and initialize an array:

```
mut sports := [ 'cricket', 'hockey', 'football' ]
```

Here, we declared a mutable array, named `sports`, and initialized the array with elements of the string type. The length of the `sports` array is 3, which is the number of elements in this array.

Declaring an empty array

An empty array must be declared with the `mut` keyword, which later allows you to append or update elements to it. The following code indicates how to declare an empty array:

```
mut <VAR_NAME> := []DATA_TYPE{}
```

The preceding syntax shows the declaration of an empty array. It starts with the `mut` keyword followed by VAR_NAME. VAR_NAME can be any meaningful name. Then, we are defining an empty [] square bracket without indicating the size of the array on the right-hand side of the := operator. DATA_TYPE could be any primitive type or advanced type such as a struct. Then, follows the {} with no properties defined.

Let's create an empty array of strings based on the previous syntax:

```
mut animals := []string{}
println(animals) //prints empty array: []
```

Now, we will append a value to the mutable array of `animals` strings:

```
animals << 'Chimpanzee'
animals << 'Dog'
println(animals) // ['Chimpanzee', 'Dog']
```

Declaring arrays using array properties

V allows you to declare an array by specifying the values of the array's properties such as `cap`, `len`, and `init`.

Declaring array with the len property

The `len` array property can be assigned to a value when declaring an array as follows:

```
mut i := []int{len:3}
println(i)
```

Here is the output:

```
[0, 0, 0]
```

In the preceding code, we declared a mutable array of integers with a default length of 3. When we print the array, we notice that the `i` array has three elements with a default integer value of 0 allocated in each of the three positions of the array. This method of declaring the array requires you to reallocate the values of the array elements, thus replacing the default value of 0.

Declaring an array with default initial values using init

We can define an array with the default value of all elements initialized to the same value using the `init` property, as follows:

```
mut j:= []int {len: 3, init: 1}
println(j)
```

Here is the output:

```
[1, 1, 1]
```

The preceding code demonstrates the usage of the `init` property, where we declare an integer array with an initial length of 3 and fill all of the three positions with a default value of 1, as specified.

Declaring an array with an initial capacity using the cap property

You can also define the array by specifying the capacity of the array during the declaration itself. This method of declaring mutable arrays generally improves the performance of element insertions into the array:

```
mut k := []int{cap: 2}
println(k)
```

Here is the output:

```
[]
```

Here, we are declaring a mutable array of integers with an initial capacity of 2 set to the `cap` array property. Note that the output when we printed the `k` array is an empty array. Therefore, it is evident that the declaration of an array with the `cap` property set reduces the number of reallocations needed.

We can append values to the array using the << operator, for example, k << 1. We will learn more about appending values to an array using the << operator in the later parts of this chapter.

Working with the len and cap array properties

Once declared, the array will expose two public read-only properties, namely, `len` and `cap`. The `len` property indicates the length of the array. Specifically, the length represents the number of elements that are actually present in the array. The other property, `cap`, denotes the capacity of the array.

Let's consider the following code, which demonstrates the usage of array properties:

```
mut sports := ['cricket', 'hockey', 'football']
println(sports.len) // Length of sports array
println(sports.cap) // Capacity of sports array
```

Here is the output:

```
3
3
```

We can observe that the `sports` string array has both a length and capacity of 3. With the `sports` array being mutable, let's examine how the length and capacity might change over the period of various operations performed on this array.

For example, if we delete an element from the `sports` array, then the lenght and capacity decreases by one:

```
sports.delete(2) // deleting football
println('Length of sports array: $sports.len')
println('Capacity of sports array: $sports.cap')
```

Here is the output:

```
Length of sports array: 2
Capacity of sports array: 2
```

We are deleting an element at index 2 from the `sports` array using the `delete` function. The `delete` function accepts the index of the element to be deleted. After the deletion of an element, both the length and capacity of the array is 2.

Now, let's add two new sports to the `sports` array using the `<<` operator:

```
sports << ['volleyball', 'baseball']
println(sports)
println('Length of sports array: $sports.len')
println('Capacity of sports array: $sports.cap')
```

Here is the output:

```
['cricket', 'hockey', 'volleyball', 'baseball']
Length of sports array: 4
Capacity of sports array: 4
```

From the preceding operation, we are adding two more elements to the sports array, such as volleyball and baseball. This operation will increase the length from 2 to 4, as we are adding two new types of sports to the array. The capacity before adding these two sports was 2; after this operation, the capacity becomes 4 because the capacity is *doubled* every time the length of elements exceeds the current capacity.

Accessing array elements using the index

Sometimes, you need to access a specific element in an array based on its position given that you know its position. V allows you to access array elements via their index. The index of an array starts from zero, and you can access any specific element of an array based on its index. The sports array has a length of three elements, so the last element's index is calculated as length of array - 1; in our case, it is 3 - 1, which becomes 2.

For example, if you want to access the second element in the sports array, you can do so as follows:

```
s := sports[1]
println(s) // hockey
```

Here, the syntax shows you how to access an item in the sports array at index position 1 enclosed between the [and] square brackets.

Accessing array elements using slices

Let's suppose you want to access a sequence of elements given a range, then you can follow the approach of slicing the array elements. The result of slicing the array provides a partial array of elements in the range provided. The syntax to slice over the elements of an array is shown here:

```
ARRAY_VAR[STARTING_INDEX .. ENDING_POSITION]
```

The preceding syntax represents slicing the elements of an array:

- ARRAY_VAR is the variable name of the array. The STARTING_INDEX, ENDING_ POSITION, and the .. operator that separates these two are wrapped in between [and] square brackets.

- STARTING_INDEX is an integer that represents the index of the element that we want to start slicing the array.

- ENDING_POSITION is also an integer that represents the actual position to which the elements are sliced, resulting in a partial array.

Similar to the majority of programming languages such as Python, C#, Java, C, and more, indexing in V starts from 0. This means the first element in the array is identified with index 0, the next element with index 1, and so on. We can assume that index + 1 is the actual number that represents the *position* of an element in an array. Let's consider the following example:

```
println(sports) // prints ['cricket', 'hockey', 'football']
println(sports[1..3]) // prints ['hockey', 'football']
```

In the preceding code, we slice the sports array to print the elements starting from index 1 to position 3. Notice the terms I have used here; the first number in the [1..3] range is 1, which indicates the *index*, and the other number, 3, indicates the *position*.

There are various conditions when slicing arrays:

- The starting index must be greater than or equal to 0.

- The starting index cannot be greater than the last index of the array, which is length - 1.

- If the starting index is not provided, then it is interpreted as 0.

  For example, the sports[..2] statement is similar to sports[0..2].

- The ending position must be greater than or equal to the starting index.

- The ending position must not be greater than the length of the array.

- If the ending position is not provided, then it is interpreted as the value of the length of an array. For example, for an array with 3 elements, the sports[1..] statement is similar to sports[1..3].

Operators used with arrays

To interact with arrays, V has various operators such as in and <<, which allow us to perform various operations on arrays. Let's try to understand these operators in more detail.

The in operator

The in operator can be used to find the presence of an element in an array. The result of the in operator is a Boolean value. So, we can also use this operator as a negation to verify if an element is not present in an array using !in.

The syntax to use the in operator with an array is shown here:

```
NEEDLE in HAY_STACK
```

The preceding statement represents the syntax for using the in operator with arrays. Here, the left operand NEEDLE represents the element that we want to verify whether or not it is present in an array. Additionally, HAY_STACK represents the variable name of the array. We must ensure that the type of left operand NEEDLE must match the type of elements held by the right operand which in our case is the HAY_STACK array.

Let's consider the following example:

```
odd := [1, 3, 5, 7]
println(3 in odd) // prints: true
println(8 !in odd) // prints: true
```

The preceding code demonstrates the usage of in and !in operators. The statement 3 in odd results in a boolean value true as the array named odd has the element 3 at index 2. Whereas, the statement 8 !in odd results in a Boolean value true as the statement reads *8 not in odd*.

The << operator

The << operator can be used to append values to the end of the mutable array. The following code demonstrates the process of appending a value to the array of integer values:

```
mut even := [2, 4, 6]
even << 8
println(even) // prints [2, 4, 6, 8]
```

The << operator also allows you to append arrays to a mutable array:

```
even << [10, 12, 14]
println(even) //prints: [2, 4, 6, 8, 10, 12, 14]
```

It is worth noting that the << operator is a multipurpose operator in V. It is used for the following purposes:

- To append values or an array of values to an array

- To perform a left shift operation on integers

We examined how to define arrays, but the arrays we declared until now allowed you to add an unlimited number of elements to them as they were not limited by size. We can also define arrays with predefined sizes, which are termed **fixed-sized** arrays in V. So, let's examine how to work with fixed-sized arrays in V.

Fixed-size arrays

V allows you to define arrays of a fixed size. This means their length cannot be altered once they are declared and, therefore, remains constant. To ensure the updating of the values of elements based on the index, it is recommended that you declare fixed-size arrays as mutable using the mut keyword.

Unlike other arrays, the memory allocation of fixed-size arrays takes place on the stack. The memory allocation on the stack allows you to use the fixed-size arrays as *buffers*.

Once you declare a fixed-size array of size *n*, all of the elements of the array are filled with a default value corresponding to the data type of array elements. That is, if the fixed array is of integers, the default value for the elements will be 0. Similarly, the default value for the string type fixed array will be an empty ' ' string.

Defining a fixed-size array

Let's consider the following code that demonstrates defining a fixed-size array of integers having four elements:

```
mut fix := [4]int{}
println(fix) // [0, 0, 0, 0]
```

Here, we can see that the default values of all the elements of the fixed-size array of integers are filled with zeros.

Updating the elements of a fixed-size array

Once you define a fixed-size array, you can add elements by referring to the index of the fixed-size array using the = sign:

```
fix[1] = 33
println(fix) //[0, 33, 0, 0]
```

As we have defined a mutable array of integers, named fix, in the preceding code, we are trying to update the value of the element at index 1 with a value of 33, using the = sign.

With fixed-size arrays, we cannot append values using the << operator. So, the fix << 44 statement will fail to execute and throw an error, saying error: invalid operation: shift on type [4]int.

The data type of a fixed-size array

Let's take a look at the data type of the fixed array we defined using the following code:

```
println(typeof(fix).name) // [4]int
```

The length of the fixed array we gave during the definition of a fixed array is embedded in its type and is presented as [4]int for a fixed array named fix.

Slicing a fixed-size array results in an ordinary array

Performing slicing on a fixed array results in an ordinary array. Let's slice the fix array, as follows:

```
s := fix[1..]
println(s) // [33, 0, 0]
```

Let's take a look at the type of s, which is obtained as a result of slicing a fixed array, as follows:

```
println(typeof(s).name) // prints: []int
```

Note that the result of slicing a fixed array is an ordinary array.

Multidimensional arrays

V allows the creation of multidimensional arrays. Let's create a two-dimensional array that holds the points on a two-dimensional plane with the coordinates of (0,0), (0,1), (1,0), and (1,1) representing a square of unit length:

```
mut coordinates_2d := [][]int{ len:4 , init: []int{len: 2}}
println(typeof(coordinates_2d).name)   // [][]int
println(coordinates_2d) // [[0, 0], [0, 0], [0, 0], [0, 0]]
```

We have initialized a mutable two-dimensional array of integers represented by type [] [] int. We initialized the array with the variable named coordinates_2d with the len property set to a value of 4. Then, we initialized each of the 4 arrays to be of length 2 with the init: []int{len: 2} statement. As we set the init property, each of the 4 arrays in the second dimension will be initialized with an array having a length of 2 elements, each with a default integer value of 0.

Let's check the length of the coordinates_2d two-dimensional array:

```
println(coordinates_2d.len) // 4
```

Let's define the arrays of length 2, which hold the point coordinates of a square of unit length:

```
point_1 := [0, 0]
point_2 := [0, 1]
point_3 := [1, 0]
point_4 := [1, 1]
```

The length of the two-dimensional array is 4, as we already defined it using the len:4 statement. So, it can accommodate 4 arrays, each having a length of 2 elements. Let's assign the coordinate values to the coordinates_2d two-dimensional array with each of the four point_1, point_2, point_3, and point_4 coordinates using the = sign, as follows:

```
coordinates_2d[0] = point_1
coordinates_2d[1] = point_2
coordinates_2d[2] = point_3
coordinates_2d[3] = point_4
println(coordinates_2d) // [[0, 0], [0, 1], [1, 0], [1, 1]]
```

Alternatively, you can add array items directly to the `coordinates_2d` multidimensional array instead of separately defining the arrays from `point_1` to `point_4`, as shown in the preceding code. The code for such an approach appears as follows:

```
coordinates_2d = [
    [0, 0],
    [0, 1],
    [1, 0],
    [1, 1],
]
```

Notice that even in this approach of adding items to an existing multidimensional array, we are using a = sign followed by the [open square bracket, and each element is a representation of integer array of length 2, as defined earlier when declaring the `coordinates_2d` multidimensional array. After specifying the individual elements, we then close the statement using the] closed square bracket.

Additionally, notice that a comma is specified after the last [1, 1] element of the `coordinates_2d` array in the preceding code. The comma after the last element is optional and can be ignored. This additional comma will be added when you perform code formatting of the file. Let's say you have a file named `file1.v` with the preceding code in the `main` function; running the `v fmt file1.v` command from Command Prompt will format your code. This makes your code look clean and readable.

Similarly, you can create a multidimensional array based on the example given for a two-dimensional array.

Performing various operations on an array

We can perform various operations on an array such as sorting, reversing, or filtering, to mention a few. We will examine the most commonly used array functions, including array cloning, sorting, filtering, and mapping techniques.

Cloning an array

To copy the array into another array, you need to use the `clone` function, which is available on the array to be copied. The traditional assignment of an array to a new variable is not allowed using `:=`, as this approach will produce unsafe code. To achieve this, we use the `clone` function, as demonstrated in the following code:

```
r := [1,2,3,4]
mut u := r.clone() // copies the array r to u
println(u)
```

Here is the output:

```
[1, 2, 3, 4]
```

In the preceding code, we can observe that the `r` immutable array is cloned to an `u` mutable array.

The direct assignment of an array to a new variable will throw an error. For example, let's consider what happens when we try to run the following code:

```
s := r // This will throw error.
```

The program will throw an error with the message that says `error: use array2 := array1.clone() instead of array2 := array1 (or use unsafe)`.

Another way to copy an array, as suggested in the previous error message, is to copy an array to a new variable using `unsafe`:

```
s := unsafe { r }
println(s)
```

Here is the output:

```
[1, 2, 3, 4]
```

Now, the `r` array has been successfully assigned to a new `s` variable using the `unsafe` block.

Sorting arrays

You can sort an array using the sort function that is available on the array. By default, the sort function that has been applied to an array will sort the elements of the array in ascending order. The sort operation alters the original order of the elements of the array. Therefore, the sorting can only be done on a mutable array.

The sort function optionally accepts a sort expression as an input argument. Generally, the sort expression indicates the order in which the elements need to be sorted. The sort expression is built using two special a and b variables and one of the > or < operators:

- The special a and b variables represent the elements of an array.
- The < operator is used to sort array elements in ascending order.
- The > operator is used to sort array elements in descending order or reverse order.

Having understood the basic principles of sorting arrays, we will demonstrate how sorting can be applied to arrays with elements of the integer, string, and struct types with examples.

Sorting the elements of an integer array

The following code demonstrates how to sort an integer array in ascending and descending order:

```
mut i := [ 3, 2, 8, 1]
i.sort() // ascending order
println(i)
i.sort(a > b) //descending order
println(i)
```

Here is the output:

```
[1, 2, 3, 8]
[8, 3, 2, 1]
```

Additionally, you can explicitly specify the sort expression as i.sort(a < b) to sort the array elements in ascending order.

Sorting the elements of an array of strings

Now, let's sort an array of strings and view what the results look like:

```
mut fruits := ['Apples', 'avocado', 'banana', 'Orange']

fruits.sort() // ascending order
println(fruits)
fruits.sort(a>b) // reverse order
println(fruits)
```

Here is the output:

```
['Apples', 'Orange', 'avocado', 'banana']
['banana', 'avocado', 'Orange', 'Apples']
```

Note that the ascending order sorts the strings based on the ASCII sequence.

Sorting the array with struct elements

The purpose of these special a and b variables will come in handy when the elements of any array have structs. In such cases, we can expand the `sort` statement to sort the array elements based on the fields of a struct.

For example, let's consider the following code that demonstrates how to sort arrays with elements as struct types:

```
module main

struct Student {
        id     int
        name   string
        class int
}

fn main() {
        // Declare an empty array
        mut students := []Student{}

        // Create students
        st1 := Student{
```

```
        id: 1
        name: 'Ram'
        class: 9
}
st2 := Student{
        id: 2
        name: 'Katy'
        class: 3
}
st3 := Student{
        id: 3
        name: 'Tom'
        class: 6
}

// Append all the students to the array
students << [st1, st2, st3]
println(students)

// Reverse Sort students by id
students.sort(a.id > b.id)

println('Students sorted in reverse order of id:')
println(students)

// Sort students by class in ascending order
students.sort(a.class < b.class)

println('Students sorted in ascending order of
        class:')
println(students)

// Sort students by name in reverse order
students.sort(a.name > b.name)

println('Students sorted in reverse order of
```

```
                         name:')
          println(students)
}
```

We created a struct named Student with three struct fields: id, name, and height. Then, we created three students and added these students to an array. Then, we sorted the students based on the id, name, and class fields. The result of sort operations performed on an array of the Student struct is shown here:

```
[Student{
    id: 1
    name: 'Ram'
    class: 9
}, Student{
    id: 2
    name: 'Katy'
    class: 3
}, Student{
    id: 3
    name: 'Tom'
    class: 6
}]
Students sorted in reverse order of id:
[Student{
    id: 3
    name: 'Tom'
    class: 6
}, Student{
    id: 2
    name: 'Katy'
    class: 3
}, Student{
    id: 1
    name: 'Ram'
    class: 9
}]
Students sorted in ascending order of class:
```

```
[Student{
    id: 2
    name: 'Katy'
    class: 3
}, Student{
    id: 3
    name: 'Tom'
    class: 6
}, Student{
    id: 1
    name: 'Ram'
    class: 9
}]
Students sorted in reverse order of name:
[Student{
    id: 3
    name: 'Tom'
    class: 6
}, Student{
    id: 1
    name: 'Ram'
    class: 9
}, Student{
    id: 2
    name: 'Katy'
    class: 3
}]
```

Filtering arrays

V allows you to filter arrays using a function, named `filter`, which has been accessed on the array variable. The `filter` function accepts a filter condition projected on each element of the array. The condition comprises an expression with the built-in `it` variable, which is used to represent the element that is being evaluated against the condition followed by the filter condition.

The filter results in a new partial array based on the filter condition and it does not act on the original array where the filter is applied. So, you can apply a `filter` function on both mutable and immutable arrays. Only the elements that satisfy the logic mentioned in the filter condition will be passed to the filtered array.

The result of a `filter` operation on an array always returns an array with elements that are of a similar type to the elements of the array where the filter is applied.

For example, if we want to filter all the numbers that are multiples of 3 in a given array of integers, we can apply the filter function, as follows:

```
f := [1, 2, 3, 4, 5, 6, 7, 8, 9]
multiples_of_3 := f.filter(it % 3 == 0)
println(multiples_of_3) // [3, 6, 9]
```

Filter functions also accept anonymous functions. It is noteworthy that such filters with anonymous functions might take more time to execute. Let's consider the following code:

```
fruits := ['apple', 'mango', 'water melon', 'musk melon']

fruits_starting_m := fruits.filter(fn (f string) bool {
        return f.starts_with('m')
})

println(fruits_starting_m)
```

Here is the output:

```
['mango', 'musk melon']
```

The preceding code applies `filter` onto the `fruits` array such that the fruit names starting with the letter m are added into the resulting array `fruits_starting_m`.

Applying mapping onto array elements

V allows you to map each of the elements of any array in order to produce a new array in another form. Unlike the `filter` function, which accepts a filter condition and only acts on the array elements that satisfy the filter condition, a map applies to all the elements of an array. The map function is available on an array variable that accepts the operation to be performed on each element of the array as an input argument. Each element of an array during the map operation is referenced by the built-in `it` variable.

Unlike the `filter` function, the result of the `map` function can produce an array that contains elements of similar or different types to that of the array on which the `map` function is performed.

Let's consider the following example that appends the salutation to each name of the string array:

```
visitor := ['Tom', 'Ram', 'Rao']
res := visitor.map('Mr. $it')
println(res)
```

Here is the output:

```
['Mr. Tom', 'Mr. Ram', 'Mr. Rao']
```

The `map` function on an array can also take anonymous functions as input arguments. For example, consider the following code that demonstrates the use of the `map` function of an array with an anonymous function:

```
colors := ['red', 'blue', 'green', 'white', 'black']

colors_with_letter_e := colors.map(fn (c string) int {
    if c.contains('e') {
        return 1
    } else {
        return 0
    }
})

println(colors_with_letter_e)
```

Here, we are mapping over the array of colors where the color name has a letter e within it. Then, we are building a resulting array of integers as a result of the map function indicating the presence of letter e with 1 and 0 otherwise. Now that we have learned all about arrays, let's move on to learning about maps.

Maps

A **map** is used to represent a collection of key-value pairs. The keys need to be of a primitive data type. A map is defined using the map keyword. By default, maps are immutable. We can define a mutable map using the mut keyword.

Maps are like dictionary types in other programming languages such as **Dictionary** in C#, **HashMap** in Java, and **dict** in Python. We will explore how to work with maps, including various ways in which to initialize maps. Then, we will look at how to add, update, or delete key-value pairs from the map.

The explicit initialization of a map

The following code presents the syntax to define a map in V:

```
mut MAP_NAME := map[KEY_TYPE]VALUE_TYPE{}
```

The preceding syntax shows the explicit initialization of an empty mutable map. Here, MAP_NAME is a variable name for the map that follows a standard variable naming convention. Then, to the right-hand side of :=, we have used the map keyword. KEY_TYPE must be a primitive data type such as string, rune, and voidptr or a numeric type. KEY_TYPE must be represented between [and] square brackets. After the key type is specified in square brackets, we need to mention the value type followed by empty { and } curly brackets.

As the explicit initialization doesn't support key-value pairs to be passed as parameters between { and }, we can initialize the map with the syntax shown here:

```
MAP_NAME[KEY_1] = VALUE_1
MAP_NAME[KEY_2] = VALUE_2
.

.

MAP_NAME[KEY_N] = VALUE_N
```

Note that the values for a map can be initialized by mentioning the key in between the [and] square brackets followed by a = sign and then the value to the right-hand side of the expression.

To demonstrate the usage of a map, let's declare a map of `books` that holds a book name as a key and the page count as a value:

```
mut books := map[string]int{}
```

We defined a mutable map of books with keys that hold the book name and the value is of the `int` type to store the page numbers. Now, let's add a couple of books to our `books` map, as follows:

```
books['V on Wheels'] = 320
books['Go for Dummies'] = 279


println(books)
```

Here is the output:

```
{'V on Wheels': 320, 'Go for Dummies': 279}
```

The short syntax initialization of a map

You can also initialize a map with key values during the declaration itself using the short syntax shown here:

```
mut MAP_NAME := {
    KEY_1: VALUE_1
    KEY_2: VALUE_2

    .

    .

    KEY_N: VALUE_N
}
```

The preceding syntax demonstrates how to define a mutable map with a variable, named `MAP_NAME`, that follows the standard variable naming convention in V. Then, the value is initialized to the right-hand side of the `:=` sign, which starts with a `{` that accepts various key-value pairs specified in each line. These key-value pairs are wrapped in `{` and `}` curly brackets. If you are defining a map in a single line, it is recommended that you separate the key-value pairs using a `,` comma symbol.

Let's create a map of marks obtained by a student in various subjects:

```
mut student_1 := {
    'english' : 90,
```

```
    'mathematics' : 96,
    'physics' : 83,
    'chemistry' : 89
}
println(student_1)
```

Here is the output:

```
{'english': 90, 'mathematics': 96, 'physics': 83, 'chemistry':
89}
```

The count of key-value pairs in a map

You can check the number of key-value pairs present in a map using `len`, which is a read-only property available on the map variable.

Let's print the total count of key-value pairs present in the `student_1` map that we defined earlier:

```
cnt := student_1.len
println('There are $cnt key-value pairs in student_1 map')
```

Here is the output:

```
There are 4 key-value pairs in student_1 map
```

Retrieving a value given the key of a map

Let's suppose we want to retrieve the marks for the `physics` subject from the `student_1` map. We can write the following code:

```
println(student_1['physics']) // 83
```

Accessing a non-existent key from a map

If we try to access a key that doesn't exist in a map, it will return 0 if the value is an integer type, and in the case of a string, an empty string will be returned:

```
println(student_1['geography']) // 0
```

In the preceding code, we are trying to access the marks for the `geography` subject that do not exist for the `student_1` map.

Handling the retrieval of missing keys in a map

We can gracefully handle the scenario in which a key being retrieved is not found in a map using the or {} block and display intuitive error messages.

Let's consider the same scenario when we try to access the marks for the geography subject; instead of returning 0, which is done by V, we can use the or {} block to show a detailed error message:

```
sub := 'geography'
res := student_1[sub] or { panic('marks for subject $sub not
yet updated')} // throws error
```

Here is the output:

```
V panic: marks for subject geography not yet updated
```

Therefore, we can customize the behavior when a key is not found in a map that we are searching for using the or {} block.

Updating the value of the key in a map

You can update the value of the key in a map by specifying the map variable name followed by the key that already exists and then specifying the value after the = sign.

To demonstrate how to update the value of a map's key-value pair, let's consider the map of student_1. We will update the marks for the english subject from 90 to 93:

```
student_1['english'] = 93
println(student_1)
```

Here is the output:

```
{'english': 93, 'mathematics': 96, 'physics': 83, 'chemistry':
89}
```

Deleting a key-value pair from a map

You can delete the key-value pair from a mutable map using the delete function that is available on the map variable. The delete function accepts the key of the map that needs to be deleted and updates the map variable with the result.

For example, if we want to delete the marks for the `physics` subject from the `student_1` map, then you can write the statement as follows:

```
println('Key-Value pairs before deleting a key: $student_1.
len')
student_1.delete('physics')
println('Key-Value pairs after deleting a key $student_1.len')
```

Here is the output:

```
Key-Value pairs before deleting a key: 4
Key-Value pairs after deleting a key: 3
```

After the deletion of the `physics` key from the `student_1` map, the length property reduced its count by 1 and the new length of `student_1` became 3.

Summary

In this chapter, we understood the concept of working with arrays and maps in detail. Regarding arrays, we understood the different types of arrays, including fixed-size arrays and multidimensional arrays, and performed various operations such as cloning, sorting, and filtering arrays.

We also learned about maps, how to initialize them, and performed various map operation techniques such as counting key-value pairs and retrieving values given keys. We also learned how to manipulate the key-value pairs of a map, including updating and deleting key-value pairs.

During the process of learning about the basic concepts of V programming, it is essential to know how to branch out the code to perform a different job using logical or relational operators and how to recursively perform operations. V will facilitate writing this type of code with the help of conditional statements, such as `if`, and to perform repeated operations or iterate over the bunch of items in a given array or map using iterative statements. So, let's jump into the next chapter, *Conditionals and Iterative Statements*, to learn more about these concepts.

6
Conditionals and Iterative Statements

Conditional programming helps you to control the execution of a program in the desired manner. This means you can write software that meets all of the scenarios for the various sets of use cases with the help of conditional branching. Thus, in each conditional branch, you can write the logic for a specific use case. In this chapter, we will learn about conditional statements, in detail, in the V programming language. We will examine how to work with conditional blocks such as `if`, `if-else`, and chaining `else-if`, along with the use of the `goto` statement supported by labels. We will also cover the `match` block in depth, which is used for conditional code branching.

In the later parts of this chapter, we will look at the various types of iterations. Writing a program using iterative code blocks allows you to access each entity in a collection. With this approach, you have focused on access to each element in the collection and, therefore, can apply special processing to the entity for each iteration. For each element in the iteration, you can perform special processing in combination with conditional branching; this will programmatically reflect the functionality of any use case. In this chapter, we will perform iterations on maps and arrays using the `for` loop, and then we will look at the different ways in which to write iterative statements using the `for` loop.

Through this chapter, we will cover the following main topics:

- Conditional blocks
- Iterative statements

By the end of this chapter, you will be able to write conditional and iterative statements in V.

Technical requirements

For those of you who would like to follow along with the code examples in this chapter, it is recommended that you install V, as mentioned in *Chapter 2, Installing V Programming*. To write V programming, you can use a command-line Terminal with editors such as **Nano** or **Vim**. Alternatively, you can also use **Notepad ++**, **Visual Studio Code**, or any other programming editor of your choice.

The full source code for this chapter is available at `https://github.com/PacktPublishing/Getting-Started-with-V-Programming/tree/main/Chapter06`.

Conditional blocks

Often, it is a requirement to perform certain routines based on the outcome of an operation. In any programming language, we can achieve this via conditionals such as an `if` statement or a `match` block. In this section, we will gain an understanding of each of the conditional blocks offered by V in further detail. We will begin our discussion with the `if` statement.

The if statement

Conditionals such as `if` and `if-else` blocks in V allow you to make decisions based on the outcome of the condition being evaluated in the statement. The evaluation might involve the result of logical or relational operators. The `if` statement in V allows you to create a special code block that will only be executed upon satisfying the condition mentioned in the `if` statement. The following is the syntax for writing an `if` block:

```
if CONDITION {
        // CONDITION evaluated to true
}
```

The preceding syntax demonstrates how to write an `if` statement. It begins with the `if` keyword and is followed by a condition that evaluates to a Boolean result of `true` or `false`. Then, the syntax follows the special code block wrapped inside curly brackets, `{` and `}`, which is only executed when the result of the condition evaluates to `true`.

This is a basic syntax that tells us how to write an `if` statement. However, the `if` statement has various flavors to it:

- The `if-else` statement
- Chaining with `else-if`
- The `if` conditions with a `goto` statement

Let's learn about each of these in further detail.

The if-else statement

The `if-else` statement allows you to decide whether to execute a certain piece of code provided the condition in the `if` statement evaluates to `true` as well as the `else` case to handle the code when the condition evaluates to `false`. In the `if-else` block, either the code inside the `if` block or the `else` block will execute based on the evaluation of the condition.

The following code shows the syntax to write an `if-else` block using the `if` and `else` keywords:

```
if CONDITION {
        // CONDITION evaluated to true
} else {
        // CONDITION evaluated to false
}
```

Chaining with else-if

As mentioned earlier, in the case of `if-else`, at least one of the code blocks will be executed. In some scenarios, you might want to have a custom check with the code being executed when the first condition of the `if` statement fails to evaluate to `true` and does not directly allow the control flow to execute the code in the `else` block. You can write an `else if` statement for such use cases.

The syntax for writing `else if` along with `if` and `else` is shown here:

```
if CONDITION_1 {
        // CONDITION_1 evaluated to true
} else if CONDITION_2 {
        // CONDITION_2 evaluated to true
} else {
        // None of the Conditions evaluated to true
}
```

Unlike the `else` block, the `else if` block requires a condition to be specified. However, it is optional to have an `else` block. You can chain many such `else if` blocks that specify different conditions in each of the `else if` blocks along with `if`. However, once the control enters any of the blocks that satisfy the condition, the code specific to that block is executed and the control comes out of the `if`, `else-if`, and `else` chains completely.

Let's consider the following code:

```
module main


fn breakfast_menu(day string) {
        if day == 'Monday' {
                println('Bread, Jam, Half boiled Egg')
        } else if day == 'Tuesday' {
                println('Bread, Jam, Juice')
        } else if day == 'Wednesday' {
                println('Milk, Bread, Fruit Bowl')
        } else if day == 'Thursday' {
                println('Bread, Jam, Juice')
        } else if day == 'Friday' {
                println('Cereals, Bread, Jam, Half boiled
                        Egg')
        } else if day == 'Saturday' {
                println('Milk, Bread, Fruit Bowl')
        } else if day == 'Sunday' {
                println('Cereals, Bread, Jam, Half boiled
                        Egg')
        } else {
```

```
                println('invalid input')
        }
}

fn main() {
        breakfast_menu('Saturday')
}
```

The output for the preceding code is as follows:

```
Milk, Bread, Fruit Bowl
```

The preceding code demonstrates the chaining of else-if statements that performs checks for various days and then prints the menu that matches the day input parameter for the breakfast_menu function. There are no limitations to the number of else-if conditions, but the code looks dirty and redundant. We will learn how to use match for such scenarios, write the reusable code, and make the code look neat using match blocks in the coming sections of this chapter.

The if conditions with a goto statement

V allows you to label code and refer to the execution control using the goto keyword. The goto statement needs to be specified with a label that indicates the control to navigate to the label when the execution flow encounters a goto statement. A label is defined with general text followed by a : colon symbol.

Note

A goto statement must be wrapped inside an unsafe block. This is because goto allows the program execution flow to move past variable initialization or return to code that accesses memory that has already been freed. As the goto statement requires an unsafe block, it should be avoided to prevent the risk of violating memory safety.

The following code shows the syntax of a goto statement wrapped inside an unsafe block:

```
sample_label:
        println('this will be called when goto is invoked')
```

```
unsafe {
    goto sample_label
}
```

Now, let's take a look at the following code that demonstrates the usage of the goto statement:

```
module main

import os

fn main() {
        improper_input_age:
        println('Invalid input. Please provide value
                greater than 0.')

        next_person:
        inp := os.input('Enter your age:')

        if inp != 'stop' {
                age := inp.int()

                if age >= 13 {
                        println('You are allowed to watch
                                this movie')
                } else if age > 0 && age < 13 {
                        println('Parental Guidance is
                                required to watch this movie')
                } else if age <= 0 {
                        unsafe {
                                goto improper_input_age
                        }
                }
                unsafe {
                        goto next_person
                }
        }
}
```

The preceding code checks the age variable provided from the standard input console. Then, it checks whether the age input is meeting certain criteria. If age is a negative number, it moves to the logic labeled as improper_input_age and executes the code that prints the Invalid input. Please provide value greater than 0 message. For all other inputs except stop, it checks for the eligibility to watch a movie with parental guidance or not. Then, it accepts the age input of the next person in the queue using another goto statement labeled next_person. Additionally, we can observe that the goto blocks are wrapped in unsafe blocks. When the input is provided as stop, the program exits from the execution.

Now that we have gone through the details of if statements and how these statements can be used with code examples, we will proceed with learning more about how the match block can be used in conditional programming.

match

A match block does the job of *pattern matching* the conditions specified inside its code block. In most scenarios, it is also used as a switch case. As V does not have a **switch case** block, similar functionality can be achieved with the help of a match block.

First, we will learn about the basic syntax of a match block, and then, in the subsequent sections, we will look at various use cases of a match block, including the following:

- A match block as a switch case
- The cascading conditions of a match block
- Using match with an else condition along with enum types
- Using match block for pattern matching

The following is the syntax for a match statement using the match keyword:

```
match VALUE {
    CONDITION_1 { /*CONDITION_1 matched.*/ }
    CONDITION_2 { /*CONDITION_2 matched.*/ }
    ..
    CONDITION_N { /*CONDITION_N matched.*/ }
    else { /*None of the patterns match. Do other routine.*/ }
}
```

In the preceding syntax, the `match` keyword expects `VALUE` to be of a similar data type to that of all the conditions defined inside it. Additionally, it is necessary to declare that all of the patterns, which we add in place of conditions in the preceding syntax, belong to a similar data type. Failing this, the program will throw an error that says `cannot match with condition`. Unless the match is being declared for `enum` types, it is mandatory to declare an `else` condition that acts as a sink when none of the conditions get a satisfactory match.

To summarize, the `match` block expects the following:

- The conditions should be of a similar type to the value being passed to the `match` block.

- The return types of all the conditional branches of a `match` block must be of a similar type.

- The `match` block must be exhaustive in the case that not all of the possible conditions are specified. This can be achieved using the `else` block at the end.

- The case of a `match` block cannot be handled more than once. This is applicable for ranges too, and V does the automatic checking of duplicate ranges or overlapping ranges of a pattern match during compile time and throws an error that says `match case is handled more than once`.

- Now that we have understood the basic syntax of a match block, we will now proceed further and examine the different ways in which you can work with a `match` block.

A match block as a switch case

A `match` block in V can be used as a traditional switch case. We can understand this by rewriting the code example that we have seen in the *Chaining with else-if* section using the `match` block. Let's take a look at the following code:

```
module main

fn breakfast_menu(day string) {
        match day {
                'Monday' {
                        println('Bread, Jam, Half boiled Egg')
                }
                'Tuesday' {
                        println('Bread, Jam, Juice')
```

```
                }
        'Wednesday' {
                println('Milk, Bread, Fruit Bowl')
        }
        'Thursday' {
                println('Bread, Jam, Juice')
        }
        'Friday' {
                println('Cereals, Bread, Jam, Half
                        boiled Egg')
        }
        'Saturday' {
                println('Milk, Bread, Fruit Bowl')
        }
        'Sunday' {
                println('Cereals, Bread, Jam, Half
                        boiled Egg')
        }
        else {
                println('invalid input')
        }
    }
}

fn main() {
        breakfast_menu('Sunday')
}
```

The following is the output of the preceding code:

```
Cereals, Bread, Jam, Half boiled Egg
```

The preceding code matches the day input provided as an argument to the breakfast_ menu function and prints the breakfast menu corresponding to the day that matches the condition defined in the match statement. When the day is provided with the value of Sunday, the match statement that has the condition defined for Sunday will be executed.

The cascading conditions of a match block

In cases where multiple conditions of a match block perform the same operation, we can cascade the conditions of a match block using a comma. In the previous example, the breakfast menu is the same for the Friday and Sunday values; similarly, the breakfast menu is the same for the Tuesday and Thursday values. So, we can merge the logic for the day that matches the days of Friday and Sunday in a single condition of the match block along with Tuesday and Thursday, as shown here:

```
module main

fn breakfast_menu(day string) string {
        return match day {
                'Monday' {
                        'Bread, Jam, Half boiled Egg'
                }
                'Tuesday', 'Thursday' {
                        'Bread, Jam, Juice'
                }
                'Wednesday' {
                        'Milk, Bread, Fruit Bowl'
                }
                'Friday', 'Sunday' {
                        'Cereals, Bread, Jam, Half boiled
                        Egg'
                }
                'Saturday' {
                        'Milk, Bread, Fruit Bowl'
                }
                else {
                        'invalid input'
                }
        }
}

fn main() {
        friday_menu := breakfast_menu('Friday')
```

```
        println(friday_menu)

        sunday_menu := breakfast_menu('Sunday')
        println(sunday_menu)

        tuesday_menu := breakfast_menu('Tuesday')
        println(tuesday_menu)

        thursday_menu := breakfast_menu('Thursday')
        println(thursday_menu)
}
```

The following is the output of our preceding example code:

```
Cereals, Bread, Jam, Half boiled Egg
Cereals, Bread, Jam, Half boiled Egg
Bread, Jam, Juice
Bread, Jam, Juice
```

After cascading the conditions of a match block using a comma, the breakfast_menu function is still the same but with less redundant code and is easier to read. Additionally, it is refactored to return a value of the string type. Now, it returns the menu that matches the day input argument with one of the conditions of the match block.

Using match with enum types

A match block in V also accepts enum types to match its enclosing conditions. The fields of an enum type are represented with field names prefixed with a (.)dot symbol. As an enum type has a defined set of fields, the use of else is *prohibited* when all the fields of enum are mentioned in the match conditions:

```
module main

enum Day {
        sunday
        monday
        tuesday
        wednesday
        thursday
```

```
          friday
          saturday
}


fn breakfast_menu(day Day) string {
      return match day {
            .monday {
                    'Bread, Jam, Half boiled Egg'
            }
            .tuesday, .thursday {
                    'Bread, Jam, Juice'
            }
            .wednesday {
                    'Milk, Bread, Fruit Bowl'
            }
            .friday, .sunday {
                    'Cereals, Bread, Jam, Half boiled
                    Egg'
            }
            .saturday {
                    'Milk, Bread, Fruit Bowl'
            }
      }
}


fn main() {
      friday_menu := breakfast_menu(Day.friday)
      println(friday_menu)

      sunday_menu := breakfast_menu(Day.sunday)
      println(sunday_menu)

      tuesday_menu := breakfast_menu(Day.tuesday)
      println(tuesday_menu)

      thursday_menu := breakfast_menu(Day.thursday)
```

```
        println(thursday_menu)
}
```

Here is the output of our code example:

```
Cereals, Bread, Jam, Half boiled Egg
Cereals, Bread, Jam, Half boiled Egg
Bread, Jam, Juice
Bread, Jam, Juice
```

To demonstrate the usage of enum fields as conditions of a match block, we have declared an enum type, named Day, with the fields representing the days of a week. The breakfast_menu function has a match block that returns the menu as a string type for the input argument of enum, named Day. Additionally, the conditions of the match block are the fields of the Day enum prefixed with a dot symbol. As we have specified all the fields of the Day enum in the conditions, that leaves us with the match block, which has exhausted all possible matches that it could cover for all of the scenarios. So, in this case, the usage of the else block is prohibited.

Using match with an else condition along with enum types

If we do not mention all of the enum fields in the list of conditions of a match block, then we have to specify the else condition for that match block.

The following code demonstrates the usage of else in a match block with enum types as conditions:

```
module main

enum Day {
        sunday
        monday
        tuesday
        wednesday
        thursday
        friday
        saturday
}

fn weekend_breakfast_menu(day Day) string {
```

```
        return match day {
            .sunday {
                    'Cereals, Bread, Jam, Half boiled
                    Egg'
            }
            .saturday {
                    'Milk, Bread, Fruit Bowl'
            }
            else {
                    'Sorry, we are closed on weekdays!'
            }
        }
    }

fn main() {
    sunday_menu := weekend_breakfast_menu(Day.sunday)
    println(sunday_menu)

    tuesday_menu := weekend_breakfast_menu(Day.tuesday)
    println(tuesday_menu)
}
```

The following is the output:

```
Cereals, Bread, Jam, Half boiled Egg
Sorry, we are closed on weekdays!
```

In the preceding code, we replaced the method and only wanted to show the menu during the weekend on saturday and sunday. As the match block doesn't utilize all of the fields but only specifies the fields as .saturday and .sunday conditions, we must use else in the match block. If we do not write else here, it will lead to an error that displays a message, saying error: match must be exhaustive (add match branches for: .monday, .tuesday, .wednesday, .thursday, .friday* or else {} at the end)*.

Pattern matching using match

So far, we have read about the usage of the `match` block as a traditional switch case. However, the actual power of `match` can be leveraged for pattern matching.

The following code demonstrates the use of `match` for pattern matching:

```
module main

fn main() {
        age := 18
        res := match age {
                0...18 { 'Person with age $age classified as a
                     Child' }
                19...120 { 'Person with age $age classified as
                     an Adult' }
                else { '$age must be in the range 0 to
                     120' }
        }
        println(res)
}
```

Here is the output:

```
Person with age 18 classified as a Child
```

The preceding code demonstrates the usage of a `match` block with ranges. Notice that the range uses . . . (that is, three dots) to define the *range* as a case inside a `match` block. The *range* defined as a conditional case of a `match` block is inclusive of the last element in the range. The code checks the value of `age`, and if it is in the range of *0 to 18* inclusive then the person is classified as a child. The other case checks for the adults whose age is in the range of *19 to 120* inclusive. If the number does not fall into any of the two conditional branches with the ranges from *0 to 18* and *19 to 120*, then a message is displayed to provide an age between *0 and 120* to classify a person properly.

In this section, we learned, in detail, about the `if` statement and the `match` block and also understood their syntax and how to use those conditional blocks with code examples. Now, it's time for us to jump onto the next part of this chapter, where we will learn about working with iterative statements in V.

Iterative statements

During software development, you might need to process or handle each element of the collection such as an array or a map. Sometimes, you will want to access each element of the collection and change its value or just read it for further processing. In V, you can achieve this by writing iterative statements using `for` loops.

The `for` loop, which is used as an iterative statement in V, is used to iterate over the elements of a collection. The collection is generally an array that has elements of a certain data type, or it could be a `map` that holds data in the form of key-value pairs.

In this section, we will examine the very basic syntax of how to write a `for` loop in V. Then, we will explore various ways in which to work with `for` loops, including how to write the following:

- A `for` loop on maps
- A `for` loop on arrays
- A `for` loop without an index on the array
- A traditional C-style `for` loop
- A reverse `for` loop
- A `for` loop on a range
- A bare `for` loop or an infinite `for` loop
- Using `break` in a `for` loop
- Using `continue` in a `for` loop
- Using the `continue` and `break` statements with `labels`

To begin, let's take a look at the following syntax that shows you how to write a `for` loop using the `for` keyword and the `in` operator:

```
for INDEX_VAR, VALUE_VAR in COLLECTION {
    // access each element's index and its value
}
```

From the preceding syntax, you can observe that the `for` loop begins with the `for` keyword, and then it declares two variables: `INDEX_VAR` and `VALUE_VAR`. Then, the `in` operator comes in; this expects the variable that holds the collection to be specified after it.

The INDEX_VAR variable is of the integer data type and the VALUE_VAR represents a variable whose type is the same as the value held by the collection.

Note that COLLECTION can be an array or a map. There are certain things you need to bear in mind when writing for loops on maps, arrays, and numeric ranges:

- A for loop on a map will generate the key and value of each item being iterated.
- An optional index variable can be declared when working with arrays using a for loop.
- A for loop on ranges will only allow you to declare the variable that holds the value of the item in the range being iterated.

Now that we have examined the basic syntax of writing a for loop, we will look at how to work with a for loop with collections such as arrays and maps. Following this, we will look at different approaches in which to implement logic using a for loop. So, let's start by learning how to use for loops on maps.

A for loop on maps

The following syntax shows you how to iterate over the key-value pairs of a map using a for loop:

```
for KEY_VAR, VALUE_VAR in MAP_VAR {
    // access key and value here
}
```

In the preceding syntax, KEY_VAR and VALUE_VAR indicate the variables that hold the key and value of the map for every iteration.

Let's consider the following code:

```
module main

fn main() {
        lottery := {
                    'First':       1000
                    'Second':      700
                    'Consolation': 200
        }

        for k, v in lottery {
```

```
                    println('$k prize lottery amount: $v USD')
        }
}
```

The following is the output of our code example:

```
First prize lottery amount: 1000 USD
Second prize lottery amount: 700 USD
Consolation prize lottery amount: 200 USD
```

The preceding code iterates over the key-value pairs of a map. In the `for` statement, the two k and v variables represent the key and the value of the elements of the map variable, named `lottery`.

Sometimes, we are interested in either the key or the value during iterations. In such scenarios, we can ignore the key or value that is being returned during the iteration of a map using a `for` loop. In order to ignore either a key or a value, use _ as a replacement in the respective position within the `for` statement. The usage of _ prevents you from assigning the key or value to a variable and is often considered a memory-efficient approach.

The following code ignores the keys of the `basket` map during the iteration using a `for` loop:

```
module main

fn main() {
        basket := {
                    'apples':  10
                    'bananas': 12
        }

        mut total := 0
        for _, v in basket {
                total += v
        }
        println('Total number of fruits: $total')
}
```

The following is the output:

```
Total number of fruits: 22
```

In the same way that we ignored the keys of a map variable named basket, we can ignore the values too, using _ in the place of the variable v.

A for loop on arrays

Performing iterations on array types will provide you with an optional index along with the value of each item being iterated. The following is a code example:

```
module main

fn main() {
        fruits := ['apple', 'banana', 'coconut']
        for idx, ele in fruits {
                println('idx: $idx \t fruit: $ele')
        }
}
```

Here is the output:

```
idx: 0    fruit: apple
idx: 1    fruit: banana
idx: 2    fruit: coconut
```

In the preceding code, the for loop iterates over an array named fruits with the values of a string data type. The block of code iterates over the array named fruits using a for loop that defines two variables: idx and ele. The idx variable will always be of the integer data type and signifies the index of each element, starting from 0, and increments by 1 for every iteration. The ele variable holds the value of the element for that iteration. In this case, the value is of a string type, which holds the name of a fruit from the fruits array. After the index and element, we specify the in operator, and then we specify the collection ... over which we are iterating. In this case, the collection is an array of fruits.

A for loop without an index on the array

The `for` loop on arrays can only have one variable defined in its syntax, which holds the value of the element. Therefore, we have the option to define a variable that indicates the index of the element.

The following code demonstrates the `for` loop on an array without declaring the index variable for each iteration:

```
module main

fn main() {
        col := [1, 2, 3, 4, 5, 6, 7]
        for val in col {
                if val % 2 == 0 {
                        println('$val is Even')
                } else {
                        println('$val is Odd')
                }
        }
}
```

Here is the output:

```
1 is Odd
2 is Even
3 is Odd
4 is Even
5 is Odd
6 is Even
```

In the preceding example, pay attention to the `for val in col` statement. This only defines the `val` variable, which holds the values of the variable for that iteration.

A traditional C-style for loop

Sometimes, we need to skip *n* number of elements using a `for` loop. You can achieve this by writing the `for` loop in a way that you generally use for most programming languages such as C# or C. V allows you to write the `for` loop in the same way that you do in C programming. The following code displays the traditional C-style `for` loop in V:

```
module main

fn main() {
        sample := [3, 4, 23, 12, 4, 1, 45, 12, 42, 17, 92,
                38]
        for i := 0; i < sample.len; i += 3 {
                println(sample[i])
        }
}
```

The following is the output:

```
3
12
45
17
```

A reverse for loop

To iterate over the elements of an array from the last element to the first, you can write the traditional `for` loop syntax just as you do in C or C#.

The following code prints the elements of an array from the last element to the first:

```
module main

fn main() {
        subjects := ['zoology', 'chemistry', 'physics',
                'algebra']

        for i := subjects.len - 1; i >= 0; i-- {
                println(subjects[i])
        }
}
```

A for loop on a range

Unlike iterating over arrays, you cannot declare an index variable when iterating over a range using a `for` loop.

You can iterate over the elements of a range using a `for` loop, as follows:

```
module main

fn main() {
        for val in 0 .. 4 {
                println(val)
        }
}
```

Here is the output:

```
0
1
2
3
```

Here, we declared a range in the `for` loop that iterated over the sequence of four numbers starting from 0. In the `for` loop, we then printed the value of each element in the range 0..4 using the `for` loop.

A bare for loop or an infinite for loop

We can also write a `for` loop without any conditions or `in` operator. Such `for` loops are often referred to as infinite `for` loops or endless `for` loops.

Infinite `for` loops, when used in console programs, are typically used to accept user input and determine the actions based on it. Generally, these types of `for` loops require external intervention to stop their execution from infinite looping. These external factors, such as forcibly stopping the program from its execution or a user input that matches the condition, are handled inside the code.

The syntax just involves a simple `for` block that loops without any conditions, as shown here:

```
module main

fn main() {
        mut count := 1
        for {
                println('Hi $count times')
                count += 1
        }
}
```

As you might have gathered, without any limiting conditions, the `for` loop, in the preceding example, keeps printing until we forcefully stop the program execution. There are no limiting conditions in the preceding code. We can introduce conditions for such scenarios using the `break` keyword.

Using break in a for loop

V allows you to abruptly exit out of a `for` loop whenever it encounters the `break` keyword.

The `break` keyword halts the iterations performed during the `for` loop and exits it. In general, the `break` statement is used to terminate the `for` loop after meeting certain criteria that we define.

Consider the following code that depicts the usage of `break` inside a `for` loop:

```
module main

import os

fn main() {
        mut count := 0
        input := os.input('Enter number of times to
                Greet:')
        limit := input.int()
        for {
                if count >= limit {
```

```
                        break
            }
        println('Hi')
        count += 1
    }
    println('Greeted Hi $count times')
}
```

The output for the preceding code is as follows:

```
Enter number of times to Greet:3
Hi
Hi
Hi
Greeted Hi 3 times
```

Note that we are limiting the number of times a loop iterates. The number of iterations are controlled by user input. Upon meeting the `count >= limit` condition, we are making an exit from the `for` loop using the `break` statement.

Using continue in a for loop

Sometimes, the program needs to decide whether to proceed with the execution of the code block or to skip and start processing the next element iteration. In such cases, you can use the `continue` keyword, which, when encountered, will halt the execution of the current iteration and proceed with the next item in the `for` loop.

The following code depicts the usage of `continue` in a `for` loop:

```
module main

fn main() {
    for i in 0 .. 10 {
        if i % 2 == 0 { // skips printing number
// that is a multiple of 2
            continue
        }
        println(i)
    }
}
```

Here is the output:

```
1
3
5
7
9
```

In the preceding code, the `for` loop is printing odd numbers. So, we are making an early exit from the iteration with the help of a `continue` statement if the value held by the `i` iteration variable is an even number. Note that the `continue` statement will be executed when the result of the `i % 2 == 0` statement equals `true`.

Using the continue and break statements with labels

Just as the `goto` statement refers to a label, you can also write `continue` and `break` statements with labels.

Let's consider the following example:

```
module main

import os

fn main() {
        input := os.input('Enter the number of
              multiplication tables to print:')
        limit := input.int()
        if limit <= 0 {
                return
        }
        first_loop: for i := 1; i <= 10; i++ {
                println('Printing multiplication table for
                        $i')
                for j := 1; j <= 10; j++ {
                        mul := i * j
                        println('$i * $j = $mul')
                        if mul >= limit * 10 {
                                break first_loop
```

```
                                    }
                        }
                    println('*********')
                }
        }
```

Here is the output:

```
Enter the number (1 to 10):2
Printing multiplication table for 1
1 * 1 = 1
1 * 2 = 2
1 * 3 = 3
1 * 4 = 4
1 * 5 = 5
1 * 6 = 6
1 * 7 = 7
1 * 8 = 8
1 * 9 = 9
1 * 10 = 10
*********
Printing multiplication table for 2
2 * 1 = 2
2 * 2 = 4
2 * 3 = 6
2 * 4 = 8
2 * 5 = 10
2 * 6 = 12
2 * 7 = 14
2 * 8 = 16
2 * 9 = 18
2 * 10 = 20
```

The preceding code prints multiplication tables between 1 and 10; however, we can limit the number of tables that are being printed using the input to the program. We break the execution after we meet the input criterion based on the evaluation of the `mul >= limit * 10` statement results to `true`. The statement breaks the execution of the `for` loop, labeled `first_loop`, when it encounters the `break first_loop` statement. Therefore, the labeled `break` or `continue` statement can be used to control the execution of nested `for` loops.

Summary

In this chapter, we learned about writing conditional blocks and iterative statements. We understood how to use the `if` conditional and its other flavors, such as `if`, `if-else`, and chaining multiple `else-if` statements. Then, we learned how the `goto` statement can help you to navigate to any labeled piece of code when working with `if` blocks. In the *Conditional blocks* section, in addition to the `if` statement, we learned about the `match` block. We refactored the code example that is used to implement a chained `else-if` statement using the `match` block; following this, the code looked more organized and readable. Additionally, we understood the usage of a `match` block as a traditional switch case and learned how to implement pattern matching with it.

This chapter also covered iterative statements in depth. We learned how to write the syntax of a basic `for` loop, and then we discovered how to deal with arrays and maps using a `for` loop. In addition to this, we explored how to reverse iterate over a collection using a `for` loop and learned how to iterate on a range of values. Then, we examined how to skip from one iteration to the next one with the help of the `continue` keyword and abruptly exit out of the `for` loop using the `break` keyword. We also learned the art of using the `continue` and `break` statements using labels and, thus, wrote a piece of code that prints multiplication tables.

Having understood the concept of conditionals and iterative statements, we will now proceed toward learning about the basic but most crucial building blocks of software programming, that is, functions. Functions are blocks of code that wrap a logical set of instructions to run a piece of work. In the next chapter, we will discover how to work with functions in V.

7
Functions

So far, throughout this book, we have learned about the basic programming features of V, including arrays, maps, conditionals, and iterative statements. It's time for us to learn about writing functions in V. Most programmers, when writing software applications, prefer to group a set of statements such as variable declarations and perform arithmetic or logical operations with them, or iterate over the elements of an array or map and then filter them according to their need. The art of wrapping or grouping a logically related set of statements, providing it with a name, and optionally providing input arguments and return types is often referred to as the process of writing a function.

Before we begin, here is a brief outline of the topics we will cover in this chapter:

- Introducing functions
- Understanding function types
- Understanding function features

By the end of this chapter, you will have a solid understanding of the various types of functions V offers. Additionally, you will be able to write basic functions, anonymous functions, and higher-order functions. This chapter will also guide you through the vast features that functions come equipped with along with code examples for each feature.

Technical requirements

The full source code for this chapter is available at `https://github.com/PacktPublishing/Getting-Started-with-V-Programming/tree/main/Chapter07`.

Introducing functions

Functions allow you to logically wrap a set of instructions inside a code block to perform a specific operation. Often, it is necessary to provide them with a name that represents the underlying logic they encompass. Functions might take arguments as an input to perform an operation. Additionally, they might return the result of the operation performed by it. Therefore, functions offer code reusability and code readability.

A function can call another function if required to do so. In some scenarios, a function can call itself to perform a recursive operation.

V facilitates working with functions. A function in V is created using the `fn` keyword. The typical syntax to create a function in V is shown here:

```
ACCESS-MODIFIER fn FUNCTION_NAME(ARGUMENT1_NAME ARGUMENT1_
DATATYPE, ARGUMENT2_NAME ARGUMENT2_DATATYPE) RETURN_DATATYPE {
    OPERATIONS
}
```

In the preceding syntax, we can identify two parts of a function:

- A method signature or a function signature
- A function body

In general, the method or function signature is identified by the first line of the method. It has an access modifier, an `fn` keyword followed by the method name, and then, in parentheses, you have the comma-separated arguments with the argument name and the argument data type. Then, the last part of the method signature indicates the return type.

The method body will have a set of routines that the function will perform with the arguments (if any are provided) and, optionally, return a value, as defined in the method signature.

As we have just learned the basic syntax to write a function, we will proceed further to understand the different types of functions that are available in V using code examples.

Understanding function types

In this section, we will examine the different types of functions that can be written in V. We will begin with the basic or most commonly written function based on the syntax that we just learned. Then, we will take a look at how to write anonymous functions that do not have any function name and explore various ways in which we can work with anonymous functions. Following this, we will learn how to create functions that accept other functions as input arguments and look at functions that return other functions as their return types, which are often referred to as higher-order functions.

The main function

To begin, let's start with the main function. This function is the entry point in a V file or a project with multiple V files or modules inside it. Whenever you run the file using v run filename.v or a project using the v run . command, the execution control looks for the presence of the main function and starts from there. However, there are certain things we need to bear in mind when we write main functions:

- The main function should not accept any input arguments.

- The main function should not have a return type.

- The main function needs to be placed in a file at the root of the directory structure.

- The module or file where we write the main function is specified with the module main statement.

The following code demonstrates the main function:

```
module main

fn main() {
    println('Welcome to the World of V!')
}
```

As stated earlier, from the preceding code, we can observe that the main function doesn't have any input arguments. Additionally, it doesn't have a return type. We can also observe that the module main statement is specified at the top. This enables V to identify and start the execution from the main module's main function.

You will learn more about input arguments and return types in the coming sections of this chapter. This section also mentions modules, but we will cover modules in more detail in *Chapter 9, Modules*.

Basic functions

Put simply, basic functions are just logically related statements wrapped inside a function body with a given function name. They can also accept input arguments that might be deemed necessary to perform operations and can specify the return type if the function returns any value as a result of the operation performed within the function. There are various features that functions, in V, offer to programmers, and we will go through them in the subsequent sections of this chapter. However, to begin, let's start with a simple function. The following code shows a simple function named `greet`:

```
fn greet(msg string) {
    println(msg)
}
```

The preceding code demonstrates the implementation of a `greet` function. The `greet` function simply does the job of printing the message provided to it as an input argument. Let's say you call the `greet('Hello, Welcome to the world of V programming')` function; it will print that message to the console. We can observe that the `greet` function has no return type. We will look at how to create and work with functions that return values in the subsequent sections of this chapter.

As we have just learned how to create a very basic function, V allows you to create various other types of functions such as anonymous functions and higher-order functions. Next, we will explain how to write anonymous functions and higher-order functions, in detail, using code examples.

Anonymous functions

Anonymous functions are function blocks that don't have any name and can be created inside another function. Anonymous functions can be declared and assigned to a variable on the fly such that they can be invoked by calling that variable. The scope of anonymous functions is within the scope of the function where they are declared. Let's start by gaining a better understanding of anonymous functions with the following code:

```
module main

fn main() {
        greet := fn (name string) {
                println('Hello, $name')
        }
        greet('Pavan')
        greet('Sahithi')
}
```

The preceding code depicts the creation of an anonymous function that greets us with `Hello`. The anonymous function is assigned to a variable, named `greet`, and accepts an input argument `name` of the `string` type. An anonymous function can also return values; however, in this case, it just prints the greeting to the standard output using the `println` statement.

Here is the output:

```
Hello, Pavan
Hello, Sahithi
```

Anonymous functions can also be used while working with arrays. For a detailed demonstration of how to use anonymous functions, please refer to the *Apply mapping on array elements* section of *Chapter 5*, *Arrays and Maps*.

Higher-order functions

V allows you to define functions that either accept or return other functions. These types of functions are often referred to as higher-order functions. In the following sections, we will examine, in detail, the higher-order functions that accept functions as input arguments and also the ones that return another function as their return type.

Higher-order functions that accept other functions as input arguments

In this section, we will understand the concept of higher-order functions that accept another function as input arguments via a detailed demonstration. Let's define three functions that return the message of a `string` type, as follows:

```
fn greet_morning() string {
        return 'Good Morning'
}

fn greet_noon() string {
        return 'Good Afternoon'
}

fn greet_evening() string {
        return 'Good Evening'
}
```

Note that the three functions are basic functions, and each of them returns the string that represents a different greeting: Good Morning, Good Afternoon, and Good Evening. Now we will create a higher-order function that accepts two input arguments. One of the input arguments is a function type, whereas the other will be of the string type:

```
fn greet(f fn () string, name string) string {
        return '$f(), $name!'
}
```

Here, the greet function is a higher-order function that accepts any function that returns a string. For the greet function to accept a function, it must follow the criterion specified in the method signature of the greet function. So, let's take a look at the f fn () string input argument. Note that the input argument named f has to be a function, as it is identified by the function of the fn () string type. In the fn () string expression, the empty brackets, (), specify that the function being passed has to be a function that doesn't accept any input arguments, and the type after fn () in the fn () string expression indicates that the function must return a value of the string type.

As greet_morning, greet_noon, and greet_evening meet the required criteria to be provided as arguments to the greet function as its first input argument, let's try passing them as follows:

```
mut res := greet(greet_morning, 'Pavan')
println(res)

res = greet(greet_evening, 'Sahithi')
println(res)
```

Here, we are passing the greet_morning and greet_evening functions as an input argument each time with the name of the person that will be greeted.

The signature of the function that is being passed as an argument to the higher-order function must match the definition specified within the input argument of the higher-order function.

Additionally, notice that when we are passing functions as arguments, we are simply specifying the name of the function without any parentheses. Any arguments that are required by the function being passed as an argument will have to be provided by the higher-order function. So, in this case, the higher-order greet function must take the responsibility of providing arguments to the function it is accepting as an input argument.

Apart from passing predefined functions as input arguments to higher-order functions, you can also pass anonymous functions. Let's take a look at the following code that shows you how to pass an anonymous function as an input argument to the higher-order function:

```
res1 := greet(fn () string {
        return 'New year greetings to you'
}, 'Sahithi')
println(res1)
```

In the preceding code, we are passing the anonymous function as an input argument to the higher-order function. Here, the anonymous function matches the `fn () string` signature that is defined for the `f` input argument in the higher-order `greet` function.

The following shows the full source code of this example along with the output:

```
module main

fn greet_morning() string {
        return 'Good Morning'
}

fn greet_noon() string {
        return 'Good Afternoon'
}

fn greet_evening() string {
        return 'Good Evening'
}

fn greet(f fn () string, name string) string {
        return '$f(), $name!'
}

fn main() {
        mut res := greet(greet_morning, 'Pavan')
        println(res)
```

```
        res = greet(greet_evening, 'Sahithi')
        println(res)


        res = greet(fn () string {
                return 'New year greetings to you'
        }, 'Sahithi')
        println(res)
}
```

Here is the output:

```
Good Morning, Pavan!
Good Evening, Sahithi!
New year greetings to you, Sahithi!
```

The higher-order greet function is invoked with greet_morning as an input argument along with the name of Pavan and greet_evening as an input argument along with the name of Sahithi. It prints the respective greetings that match the inputs arguments provided to it. The higher-order greet function, when passed with an anonymous function that matches the type of its first input argument which is fn () string. The greet function thus processes the result and greets us with the message returned by the anonymous function.

Higher-order functions that return other functions

In this section, we will examine a detailed demonstration of higher-order functions that return other functions.

For this kind of higher-order function, note that the function that is being returned by the higher-order function must match the return type specified by the signature of the higher-order function. Specifically, it must match the following:

- **The number of input arguments**: The returning function must accept the same number of input arguments as specified in the return type of the higher-order function.

- **The type of input arguments**: The input arguments of the function being returned must match the data type of arguments specified in the return type function signature of the higher-order function.

- **The return type of the function**: The returning function must return the same type as specified in the return type function signature of the higher-order function.

For the purposes of a demonstration, we are trying to create a function that returns the operation of the desired type by accepting an input argument that indicates the operation.

Let's define an enum, named `Operation`. The `Operation` enum defined next represents its fields as the list of operations that we want to perform:

```
enum Operation {
        add
        sub
        mul
}
```

Next, we will define three functions, `adder`, `subtractor`, and `multiplier`, that perform the logic representing their respective function names, as follows:

```
fn adder(i int, j int) int {
        return i + j
}

fn subtractor(i int, j int) int {
        return i - j
}

fn multiplier(i int, j int) int {
        return i * j
}
```

Now, we will define a higher-order function that accepts the `Operation` enum. This function returns one of the functions among `adder`, `subtractor`, and `multiplier` based on the matching operation handled by a `match {}` block, as follows:

```
fn fetch(op Operation) fn (int, int) int {
        return match op {
                .add {
                        adder
                }
                .sub {
                        subtractor
                }
```

```
        .mul {
            multiplier
        }
    }
}
```

The fetch function is a higher-order function that returns another function having a fn (int,int) int signature.

In our case, the return type specified on the higher-order fetch function is fn (int, int) int. This means that the higher-order fetch function can only return functions that meet the following criteria:

- The returning function must accept two input arguments.
- Both of the input arguments must be of the int type.
- The returning function must return an int type.

So, the return type specified on the higher-order fn(int, int) int function matches with the adder, subtractor, and multiplier functions, which we defined earlier. Now, we will declare two integer variables and perform various operations by querying the higher-order fetch function to return the function by passing the field of the Operation enum:

```
i := 2
j := 5

// get adder function and execute it
mut f := fetch(.add) // return adder function
mut res := f(i, j) // calls adder(2, 5)
println('sum of $i and $j: $res')
```

The preceding code calls a higher-order fetch function with the add field of the Operation enum passed as an input argument. In this scenario, fetch(.add) will return the adder function, which is then assigned to the f variable. As we gain access to the adder function in the form of a variable, we will execute the adder function stored in the f variable by passing the i and j integers as input arguments, which match the type of the input arguments, as defined in the signature of the adder function.

Similarly, we can perform subtraction and multiplication by fetching the respective function after passing the respective sub and mul enum fields of the Operation enum as an input argument to the fetch function. The following is the main function that invokes all of the higher-order functions:

```
fn main() {
        i, j := 2, 5
        mut f := fetch(.add) // return adder function
        mut res := f(i, j) // calls adder(2, 5)
        println('sum of $i and $j: $res')


        f = fetch(.sub) // returns subtractor function
        res = f(i, j) // calls subtractor(2, 5)
        println('difference of $i and $j: $res')


        f = fetch(.mul) // returns multiplier function
        res = f(i, j) // calls multiplier(2, 5)
        println('product of $i and $j: $res')
}
```

Here is the output:

```
sum of 2 and 5: 7
difference of 2 and 5: -3
product of 2 and 5: 10
```

From the preceding code, we can observe that the fetch(.sub) statement returns the subtractor function, which is assigned to f, which is a mutable variable. At this point, we have access to the subtractor function. To execute, we then pass the i and j integers that hold the values of 2 and 5, respectively. As we have defined the subtractor function that returns the integer value of the operation performed, we will store that value in res, which is a mutable variable. The previous code also indicates how to fetch the multiplier function in a similar fashion, and the output shows the respective results of the operation performed by the adder, subtractor, and multiplier functions. Now that we have learned about the various types of functions in V, let's gain an understanding of the features of functions in V.

Understanding function features

In the previous sections, we learned about various types of functions and discovered how to write basic functions, anonymous functions, and higher-order functions. As a V programmer, it is important to know the various features of functions that will enable you to work with them smoothly while programming. The following is a list of the features of functions in V:

- Functions can return values or simply perform operations.
- Functions can take zero or more input arguments.
- Functions can return multiple values.
- Functions can call other accessible functions.
- Functions allow only arrays, interfaces, maps, pointers, and structs as mutable arguments.
- Function declarations in script mode should come before all script statements.
- Functions do not allow access to module variables or global variables.
- Functions do not allow default or optional arguments.
- Functions can have optional return types.
- Functions are private by default and can be exposed to other modules using the pub access modifier keyword.
- Functions allow you to defer the execution flow using a defer block.
- Functions can be represented as elements of an array or a map.

Let's understand each of these features of the functions offered in V in detail.

Functions can return values or simply perform operations

By default, functions in V are pure. This means that return values are a function of their arguments only, and their evaluation has no side effects (besides I/O). This means that functions are responsible for what they are intended to do and nothing else. To demonstrate this, consider the sum function, as follows:

```
fn sum(a int, b int) int {
    return a + b
}
println(sum(2, 3))
```

In the preceding code, the `sum` function that adds 2 numbers provided to it as input arguments can easily replace the number 5 with the function call `sum(2, 3)`. So, the `sum` function just does the addition of the two numbers and returns the value and nothing else. This indicates that pure functions offer consistent results for the same input no matter how many times we call them.

For a function to return the results of an operation, you need to specify the return type in the method signature that matches the data type of the value being returned by the method. Functions use the `return` keyword to pass values to their callers:

```
fn say_hello() string {
        return 'Hello!'
}

// call the method
res := say_hello()
println(res) // prints: Hello!
```

In the preceding code, the function named `say_hello` is returning a string `Hello!` The value 'Hello!' is specified after the `return` keyword that matches with the return type specified in the method signature as a `string` data type.

In contrast to the preceding example, some methods do not have to acknowledge their callers and can just perform operations, such as I/O operations such as printing to the console, file operations, insert, update, or delete records from a database table, or set environment variables. For example, consider the following method:

```
fn console_greeter() {
        println('Hello!')
}

console_greeter() // prints: Hello!
```

The callers of this function do not expect a return value from the `console_greeter` method. This is because it does not specify any return type in its method signature. This method just prints the `Hello!` text to the console and does not return anything to the callers.

Functions can take zero or more input arguments

Functions can be passed with input arguments that might help you to achieve the underlying operation. Input arguments need to be passed after the method name is in rounded brackets. One input argument is represented by its name followed by the data type of the input argument. If you have multiple input arguments, you must separate those with a comma, as follows:

```
fn add(a int, b int) int {
        return a + b
}


res := add(2, 4)
println(res) // prints: 6
```

In the preceding code, we have declared a function named add that returns the sum of two integers. The two integers are provided as input arguments to the add method.

Functions can return multiple values

V enables you to provide multiple return values as the result of operations performed inside a function. The syntax uses the return keyword with the values to be returned separated by a comma. Additionally, it is necessary to indicate the return types in the method signature after the input arguments. The multiple return types need to be enclosed in rounded brackets with just the data types separated by a comma in the order that they are returned:

```
fn greet_and_message_length(name string) (string, int) {
        mut greeting := 'Hello, ' + name + '!'
        return greeting, greeting.len
}


i, j := greet_and_message_length('Navule')
println(i)
println(j)
```

In the preceding code, the greet_and_message_length function returns multiple values of different data types. It accepts the name input argument of the string data type. Then, it performs string concatenation and, finally, returns the greeting of the string data type followed by the length of the string, which is of the int data type. This follows the order of the sequence, as mentioned in the (string, int) method signature.

The callers receive the values in the variables separated by a comma, as shown in the following code:

```
i, j := greet_and_message_length('Navule')
```

Here is the output:

```
Hello, Navule!
14
```

Ignoring return values from functions

If you are only interested in one or a few return values from a function, then you can ignore the initialization of unwanted return types with the underscore for the respective value.

For example, the following code shows the caller is only interested in capturing the greeting message and is not interested in the length of the message and, therefore, skips initializing it by mentioning _ for the position where the message length is being returned:

```
i, _ := greet_and_message_length('Navule')
```

This technique of ignoring a return value can also be applied to methods that return a single value.

Functions can call other accessible functions

A function can call other functions that it has access to. The access includes the functions of the same module or the public functions of the imported modules. **Modules** in V allow you to group related functionality together and, therefore, help you to modularize the code. We will learn more about modules in *Chapter 9, Modules*.

In the following example, the greet function is being called by the welcome function and appending the result of the greet function with the Welcome message:

```
fn greet(p string) string {
        return 'Hello, $p!'
}


fn welcome(p string) string {
        msg := 'Nice to meet you!'
        mut g := greet(p)
        g = g + ' $msg'
```

```
        return g
}
```

```
res := welcome('Visitor')
println(res)
```

Here is the output:

```
Hello, Visitor! Nice to meet you!
```

Functions allow only arrays, interfaces, maps, pointers, and structs as mutable arguments

Sometimes, you need to modify a variable, for instance, a primitive type, an array, or a struct. And you have gathered that the modification routine of such a variable can be moved to a reusable code block as a function. The general tendency is that you create a function that accepts the variable to be modified as an argument. Inside the function, you assign it to a new mutable variable and then perform updates. Finally, you return the updated variable having marked the function's method signature with the return type of the variable being updated.

To demonstrate the situation of variable modification, let's understand the following use case. Suppose you want to increment all the elements of an integer array by a specified number; generally, you write a function that takes an array and the increment factor as two arguments for the new function. Let's call it increment_array_items. As the function also has to return the array, we need to specify [] int in the method signature, as follows:

```
fn increment_array_items(arr []int, inc int) []int {
        mut tmp := arr.clone()
        for mut i in tmp {
                i += inc
        }
        return tmp
}

a := [5, 6]

res := increment_array_items(a, 100)
```

```
println('a: $a')
println('res: $res')
```

From the preceding code, we can observe that we are cloning the `arr` input argument into the `tmp` mutable variable and then incrementing the values of the elements of the `tmp` array. Finally, we return the `tmp` array. In this approach, we end up having different arrays that are evident from the output:

```
a: [5, 6]
res: [105, 106]
```

The `increment_array_items` function can be modified to accept a mutable argument, and we will examine how to achieve that now. V allows you to update variables by passing them as mutable arguments to the functions without having to specify any return type. Before we modify `increment_array_items` to accept mutable arguments, there are certain rules to bear in mind in order to work with functions that accept mutable arguments. They are as follows:

- Mutable arguments are only allowed for arrays, interfaces, maps, pointers, and struct types.

- The arguments that are being passed to the function that accepts mutable arguments must also be declared as mutable.

- Calling a function with mutable arguments requires you to specify the `mut` keyword during the function call. That is, you must specify the `mut` keyword when sending a value in the place of a mutable argument to a function.

Let's modify `increment_array_items` to reflect the functionality of updating variables passed to it as mutable function arguments:

```
fn increment_array_items(mut arr []int, inc int) {
        for mut i in arr {
                i += inc
        }
}

mut a := [5, 6]
increment_array_items(mut a, 100) // Must specify mut
// keyword when sending value to mut arg of a function
println('a: ${a}')
```

As you can see, the updated `increment_array_items` function doesn't have to specify any return type in its method signature. Additionally, notice that the `arr` argument is marked with the `mut` keyword.

The following is the output:

```
a: [105, 106]
```

Function declarations in script mode should come before all script statements

If you are writing scripts in V or trying out various quick and dirty outcomes of program behavior in a V file, you need to have all the functions defined before declaring the variables.

Copy the following V script and place it inside a file named `script_functions.vsh`:

```
#!/usr/local/bin/v run
cnt := 2

for i in 0 .. cnt {
        log('iteration $i')
}

fn log(msg string) {
        println(msg)
}
```

If you are on Windows, run the following command to execute the V script:

```
v run script_functions.vsh
```

If you are on any of the Unix platforms, you need to run `./script_funtioncs.vsh` in the command-line Terminal. However, before you run the `.vsh` script, you need to make it an executable. To mark it as an executable file, run the following command to execute the V script:

```
chmod u+x: ./script_functions.vsh
```

Here is the output:

```
error: function declarations in script mode should be before
all script statements
```

Note that the Terminal will print an error. For the `vsh` script to execute without any errors, we should define all the function declarations before all other script statements as follows:

```
#!/usr/local/bin/v run

fn log(msg string) {
        println(msg)
}

cnt := 2

for i in 0 .. cnt {
        log('iteration $i')
}
```

Here is the output:

```
iteration 0
iteration 1
```

We can observe that the script executes successfully when the `log` function is moved to the top of the `vsh` script before any other expression or variable declaration.

Functions do not allow access to module variables or global variables

As mentioned earlier, functions in V are pure by default. This means that functions can only process the arguments they are passed with and return the processed output. The functions cannot access variables that are defined outside of the function body.

However, V enables us to declare global variables. When it comes to the implementation of low-level applications such as programming OS kernels or system drivers, you might need to have the variables accessed globally. In such situations, you can declare variables as global and run the V program with the `-enable-globals` argument.

Now, we will examine how to declare global variables and run V programming using the -enable-globals flag. The code that we are going to work on will be structured in the following directory hierarchy:

```
E:.
│    main.v
│
└──mymod
        mymod.v
```

From a blank directory, let's create a file named main.v that contains the following code:

```
// file: main.v
module main

import mymod

fn main() {
        mymod.msg := 'global variable demo'
        println(mymod.msg)
}
```

In the preceding code, we are importing a module named mymod, which we will be developing further. In the main method, we are setting the value to the variable named msg of the string data type that we are going to define in mymod as a global variable.

The syntax to create a global variable in V is as follows:

```
__global(
<variable_name> <data_type>
)
```

Now, let's create a module named mymod and add some code to it. For that, we will create a directory named mymod, and inside the directory, create a file named mymod.v using the following code:

```
// file: mymod/mymod.v
module mymod

__global (
        msg string
)
```

In the `mymod.v` file, we defined a `msg` global variable of the string data type. From the command-line Terminal, navigate to the parent directory where we have `main.v` located. To run `main.v`, you need to provide `-enable-globals` as an argument to V, as follows:

```
v -enable-globals run main.v
```

You will see the following output:

```
global variable demo
```

Functions do not allow default or optional arguments

V does not allow you to declare functions with its arguments set to default values. This indicates that V does not support optional arguments. However, it is interesting to know that structs in V can be defined with default values assigned to their fields. To achieve this functionality, you can overcome this limitation by creating a function that accepts a struct as an argument. We will learn more about structs in *Chapter 8*, *Structs*. Additionally, we will observe the code that allows you to pass a struct with default values assigned to its fields as an argument to a function in *Chapter 8*, *Structs*. There we will learn about structs as trailing literal arguments to a function.

Functions can have optional return types

Functions can also be declared with optional return types. This is achieved by simply placing the ? symbol prefixed to the return type specified in the signature of the function, as shown in the following example. With functions having optional return types, the optional type other than the actual return type will be `none`. The caller of the function that has an optional return type must specify the `or  {}` block, as follows:

```
module main

fn is_teen(age int) ?string {
        if age < 0 {
                return none
        } else if age >= 13 && age <= 19 {
                return 'teenager'
        } else {
                return 'not teenager'
        }
```

```
        }
```

```
fn main() {
        x := is_teen(-3) or { 'invalid age provided' }
        println(x)
}
```

In the preceding example, `is_teen` is a function that optionally returns a string, indicating whether the input age is a teenager or not. As age cannot be a negative value, the method does not return anything in this case, which is indicated by the `return none` statement. Additionally, note that the caller of the function with an optional return type is the main method, and we are specifying the `or  {}` block, which is indicated by the `or { 'invalid age provided' }` statement.

Here is the output:

```
invalid age provided
```

Alternatively, you can also specify an error instead of none for functions with optional return types, as follows:

```
module main

fn is_teen(age int) ?string {
        if age < 0 {
                return error('invalid age provided')
        } else if age >= 13 && age <= 19 {
                return 'teenager'
        } else {
                return 'not teenager'
        }
}

fn main() {
        x := is_teen(-3) or { err.msg }
        println(x)
}
```

```
invalid age provided
```

The preceding code depicts the use of error for a function with the optional return type. This indicates that you can also return the `error()` function that accepts a message of the `string` type, which you want to return to the callers by replacing `return none` with `return error('invalid age provided')`. Additionally, notice that the callers, in this case, can access the error message using `err`, which is a built-in variable of the `IError` type that is created in this scope.

The `or` block must return the type that matches the non-optional return type of the function that it is clubbed in an expression. In our case, the `or` block is used along with the `is_teen` function whose return type is `?string`. So, the functionality enclosed in the `or` block should return a string. Alternatively, in the `or` block, you can write `or { panic(err) }`. You can also write `or { exit(1) }`. The `exit` function accepts an input argument of the `int` type. In general, `exit(0)` indicates the program has run smoothly, and any other input argument for the exit function such as `exit(1)` indicates the program execution has failed.

Functions are private by default and can be exposed to other modules using the pub access modifier keyword

By default, all of the functions declared in V are private and are only accessible within the default scope that they are defined in. To expose the methods to the outside world, they are decorated with the `pub` keyword, which denotes public access.

To demonstrate this, we can assume the following folder structure for a demo V application:

```
E:\v_demo
|    public_function_demo1.v
|    public_function_demo2.v
|    public_function_demo3.v
|
└──mod1
        mod1.v
```

Note that the demo V project has two v files that call various functions defined in the `mod1` module.

Let's take a look at the mod1.v file:

```
// file: mod1/mod1.v

module mod1

fn greet1() string {
        return 'Hello from greet1'
}

pub fn greet2() string {
        return 'Hello from greet2'
}

pub fn greet_and_wish() string {
        wish := 'Have a nice day!'
        return greet1() + ', ' + wish
}
```

The mod1.v file has three functions defined, namely, greet1, greet2, and greet_and_wish. Out of these three functions, only greet2 and greet_and_wish are marked with the pub access modifier. The pub access modifier makes the functions available to the parent modules. As per the definition of the greet1 function, it is private by default.

Now, let's take a look at the public_function_demo1.v file:

```
// file: public_function_demo1.v

import mod1

g := mod1.greet1()
println(g)
```

In public_function_demo1.v, we are importing the module named mod1. Following this, we are trying to store the value returned by the greet1 method, which is a private function, in a variable.

Now, let's run the command to execute the code in `public_function_demo1.v`, as follows:

```
v run public_function_demo1.v
```

After running the preceding command, you will see the following message:

```
error: function 'mod1.greet1' is private
```

Now, let's take a look at the `public_function_demo2.v` file:

```
// file: public_function_demo2.v

import mod1

g := mod1.greet2()
println(g)
```

In `public_function_demo2.v`, we are importing the `mod1` module. We are calling the `greet2` function that has been exposed as a public function of `mod1`. Following this, we are trying to store the value returned by the `greet2` function in a variable, and then we are printing the value to the console.

Now, let's run the command to execute the code in `public_function_demo2.v`, as follows:

```
v run public_function_demo2.v
```

After running the preceding command, you will see the following output:

```
Hello from greet2!
```

Additionally, let's take a look at the `public_function_demo3.v` file:

```
// file: public_function_demo3.v

import mod1

g := mod1.greet_and_wish()
println(g)
```

In `public_function_demo3.v`, we are importing the module named `mod1`. We are calling the `greet_and_wish` function, which is exposed as the public function of `mod1`. Following this, we are trying to store the value returned by the `greet_and_wish` function in a variable, and then we are printing the value to the console.

Before we execute the file, let's take a look at the `greet_and_wish` function one more time:

```
// file: mod1/mod1.v

/*full code of this file omitted for brevity*/

pub fn greet_and_wish() string {
        wish := 'Have a nice day!'
        return greet1() + ', ' + wish
}
```

The `greet_and_wish` function marked with the `pub` access modifier is accessible to its parent modules. Additionally, note that it is making another function call in its list of routines to a private `greet1` function. As `greet1` and `greet_and_wish` belong to the same module, `greet_and_wish` can call `greet1` as a part of the routines performed by it. And the callers of the `greet_and_wish` method will be able to access the method successfully and consume the result without any error.

Now, let's run the command to execute the code in `public_function_demo3.v`, as follows:

```
v run public_function_demo3.v
```

After running the preceding command, you will see the following output:

```
Hello from greet1, Have a nice day!
```

By default, all of the functions declared in V are private and only accessible within the default scope they are defined in.

Functions allow you to defer the execution flow using the defer block

V allows you to defer the execution flow wrapped inside a defer { } block. A defer block is created using the defer keyword, and the functionality is wrapped inside curly braces that follow the defer keyword. The defer block gets executed differently for different function types. For instance, if a function returns a value of a certain type, then the defer block gets executed after the return statement has been evaluated. Alternatively, if a function returns nothing, then the defer block is executed just before the execution flow exits from the function it is defined in:

```
module main

fn void_func_defer() {
        println('Hello')
        defer {
                println('Hi from defer block')
        }
        println('How are you?')
        // the defer block will be executed when the
// execution control reaches here
}

fn main() {
        void_func_defer()
}
```

Here is the output:

```
Hello
How are you?
Hi from defer block
```

The void_func_defer function has no return type. Based on the print statements, we can observe that the defer block has run the statements wrapped inside it, after printing the Hello and How are you? messages and just before exiting out of the function.

Functions can be represented as elements of an array or a map

V allows you to define an **array** or a **map** of functions provided that all of the functions have the same signature. Let's reuse the adder, subtractor, and multiplier functions that we defined in the *Higher-order functions that return other functions* section. As these three functions have the same signature, we can define an array of these functions as follows:

```
funcs := [adder, subtractor, multiplier]
```

It is not necessary to specify the arguments or return types when adding functions as elements to an array. The arguments will be passed when we access the elements of the funcs array, which will be presented in the following code. Now, we can iterate over this array of functions that performs respective mathematical operations underlying these functions, as follows:

```
i, j := 2, 5

for f in funcs {
        res := f(i, j)
        println(res)
}
```

Here is the output:

```
7
-3
10
```

In the preceding code, for every iteration over the elements of an array variable named funcs, the f iteration variable represents one of the three functions. In every iteration, we are passing the i and j integer variables to the f iteration variable, which represents the function that we defined earlier.

The problem with the previous output is that it's not intuitive. We are not able to identify what operation was performed on the i and j integer variables. So, let's make it more intuitive by defining a map that holds these functions. We will define a map such that the keys represent the one-word description of what the function does and the value is the actual function itself:

```
d := {
        'sum':       adder
        'difference': subtractor
        'product':   multiplier
}
```

It is not necessary to specify the arguments or return types when adding functions as elements to the map.

We have declared a d map variable with the *key-value* pairs that represent the one-word descriptive name as *key* and the function name as *value*:

```
for key, val in d {
        res := val(i, j)
        println('$key of $i and $j: $res')
}
```

The full source code that demonstrates how to use functions as elements of an array and a map is shown here:

```
module main

fn adder(i int, j int) int {
        return i + j
}

fn subtractor(i int, j int) int {
        return i - j
}

fn multiplier(i int, j int) int {
        return i * j
}
```

```
fn main() {
        i, j := 2, 5
        println('Functions as elements of an Array')
        funcs := [adder, subtractor, multiplier]

        for f in funcs {
                res := f(i, j)
                println(res)
        }
        println('Functions as elements of Map')
        d := {
                'sum':        adder
                'difference': subtractor
                'product':    multiplier
        }

        for key, val in d {
                res := val(i, j)
                println('$key of $i and $j: $res')
        }
}
```

Here is the output:

```
Functions as elements of an Array
7
-3
10
Functions as elements of Map
sum of 2 and 5: 7
difference of 2 and 5: -3
product of 2 and 5: 10
```

Here, the functions can be easily constructed as the elements of an array or a map. However, having them defined as the elements of a map makes the code more readable. Also, it is evident from the code that these functions and their corresponding keys in a map allow printing the information, which makes it easier to understand. Additionally, it is evident from the preceding output that it is possible to intuitively express the operation being performed at each iteration of the map in contrast to an array.

Summary

So, we have successfully understood the concept of functions in V. To briefly summarize, we began our chapter by detailing the need to write functions. Then, we looked at the syntax of a basic function and understood various terms related to defining functions. Following this, we learned how to write different types of functions such as basic functions, anonymous functions, and higher-order functions along with detailed code examples.

In the later parts of this chapter, we discovered various features such as how to define and work with functions that accept arguments, functions that return values, and function scopes, to mention a few. We also looked at how to write functions in V script files that have the `.vsh` extension.

Additionally, we looked at advanced features such as how to create functions and mutable arguments and the various things to bear in mind when defining such functions. We learned how to defer the function execution flow using `defer` blocks.

Having gained an in-depth knowledge of functions in V, it is time for us to move on to the next chapter, where we will learn about structs in V.

8
Structs

When writing software applications, you might need to represent objects in the form of a structure that holds all their properties. For example, if you are writing a software application that deals with taking notes or a list of to-do items, you need to represent each note in the form of a structure. Assuming the most essential properties of a note are the text content of the note, the time of its creation, and a note ID to uniquely identify a note, these properties can be collectively placed inside a structure that represents a note. In **V**, you can create blueprints for representing objects using the `struct` keyword. In this chapter, we will learn about these blueprints that are often referred to as **structs**. The following is the list of topics that we are going to learn in this chapter:

- Introducing structs
- Updating the fields of a struct
- Approaches to defining struct fields
- Defining methods for a struct
- Adding a struct as a field inside another struct
- Structs as trailing literal arguments to a function

By the end of this chapter, you will be able to write structs that involve struct fields having different access modifiers, and will be able to define struct fields with default values. In addition to gaining the skill of defining and initializing structs, you will also have an understanding of how to add methods that belong to a struct and how to create functions with structs as input arguments.

Technical requirements

The full source code of this chapter is available on GitHub:

https://github.com/PacktPublishing/Getting-Started-with-V-Programming/tree/main/Chapter08

Introducing structs

Structs in V allow you to define composite objects. They facilitate you to create complex data structures, allowing its fields to have different data types. The fields of the struct can be primitive data types, enums, or could be another struct.

We will start understanding structs by observing their basic syntax. Later, we will learn how to define a struct based on this syntax, initialize a struct with values assigned to its fields, and access those fields. We will then discuss what heap structs are and illustrate this with detailed code examples.

Defining a struct

You can define a struct in V by using the `struct` keyword followed by the name of the struct. The basic syntax of a struct in V is of the form shown here:

```
struct STRUCTNAME {
        FIELDNAME1  DATATYPE
        FIELDNAME2  DATATYPE
}
```

For example, let's define a `Note` struct to understand how a real-world example of a struct would look in V:

```
struct Note {
        id       int
        message string
}
```

From the preceding code, we can understand the `Note` struct has two fields, `id` and `message`, of data types integer and string respectively.

Initializing a struct

We will now initialize the struct, as shown here:

```
n := Note{1, 'a simple struct demo'}
```

Arguments passed to the struct need to be ordered as they appear in the definition of the struct. We notice that we initialized a `struct` of a `Note` type with values assigned to its fields. Notice that the values for the struct field are mentioned implicitly and they get assigned to the struct fields in the order they were defined in the struct definition. In this case, `id` will be implicitly assigned a value of `1` and `message` with the value of `'a simple struct demo'`:

```
n := Note{
    message: 'a simple struct demo'
    id: 1
}
```

You can also explicitly initialize the fields of a struct in V with the field name followed by a colon (`:`) and then the value you want to assign that suits the data type of the struct field.

The type of the struct n variable is `Note`, which can be confirmed by running the following code:

```
println(typeof(n).name) // Note
```

Accessing the fields of a struct

You can access the fields of a struct that are directly available on the value object of the struct.

For example, to print the value of `message` of the `Note` struct, you can use `.field` on the value object, as shown here:

```
n := Note{1, 'a simple struct demo'}
println(n.message)
```

The output will print the value held by the `message` field of the `Note` struct as shown next:

```
a simple struct demo
```

Understanding heap structs

When a struct is initialized, its memory is allocated on the stack by default. V allows you to initialize a struct and allocates its memory on the heap, provided that you specify & before the struct name during initialization, as shown here:

```
n1 := &Note{1, 'this note will be allocated on heap'}
```

The preceding code example demonstrates the initialization of the **heap struct**, which is identified by adding & before the name of the struct. Accessing the fields of a heap struct can be done in a similar way to with a normal struct.

The type of heap struct variable n1 is &Note, which can be confirmed by running the following code:

```
println(typeof(n1).name) // &Note
```

Heap structs are particularly useful when dealing with structs that carry large amounts of data. Therefore, opting for heap structs can reduce explicit memory allocations.

Now that we have understood the basic syntax of structs and tried to initialize and access the struct fields along with creating heap structs, we will discuss different ways to update the values of struct fields.

Updating the fields of a struct

While working with structs, sometimes we might need to update specific fields of a struct in order to change the existing or default value that a field holds. V has certain specifications when it comes to updating struct fields. In this section, we will see different approaches to updating the fields of structs and understand all the prerequisites that are needed in order to make changes to the values of struct fields.

All the fields of a struct are immutable by default. They can only be initialized once. To change the value of a field of a struct, it needs to be specified under the section marked with mut :. All the fields defined in a line below the mut : will be mutable fields.

We will change the struct Note so that the message field can be mutable:

```
struct Note {
        id      int
mut:
        message string
}
```

Now, we will declare and initialize the `Note` struct, as shown next:

```
n := Note {1, 'a simple struct demo'}
println(n)
```

The output will print the `Note` object to the console on a new line, as shown here:

```
Note{
    id: 1
    message: 'a simple struct demo'
}
```

Let's update the `message` field of the `Note` struct, as shown here:

```
n := Note {1, 'a simple struct demo'}
n.message = 'a simple struct updated'
```

You will be surprised to see there is an error that says the following:

```
error: 'n' is immutable, declare it with 'mut' to make it
mutable
```

Let's update the variable declaration to be mutable in nature. Also, we will try to update the value of the `message` field, as shown next:

```
mut n := Note { 1, 'a simple struct demo' }
n.message = 'a simple struct updated'
```

To update a field of a struct, it is necessary that both the field and the variable to which the struct is initialized are mutable.

At this point, the complete code appears as follows:

```
module main

struct Note {
        id int
mut:
        message string
}
```

```
fn main() {
        mut n := Note{1, 'a simple struct demo'}
        println('before update')
        println(n)

        n.message = 'a simple struct updated'
        println('after update')
        println(n)
}
```

The output of the preceding code is shown here:

```
before update
Note{
    id: 1
    message: 'a simple struct demo'
}
after update
Note{
    id: 1
    message: 'a simple struct updated'
}
```

Now, let's see what happens if we try to update the immutable id field of the Note struct:

```
mut j := Note{1, 'a simple struct demo'}
j.id = 2
```

You will see the error reminding us of the immutable nature of the id field in the Note struct as follows:

```
error: field 'id' of struct 'Note' is immutable
```

There are a few things to remember while you update the values of struct fields:

- The variable to which the struct is declared must be mutable.

- You must specify the struct name to the right-hand side of the = operator followed by the struct fields that you wish to update. The values must be enclosed in curly braces ({ }).

- The field names must be specified as literals and only then can they be assigned values separated by a : sign.

- The unspecified fields in the update statements are assigned zero by default.

The fields not specified in the update statement are assigned zero by default, even if they had some values in the previous initialization. Let's look at the following example:

```
module main

struct Note {
        id int
mut:
        message string
}

fn main() {
        // declare
        mut n := Note{}

        // populate
        n = Note{
                id: 1
                message: 'updating struct fields demo'
        }
        println(n)

        // unspecified fields zeroed by default
        // id being type of int, will become 0 here
        println('unspecified id zeroed during short struct
                type initialization')
        n = Note{
                message: 'updating struct fields demo 2'
        }
        println(n)
}
```

In the preceding code, notice that the id field is ignored when we update the message for the second time.

Here is the output:

```
Note{
    id: 1
    message: 'updating struct fields demo'
}
unspecified id zeroed during short struct type initialization
Note{
    id: 0
    message: 'updating struct fields demo 2'
}
```

From the preceding output, we can observe that the value of the id field got zeroed to the default integer value 0 after we updated it for the second time, even though it was assigned a value of 1 when the n variable was populated with id set to 1. It is worth mentioning that if you had other field data types like bool or string, the zero value of such types would be false and ' ' respectively.

Approaches to defining struct fields

When declaring structs, you often need to limit or control the behavior of its field members. In this section, we will see how to implement such behavior, which includes the following:

- Adding multiple mutable fields to a struct
- Grouping fields in a struct using access modifiers
- Defining required fields in a struct
- Defining struct fields with default values

Let's discuss each of these in detail in the following subsections.

Adding multiple mutable fields to a struct

We can define all the mutable fields of a struct using the mut keyword followed by : on a separate line. The syntax for defining mutable fields in a struct is shown here:

```
struct Note {
        id      int
mut:
        message string
        status  bool
}
```

In the preceding code example, we specified a new field for the Note struct named status with bool as its data type. The significant thing to notice here is that all the mutable types are declared under the mut keyword with a colon (:) symbol. The indent is optional and to help readability. The only thing that is noteworthy is that the syntax mut : to declare mutable fields has to be on its own separate line.

So, it is evident that all the fields of a struct declared before the mut : syntax are immutable and the ones after mut : are mutable.

Grouping fields in a struct using access modifiers

A struct allows the filtering of its fields at various access levels. With the help of the keywords pub, for public access of fields, and mut, to indicate mutable fields, you can control the way the fields of a struct can be accessed.

The various access control levels that could be applied to the fields of a struct are tabulated here:

Access modifier	Within module	Outside module
pub	public	public
mut	mutable	immutable
pub mut	public, mutable	public, mutable
__global	public, mutable	public, mutable

Table 8.1 – Understanding access control for struct fields

Let's apply the various access modifiers to the fields of the Note struct and discuss what we are doing in detail:

```
pub struct Note {
pub:
        id int
pub mut:
        message string
        status  bool
}
```

We have marked the Note struct as pub. We also marked the id field as public by declaring it under the pub group. The fields under the pub group are public and are read-only outside the module. Also, the message and status fields are marked with the pub and mut access modifiers. Defining struct fields under the pub mut group indicates that the struct fields are accessible and mutable within and outside the module where Note is defined.

Defining required fields in a struct

Sometimes it is obvious that a structure's existence does not make sense if it doesn't hold a value for a few struct fields. For example, a Note struct without a message looks obsolete. In order to prevent such situations, you can enforce a requirement to mark certain fields by enclosing the required keyword between square brackets ([]) to the right of the field. This is often referred to as *annotating the struct fields as required*. Using this annotation flag, the compiler will know that the specific field is marked as required. The following code shows the message field marked with the [required] annotation in the Note struct, as shown here:

```
pub struct Note {
pub:
        id      int
pub mut:
        message string [required]
        status  bool
}
```

Now, let's create a `Note` struct without actually initializing any value to the `message` field, as follows:

```
_ := Note{
    id: 1
    status: false
}
```

You will notice that V will throw an error, as shown here:

```
error: field 'Note.message' must be initialized
```

As we have marked the `message` field as `[required]`, we must initialize the `message` field going forward. The full code, along with the `message` field being initialized, will appear as shown here:

```
module main

pub struct Note {
pub:
    id int
pub mut:
    message string [required]
    status  bool
}

fn main() {
    n := Note{
        id: 1
        message: 'a simple struct demo'
        status: false
    }
    println(n)
}
```

Defining struct fields with default values

Sometimes it is required to have a struct field defined and initialized with some default value. This allows the programmers to prevent such fields from being explicitly initialized unless there is a need to do so. V allows you to define struct fields with default values assigned to them. Let's say we want to capture the time of the creation of a note every time we initialize and assign values to the other fields of the Note struct. In such a case, we can define an immutable field to hold the time information and assign it with a default value that holds the time of the creation of the note within the definition of the struct.

To illustrate this use case, we will modify the Note struct to accommodate two new fields, namely created and due. The syntax for creating struct fields with default values assigned to them is shown here:

```
import time


pub struct Note {
pub:
        id       int
        created time.Time = time.now()
pub mut:
        message string       [required]
        status   bool
        due       time.Time = time.now().add_days(1)
}
```

The newly introduced fields in the Note struct (created and due) are of type, Time. The Time type is available as a part of the built-in time module.

In the Note struct, the field named created is an immutable field with the default value assigned with the time at which the Note was created. The other field named due will be set to the default value time.now().add_days(1), such that it identifies that the particular Note is due by 1 day from the time of the creation of Note.

Now, we will create a Note struct. Let's say to *order groceries* and then print Note, as shown here:

```
n := Note{
        id: 1
        message: 'order groceries'
}


println(n)
```

Here is the output:

```
Note{
    id: 1
    created: 2021-03-04 02:02:33
    message: 'order groceries'
    status: false
    due: 2021-03-05 02:02:33
}
```

The output will appear with the default values for the created, status, and due fields of Note as defined in the definition of the Note struct.

Notice that the status field has been assigned false, even though we didn't assign any value. This is due to the fact that, in V, *the values of struct fields are zeroed by default during the creation of struct*. In this case, the default value for status is assigned with the default value of the bool data type, which is false. Therefore, the value of the status field, even when it is not assigned any value, will be displayed as false.

The full source code will now appear as shown here:

```
import time


pub struct Note {
pub:
        id      int
        created time.Time = time.now()
pub mut:
        message string      [required]
        status  bool
        due     time.Time = time.now().add_days(1)
}


fn main() {
        n := Note{
                id: 1
                message: 'order groceries'
        }
```

```
        println(n)
}
```

So far, we have learned different methods to define struct fields, such as defining mutable fields, defining fields with access modifiers, marking the fields as required members, and defining struct fields with default values. We will now look at creating methods for structs. The methods for a struct allow us to define a behavior that is specific for the struct and allow us to update struct fields. Let's learn about defining methods in the following section.

Defining methods for a struct

V allows us to define methods for a struct. A **method** is a function with a special receiver argument that appears between fn and the method name. They allow us to add functions to a struct in a convenient manner. Methods are the kind of functions that access the properties of the struct to perform some routine. To define a method for a struct, follow the syntax shown here:

```
fn (r RECEIVER_TYPE) METHOD_NAME(OPTIONAL_INPUT_ARGUMENTS)
RETURN_TYPE {
        METHOD BODY
}
```

In the preceding syntax, the RECEIVER_TYPE indicates the name of the struct to which the method belongs. If you are familiar with the **C#** programming language, this feature is similar to the concept of extension methods in C#. During runtime, the methods of a struct have access to the values held by the fields of the struct. Therefore, the methods help to evaluate logic or perform desired operations with the struct fields.

> **Note**
> The methods that belong to a struct need to be placed in the same module where the struct belongs.

Let's look back at the Note struct and we will create a method to check if the message field is empty. Even though we can enforce struct fields to be [required], there is a chance that the message can be provided with an empty string. To verify this, let's create a method for the Note struct, as shown next:

```
pub fn (n Note) is_empty_message() bool {
        return n.message.len < 1
}
```

Now, we can call this method on an initialized `Note` struct to check whether the `message` field is empty or not. For demonstration purposes, the `message` field is set to empty, as shown in the following code:

```
module main

import time

pub struct Note {
pub:
    id        int
    created time.Time = time.now()
pub mut:
    message string      [required]
    status   bool
    due        time.Time = time.now().add_days(1)
}

// is_empty_message is a method that belongs to Note
pub fn (n Note) is_empty_message() bool {
    return n.message.len < 1
}

fn main() {
    mut n := Note{
        id: 1
        message: ''
    }

    if n.is_empty_message() {
        println('message is empty')
    } else {
        println('message not empty')
    }
}
```

Here is the output:

```
message is empty
```

Executing the preceding code will print `message is empty` to the standard output of the console.

As we just learned how to write methods for a struct, let's move ahead and learn how to add a struct inside another struct.

Adding a struct as a field inside another struct

Imagine a situation where you need to create a new struct. During the creation of the struct, you end up identifying more fields that become a part of the struct you are defining. There might be a chance that a few fields are related to each other, but they might not play a significant role in representing the struct you are declaring. In such cases, those fields can be moved to a separate struct and represent that separate struct inside the main struct as one of its fields. In such cases, V allows adding a struct as a field inside another struct. The only prerequisite to adding a struct inside of another struct is that the fields of type `struct` must be declared at the beginning of the struct body.

To illustrate, let's take the `created` and `due` fields out of the `Note` struct and move them to another struct (let's say `NoteTimeInfo`), as shown next:

```
import time


// NoteTimeInfo is a struct to store time info of Note
pub struct NoteTimeInfo{
pub:
        created time.Time = time.now()
pub mut:
        due      time.Time = time.now().add_days(1)
}


// Note is a struct with struct NoteTimeInfo as a field,
// along with other fields
pub struct Note {
        NoteTimeInfo // Struct as another struct field
pub:
        id      int
```

```
pub mut:
        message string [required]
        status  bool
}
```

We notice that the `NoteTimeInfo` struct is added as a field to the `Note` struct. Also, notice that the `NoteTimeInfo` field, which is a type of struct, is declared at the beginning of the `Note` struct body before any other field.

Now, let's initialize the `Note` struct and access the `due` property, which is actually a part of `NoteTimeInfo`:

```
n := Note{
    id: 1
    message: 'adding struct as struct field demo'
}
println('Due date: $n.due')
```

We see that `due` is the field of `NoteTimeInfo`, but it is accessible on the property of the `Note` struct n variable using the statement `n.due`. This is because the `NoteTimeInfo` struct is a struct field of `Note`.

Let's try to print the entire note using the following code:

```
println(n)
```

Here is the output:

```
Note{
    NoteTimeInfo: NoteTimeInfo{
        created: 2021-04-21 22:55:29
        due: 2021-04-22 22:55:29
    }
    id: 1
    message: 'adding struct as struct field demo'
    status: false
}
```

Modifying the fields of struct type inside another struct

To update the fields of a struct type, there are two approaches:

- The first approach is the implicit way to access the fields of a struct which is a field of parent struct value. We then use equals (=) sign to modify its value.

- The other approach is that you can explicitly specify the name of the struct field and then specify the corresponding fields of the struct and update the value using the equals (=) sign.

For example, if we want to extend the due date of an existing note by two more days from now, one approach is to directly access the fields of `NoteTimeInfo`, without having to explicitly specify the `NoteTimeInfo` field, and update the fields, as shown here:

```
n.due = n.due.add_days(2)
```

Another approach is to explicitly specify the name of the field that is of type `struct`, which is `NoteTimeInfo` in this case, and then specify its field, as shown here:

```
n.NoteTimeInfo.due = n.NoteTimeInfo.due.add_days(2)
```

Following is the full code demonstrating the two approaches of accessing the fields of a struct which are of type `struct`:

```
module main

import time

// NoteTimeInfo is a struct to store time info of Note
pub struct NoteTimeInfo {
pub:
    created time.Time = time.now()
pub mut:
    due time.Time = time.now().add_days(1)
}

// Note is a struct with struct NoteTimeInfo as a field,
// along with other fields
```

```
pub struct Note {
    NoteTimeInfo
pub:
    id int
pub mut:
    message string [required]
    status  bool
}

fn main() {
    mut n := Note{
        id: 1
        message: 'adding struct as struct field demo'
    }

    println('Due date: $n.due')
    // approach 1: implicit access of struct fields of
    // fields of type struct
    n.due = n.due.add_days(2)
    println('Due date after update: $n.due')

    // approach 2: explicitly specifying the field of type
    // struct and its fields
    n.NoteTimeInfo.due =
     n.NoteTimeInfo.due.add_days(2)
    println('Due date updated second time: $n.due')
    println(n)
}
```

Here is the output:

```
Due date: 2021-04-22 23:00:49
Due date after update: 2021-04-24 23:00:49
Due date updated second time: 2021-04-26 23:00:49
Note{
    NoteTimeInfo: NoteTimeInfo{
        created: 2021-04-21 23:00:49
```

```
        due: 2021-04-26 23:00:49
    }
    id: 1
    message: 'adding struct as struct field demo'
    status: false
}
```

Having learned the approaches to define and update the structs that have fields of type `struct`, we will now learn how to pass structs as trailing literal arguments to a function.

Structs as trailing literal arguments to a function

As V does not support default function arguments or named arguments, we can use trailing struct literal syntax. In V, you can define functions that accept structs as input arguments. Therefore, we can pass a struct with default values to a function that accepts the struct as an input argument.

For example, let's create a function that creates a `Note` struct to remind us to buy groceries. This function will take the `Note` struct provided as an input argument and create a new `Note` struct that prepends a phrase, `Buy Groceries:`, to the `message` field of every new note being created, as follows:

```
fn new_grocery_note(n Note) &Note {
    return &Note{
        id: n.id
        message: 'Buy Groceries: ' + n.message
    }
}
```

Now, we can create a note of groceries to buy, as follows:

```
g := new_grocery_note(id: 1, message: 'Milk')
println('$g.message is due by $g.due')
```

The preceding code snippet demonstrates the method of passing values to a function that accepts a struct as its input argument. Notice that the arguments are the fields of a struct, along with the values that we want to assign to those fields. Also notice that the multiple *field-name: value* pairs are separated by a comma (,) sign. It is optional to specify the name of the struct, as we saw in the preceding code. Alternatively, you can explicitly mention the name of the struct, as shown here:

```
g := new_grocery_note(Note{id: 1, message: 'Milk'})
println('$g.message is due by $g.due')
```

Let's say we want to delay the due date of a note by a day. To do this, we can create a function so that we do not have to re-write the full field assignment every time we want to extend the due date. This reusable code can be invoked by just passing an existing note and it does the job of extending the due date by a day:

```
fn extend_due_by_a_day(n Note) &Note {
        return &Note{
                NoteTimeInfo: NoteTimeInfo{
                        due: n.due.add_days(1)
                }
                id: n.id
                message: n.message
        }
}
```

You can call this method on an already created Note struct that extends the due date by one more day or you can directly create a new Note that has a default due date as two days from the time of creation:

```
n := extend_due_by_a_day(g)
println('After extending due date by a day')
println('$n.message is due by $n.due')
```

The preceding code demonstrates another approach of passing a struct to a function. Here, we are directly passing the new grocery variable, g, that we obtained earlier as a result of the new_grocery_note function, as an argument to the extend_due_by_a_day function.

Combining all these, we will see the following program that demonstrates working with functions with trailing struct literals:

```v
module main

import time

// NoteTimeInfo is a struct to store time info of Note
pub struct NoteTimeInfo {
pub:
        created time.Time = time.now()
pub mut:
        due time.Time = time.now().add_days(1)
}

// Note is a struct with struct NoteTimeInfo as a field,
// along with other fields
pub struct Note {
        NoteTimeInfo
pub:
        id int
pub mut:
        message string [required]
        status  bool
}

fn new_grocery_note(n Note) &Note {
        return &Note{
                id: n.id
                message: 'Buy Groceries: ' + n.message
        }
}

fn extend_due_by_a_day(n Note) &Note {
        return &Note{
                NoteTimeInfo: NoteTimeInfo{
                        due: n.due.add_days(1)
```

```
            }
            id: n.id
            message: n.message
        }
}

fn main() {
        g := new_grocery_note(Note{ id: 1, message: 'Milk' })
        println('$g.message is due by $g.due')
        n := extend_due_by_a_day(g)
        println('After extending due date by a day')
        println('$n.message is due by $n.due')
}
```

In this section, we learned how to define a function that accepts a struct as an argument. We then saw different approaches to pass a struct to a function. We saw how to pass struct fields directly as input arguments and also saw how to pass a struct variable to a function that accepts the struct as an input argument. Understanding these approaches helps programmers to become hands-on while working with structs and also helps them write programs that involve structs with ease and comfort.

Summary

In this chapter, we learned how to declare structs. We started with the syntax to define a struct and then learned about initializing and accessing the struct fields. Then, we learned how to update the fields of a struct after initializing it.

After that, we discussed various methods of defining struct fields, which included fields with mutability, access scope, required attributes, and default values assigned. You are also able to define methods that belong to a struct and learned how to specify a struct as a field of another struct. Finally, we saw various approaches to pass struct fields and struct variables to a function that accepts a struct as an input argument, along with code examples.

The next chapter will help you to write and maintain modular code in V.

9
Modules

Modular programming is the concept of logically grouping related functionalities together into modules and working with them. This approach enables you to wrap the related functionality into modules and allows you to import the required functionality that is available in those modules. V offers the concept of modular programming, allowing you to create and import modules that comprise code that is functionally or logically relevant in nature. To help you understand how to work with modules, in this chapter, we will cover the following topics:

- Introducing modules
- Working with modules

To begin, you will learn about the basic syntax to define and import modules. In the later sections, you will explore how to create a simple project in V and then learn how to create and import modules defined in our simple project. Following this, you will learn how to create multiple files and work with them in a module, along with gaining an understanding of the access scope.

You will also learn about best practices, including the benefits of the initializer function and conditions to define the initializer function for a module. This chapter also covers problems that arise in V when we have cyclic imports when creating modules. In addition to this, you will explore member scopes and the accessibility of members, including constants, structs, and embedded structs across modules. By the end of this chapter, you will be well-versed with the concepts of modules and how to leverage them while writing software applications in V.

Technical requirements

The full source code for this chapter is available at `https://github.com/PacktPublishing/Getting-Started-with-V-Programming/tree/main/Chapter09`.

Introducing modules

Modules in V allow you to logically group related blocks or pieces of functionality. The concept of modules offers you the ability to structure the code base and makes the code look well organized and easily identifiable. Let's begin learning about the modular approach in V by looking at the syntax to define and import the module. We will also learn how to create a module with public functions and access them from outside the module.

The syntax to define a module

V allows you to define a module using the `module` keyword followed by the name of the module. The following code specifies the syntax of how to define a module:

```
module MY_MODULE
```

In the preceding syntax, `MY_MODULE` can be any name that signifies the functionality that is present inside the module. The module naming convention is similar to that of variables, as detailed in the *Variable naming convention* section of *Chapter 3*, *Variables, Constants, and Code Comments*.

The syntax to import a module

V allows you to consume a module using the `import` keyword, and the syntax to import a module is shown in the following code:

```
import MY_MODULE
```

The preceding syntax shows you how to consume a module named `MY_MODULE`. We can observe that the name of the module must be specified after the `import` keyword. Let's take a look at the syntax to access members of the imported module.

The syntax to access module members

Once you import any module, it must be consumed. This means we must call at least one of the public members such as functions, structs, constants, or enums marked with the `pub` keyword in the module.

The following syntax shows you how to consume the public members such as functions or structs of an imported module:

```
MY_MODULE.PUBLIC_MEMBERS_OF_MY_MODULE
```

The public members of the imported module can be accessed by specifying the name of the imported module followed by a . (dot) and then we specify the members that are marked as public using the pub keyword inside the module.

If the imported module is not used anywhere in the code, the V compiler will warn you with the `warning: module 'MY_MODULE' is imported but never used` message when we run the program.

Now that we have understood the basics of a module, in the following section, let's take a look at the things to bear in mind when working with modules.

Working with modules

The modular programming approach offers maintainability and code re-usability. It also helps you to add abstractions and allows you to expose only necessary functionality to the consumers of the module. It is recommended that you learn how to work with modules and examine how to efficiently create and organize applications whose functionality span across modules. In this section, you will learn about the various principles to define and work with modules:

- The directory name must match the module name.
- Imported modules must be consumed in the code.
- Multiple V files in the module must define the same module.
- Both private and public members of a module can be accessed from anywhere within the module.
- Only public members of the module are accessible outside of the module.
- Cyclic imports are not allowed.
- Define init functions to execute one-time module-level initializer functionality.

All of the V code that is shown later in this chapter will begin with a comment that indicates the filename along with the relative path of the file concerning the project we are working on. This is exempt for typical commands and snippets of V that show a piece of V code:

```
// file: hello/file_name.v
```

For example, if you find the comments at the beginning of the code block, as shown in the preceding code block, this indicates that the code belongs to `file_name.v` under the directory named `hello`.

Also please be noted that when it is mentioned to run the project from the Terminal, it is necessary to run the project with the `v run .` command from the `root` directory of the project.

Let's understand each of the principles that apply when working with modules using examples.

Creating a simple V project

Before we begin, we will create a demo V project, named `modulebasics`. We will then gain an understanding of all the aforementioned principles by implementing them in this project through examples. The following are the steps to create the demo project:

1. From the Terminal, navigate to the directory of choice and run the following command:

    ```
    v new modulebasics
    ```

    You will be prompted with inputs for the project description, version, and license information, as follows:

    ```
    Input your project description: Understanding Modules in
    V
    Input your project version: (0.0.0)
    Input your project license: (MIT)
    Initialising ...
    Complete!
    ```

2. Provide the description, version, and license information, or skip this by hitting the *Enter* key, and you will see that the prompt shows the status of project creation as `Complete!`.

3. Now, from Command Prompt, set the current directory to the new project that we just created by running the command as follows:

    ```
    cd modulebasics
    ```

Once you have done this, you will have a new V project with three files in a directory named `modulebasics`. The three files are as follows:

a) `.gitignore`

b) `modulebasics.v`

c) `v.mod`

The `.gitignore` file is for Git and will hold the list of files, file extensions, and directories that need to be ignored when pushing our project to Git-based source controls such as GitHub, GitLab, or BitBucket.

The `modulebasics.v` file is the entry point for the application that we have just created. The `v new` command has also added the boilerplate code to the `modulebasics.v` file as follows:

```
// file: modulebasics.v
module main

fn main() {
        println('Hello World!')
}
```

Here, `modulebasics.v` is the entry point to our project and is identified by the main module definition present in the `module main` file. It is also identified by the presence of `fn main()`, which indicates the main entry point function.

The `v.mod` file has module information that will expose details such as the name, description, version, license, and dependencies to the other projects that import this module. Now, we will proceed to create a module in our existing project.

4. We will run the `modulebasics` project by running the following command from the Terminal:

```
v run .
```

The preceding command shows the following output:

```
Hello World!
```

Now that we have set up a project to work with modules, we can go ahead and create a module.

Creating a module

We will create a module in our `modulebasics` project. The first principle to note when creating a module is that the *Directory name must match the module name.* Failing to have a similar name for the directory and module will lead to an error with a message that says `builder error: bad module definition`.

Let's create a module named `mod1` by running the following command from the Terminal:

```
mkdir mod1
```

The preceding command creates a directory named `mod1`, which will be the name of the module. Create a file named `file1.v` in the `mod1` directory with the following code:

```
// file: mod1/file1.v
module mod1


pub fn hello(){
        println('Hello from mod1!')
}
```

In the preceding code, we can observe that the module definition is identified by the `module mod1` statement in `file1.v`. This indicates that the module name is the same as the directory name, which is `mod1`. Additionally, in the `file1.v` file, we have created a public function named `hello`. The `hello` function is marked as public using the `pub` keyword and is accessible inside and outside the module. This allows the `hello` function to be available for the code that imports the `mod1` module.

At this stage, the directory structure of our project will appear as follows:

```
E:\MODULEBASICS
|    .gitignore
|    modulebasics.v
|    v.mod
|
\---mod1
        file1.v
```

Now, we will proceed by importing this module, which is demonstrated in the next section.

Importing a module

As we have successfully created a module named `mod1`, we will go ahead and import this module in the main module from the `modulebasics.v` file. Update the code in the `modulebasics.v` file to import the `mod1` module, as shown here:

```
// file: modulebasics.v
module main
import mod1


fn main() {
        println('Hello World!')
}
```

Note that the `modulebasics.v` now imports the `mod1` module, which is identified by the `import mod1` statement. Now, let's run the project from the Terminal by providing the following command:

```
v run .
```

Running the preceding command will show the following output along with a warning:

```
.\modulebasics.v:3:8: warning: module 'mod1' is imported but
never used
    1 |  // file: modulebasics.v
    2 |  module main
    3 |  import mod1
      |         ~~~~
    4 |
    5 |  fn main() {
Hello World!
```

We can observe that the last line is the output of the program that prints the `Hello World!` message of the `main` function. The rest of the output from the beginning is a warning that details `module mod1 is imported but never used`. So, in the next section, let's take a look at how to access the members of an imported module.

Accessing members of a module

As we have already learned, the second principle says *Imported modules must be consumed in the code*, so let's go ahead and consume the public members of the mod1.

We have already defined a public hello function in the mod1 module. The public hello function of mod1 can be accessed with the help of the imported mod1 module with the mod1.hello() syntax. Now, the code in the modulebasics.v file will be changed as follows:

```
// file: modulebasics.v
module main

import mod1

fn main() {
        mod1.hello()
        println('Hello World!')
}
```

The modulebasics.v file imports the mod1 module and also consumes the public hello function with the mod1.hello() statement. Now with these changes in place, let's run the project with the command from the command-line Terminal, as follows:

```
v run .
```

The output of the preceding command will appear as follows:

```
Hello from mod1!
Hello World!
```

The mod1.hello() statement is executed and the program prints an output Hello from mod1! to the console, which is the functionality enclosed in the hello function of the mod1 module. The output also prints Hello World! to the console, which is as per the sequence of the execution mentioned in the main function of the modulebasics.v file.

Working with multiple files in a module

So far, we only had a single file in the mod1 module. Now we will understand the details of working with multiple files in a single module.

If there are multiple files in a module, then all of the files must define the same module definition. Failing to define the same module for all the files within a module will lead to an error that is similar to `builder error: bad module definition`.

Let's create another file, named `file2.v`, in the `mod1` module with the following code:

```
// file: mod1/file2.v


fn hello2() {
    println('Hello 2 from mod1!')
}
```

At this stage, the directory structure of our project will appear as follows:

```
E:\MODULEBASICS
|    .gitignore
|    modulebasics.v
|    v.mod
|
\---mod1
        file1.v
        file2.v
```

Here, the `file2.v` file has a private function named `hello2`. The `hello2` function just prints the message to the standard output. With these changes in place, let's run the project with the following command:

```
v run .
```

The output of the preceding command will show an error, as follows:

```
.\modulebasics.v:4:1: builder error: bad module definition: .\
modulebasics.v imports module "mod1" but E:\modulebasics\mod1\
file2.v is defined as module 'main'
    2 |  module main
    3 |
    4 |  import mod1
       |  ~~~~~~~~~~~
    5 |
    6 |  fn main() {
```

This is because the code in `file2.v` doesn't define `module mod1`. By default, V assumes that a module will be the main module for the files that do not have a module definition. We have already defined the main module, which could be identified with the `module main` statement in `modulebasics.v`.

When we run the project, the V compiler encounters the `file2.v` file, which doesn't have any module definition. The compiler treats it as the `main` module, and hence, it will throw an error with a message that says `builder error: bad module definition: ..v imports module "mod1" but E:12.v is defined as a module`.

As per the third principle, *Multiple V files in the module must define the same module*, we can get rid of this error by defining the module definition in `file2.v` as `module mod1`, which is similar to that of `file1.v`. Now, the updated `file2.v` file will appear as follows:

```
// file: mod1/file2.v
module mod1


fn hello2() {
    println('Hello 2 from mod1!')
}
```

Here, `file2.v` also has a similar module definition statement of `module mod1`, as identified in `file1.v`. Now, if we run the project with the `v run .` command in the Terminal, the output will appear as follows:

```
Hello from mod1!
Hello World!
```

We can observe that the output is printing the `println` statements of the `hello` and `main` functions. This is because we haven't currently started consuming the new `hello2` function that we just defined. Additionally, notice that the `hello2` function is not marked as public and can only be accessed from inside the `mod1` module.

In the next section, we will examine how we can access the `hello2` function from within the `mod1` module. We will explore, in detail, the member scope of the module members inside and outside of the module.

Member scope in the module

The default scope for members of a module is `private`. These private members can be accessed internally within the module. Specifically, members such as functions, structs, constants, or enums defined in the module are accessible across the module. Only the members that are marked as public using the `pub` keyword are accessible outside the module.

So far, our `modulebasics` project has a module named `mod1` that has two files: `file1.v` and `file2.v`. The tree structure of the project looks like this:

```
E:\MODULEBASICS
|     .gitignore
|     modulebasics.v
|     v.mod
|
\---mod1
          file1.v
          file2.v
```

Let's go ahead and try to access the `hello2` function from the `main` module, as follows:

```
// file: modulebasics.v
module main

import mod1

fn main() {
    mod1.hello()
    mod1.hello2()
}
```

Here, `hello2` is not marked as public, and accessing it from the main module throws an exception with the `error: function mod1.hello2 is private` message.

As per the fourth principle of working with modules, *Both private and public members of a module are accessible from anywhere within the module.* So, let's try to understand this principle by updating the public `hello` function of the `mod1` module to call `hello2`, which is a private function:

```
// file: mod1/file1.v
module mod1


pub fn hello() {
    println('Hello from mod1!')
    // hello2 is not a public but accessible within mod1
    hello2()
}
```

As per the fifth principle of working with modules, *Only public members of a module are accessible outside of the module.* So, let's update the `modulebasics.v` file, such that it calls the public `hello` function, as follows:

```
// file: modulebasics.v
module main

import mod1

fn main() {
    mod1.hello()
}
```

Here is the output:

```
Hello from mod1!
Hello 2 from mod1!
```

The `hello2` function, though not marked as public, is accessible across the `mod1` module. Hence, it is called in the `hello` function, which is already accessible to the main module as it has been marked as public by using the `pub` keyword.

Implications of cyclic imports

There are few instances in which programmers end up having two modules that use each other's functionality. In such situations, there is a chance that the imports of these modules end up being cyclic in nature. For instance, let's say you have two modules, m1 and m2, in a `modulebasics` project with the following code:

```
// file: m1/file1.v
module m1

import m2

pub const greet_from_m1 = 'Greetings from m1'

pub fn hello() {
        println(m2.greet_from_m2)
}
```

Here, the preceding code belongs to the m1 module that has a `greet_from_m1` constant marked with the `pub` keyword. It also has a public `hello` function that prints the constant from the imported m2 module.

Now, let's take a look at the m2 module with the following code:

```
// file: m2/file1.v
module m2

import m1

pub const greet_from_m2 = 'Greetings from m2'

pub fn hello() {
        println(m1.greet_from_m1)
}
```

The aforementioned code belongs to the m2 module, which has a `greet_from_m2` constant marked with the pub keyword. It also has a public `hello` function that prints the constant from the imported m1 module. So the m1 module is referring to m2, and m2 is referring to m1, which introduces a circular or cyclic reference. Now, if we update our `modulebasics.v` file, it looks similar to the following:

```
// file: modulebasics.v
module main

import m1
import m2

fn main() {
        m1.hello()
        m2.hello()
}
```

The `modulebasics.v` file imports both of the m1 and m2 modules and calls the `hello` function that is available in each of these modules in the main function. Now, let's run `modulebasics.v` with the `v run .` command and see what the output will be. As per the sixth principle of working with modules, which says *Cyclic imports are not allowed*, you will observe that the output appears with an error detail, as follows:

```
builder error: error: import cycle detected between the
following modules:
 * main -> m1 -> m2 -> m1
 * m1 -> m2 -> m1
 * m2 -> m1 -> m2
```

From the output, we can see that the execution control first enters the `main` module and has the following flow of execution control:

- `m1 -> m2 -> m1`: The execution control enters the `hello()` function of the m1 module. It then accesses the `greet_from_m2` constant from m2. Following this, the control flows back to m1 and prints the constant.

- `m2 -> m1 -> m2`: The execution control enters the `hello()` function of the m2 module. It then accesses the `greet_from_m1` constant from m1. Following this, the control flows back to m2 and prints the constant.

These two flows are circular in nature. The two m1 and m2 modules are trying to import and access each other's members, and this has led to an error with the builder error: error: import cycle detected between the following modules message.

The init function for a module

The last principle of working with modules requests you to *Define init functions to execute one-time module-level initializer functionality*. Modules in V allow you to define a function named init that is automatically executed when you import the module where it is defined. The init functions of a module act as an initializer of certain functionality, such as establishing database connections or initializing C libraries or module-specific settings, if any. To define the initializer function, you must meet the following conditions:

- The init function must only be defined once inside the module.

- The init function must not be marked as public.

- The init function must not accept any input arguments.

- The init function must not have a return type.

Although you can define a public function named init with at least one input argument, it doesn't act like a module initializer function.

Let's explore the init() function using an example. In our demo project, modulebasics, let's modify the mod1 module to have file1.v with the following code:

```
// file: mod1/file1.v
module mod1

pub fn hello() {
        println('Hello from mod1!')
}

fn init() {
        println('Initializing mod1')
}
```

Here, the new private init function is added to the file1.v file of the mod1 module. In this case, we are simply printing a message that says Initializing mod1 to the console. We will now update the code of the modulebasics.v file, indicating the following main module:

```
// file: modulebasics.v
module main

import mod1

fn main() {
        mod1.hello()
}
```

In the main module, we are calling the hello function that is marked as public using the pub keyword. The private init function is defined in mod1, as we learned that this will be the initializer function that is executed before any other function of the mod1 module. To view this, we will run the project by running the v run . command. The output of the preceding code will appear as follows:

```
Initializing mod1
Hello from mod1!
```

Note that before any other function is executed, the output prints the Initializing mod1 message from the init function. Only then will it print the Hello from mod1! message from the hello function.

Accessing the constants of a module

Accessing the constants of a module from another is a straightforward approach. You can access the constants of the module provided that they are marked as public using the pub keyword.

In our sample modulebasics project, let's consider the mod1 module with file1.v with the following code:

```
// file : mod1/file1.v
module mod1

pub const greet_msg = 'Greeting from mod1!'
```

In the preceding code, we have defined a constant named `greet_msg` in the `mod1` module. Additionally, we marked the constant as public using the `pub` keyword. We will learn how to access this constant from the main module. Change the code in the main module so that it looks like the following:

```
// file: modulebasics.v
module main


import mod1


fn main() {
        println(mod1.greet_msg)
}
```

The preceding code imports the `mod1` module. In the `main` function, which is the entry point of our execution control, we are accessing the `greet_msg` constant from the `mod1` module and printing it to the console:

```
Greeting from mod1!
```

The preceding output shows the value assigned to the `greet_msg` constant of the `mod1` module being printed from the main module.

Accessing structs and embedded structs of a module

In this section, we will explore, in detail, how to access the struct fields and embedded structs fields of a `mod1` module from the main module. We will update the `modulebasics` project such that, in the `mod1` module, we will have two structs, `NoteTimeInfo` and `Note`, defined as follows:

```
"// file : mod1/file1.v
module mod1


import time


// NoteTimeInfo is a struct to store time info of Note
pub struct NoteTimeInfo{
pub:
        created time.Time = time.now()
pub mut:
```

```
        due        time.Time = time.now().add_days(1)
}
```

```
// Note is a struct with embedding struct NoteTimeInfo
// along with other fields
pub struct Note {
        NoteTimeInfo // Embedded Struct
pub:
        id        int
pub mut:
        message string [required]
        status  bool
}
```

Both of these structs, NoteTimeInfo and Note, are marked as public using the pub keyword. For the NoteTimeInfo struct, the created struct field is marked as public, and due is marked as both public and mutable using the pub mut keywords. Both of the created and due fields of the NoteTimeInfo struct have the default value initialized.

Similarly, for the Note struct, the id struct field is marked as public and the message and status fields are marked as public and mutable.

Now, let's update the main module to access the struct fields and embedded struct fields as follows:

```
// file: modulebasics.v
module main

import mod1

fn main(){

        n := mod1.Note {
                id: 1
                message: 'Accessing structs of module demo'
        }
        println('Accessing struct field value Note id:
                $n.id')
```

```
        println('Accessing embedded struct field value
                NoteTimeInfo: $n.NoteTimeInfo')
}
```

The preceding code shows that we accessed the mod1 module's Note and NoteTimeInfo structs in the main module and are initializing the Note struct. Then, we are printing its id field and embedded struct field, NoteTimeInfo. The preceding code provides the following output:

```
Accessing struct field value Note id: 1
Accessing embedded struct field value NoteTimeInfo: mod1.
NoteTimeInfo{
    created: 2021-05-30 01:45:36
    due: 2021-05-31 01:45:36
}
```

The preceding output shows the result of accessing the id struct field and the embedded NoteTimeInfo struct field of the Note struct, which is defined with a public pub access specifier in the mod1 module.

Summary

In this chapter, we clearly understood the concept of modular programming in V. We learned how to create and import modules along with various concepts that help us to work with them. We learned, through code examples, that having modules makes the code that belongs to the project look more accessible and organized. We also learned about the various ways to work with modules, including accessing module members such as structs, functions, and constants.

Additionally, we covered how to work with multiple files inside a module and understood the scope for the members defined inside and outside of a module. Following this, we learned about initializer functions and also understood the implications of creating cyclic imports. Finally, we covered how to access the structs and embedded structs of a module using code examples.

Having understood modules, in the next chapter, we will proceed to explore concurrency in V.

Section 3: Advanced Concepts in V Programming

This section covers advanced concepts in V that include writing highly concurrent code, where you will learn about the go keyword and its usage as well as the thread data type. This section will provide detailed info about various concurrency patterns that enable you to share data between concurrent routines using locks and also has a detailed chapter on an advanced concurrency pattern called Channels. In the detailed chapter on Channels, you will learn how to share data by establishing communication among concurrently running routines in V.

The last chapters of this section focus on writing tests in V. In addition to this, you will be introduced to the built-in **JSON** and **Object-Relational Mapper** (**ORM**) libraries, and we'll cover building an end-to-end project that has a RESTful microservice using the vweb web server.

This section has the following chapters:

- *Chapter 10, Concurrency*
- *Chapter 11, Channels – An Advanced Concurrency Pattern*
- *Chapter 12, Testing*
- *Chapter 13, Introduction to JSON and ORM*
- *Chapter 14, Building a Microservice*

10
Concurrency

Concurrency is a crucial topic when it comes to V. The main essence of V lies in the concurrency capabilities that it offers to programmers. In this chapter, you will learn about the concept of concurrency via detailed code examples. This chapter will begin by explaining a simple real-life scenario about performing daily morning routines. In the real-life scenario that I chose to explain concurrency, you will be presented with a situation where you perform tasks without knowing that you are performing those tasks concurrently. You will also compare the results of the tasks when they were performed sequentially and see the benefits when similar tasks are performed concurrently.

In addition to the more intuitive explanation of concurrency provided in this chapter, you will gain foundational knowledge of concepts such as the `time` module and the `thread` type to get you started programming concurrent code in V.

We will cover the following topics in this chapter:

- Introducing concurrency
- Understanding parallelism
- Learning the basic terminology
- Getting started with concurrency
- Implementing concurrency in V
- Spawning a void function to run concurrently
- Implementing a real-life concurrency scenario programmatically
- Learning different approaches to implement concurrent programs
- Sharing data between the main thread and concurrent tasks

By the end of this chapter, you will be confident enough to write concurrent code in V using the go keyword and handle concurrent functions using the `thread` type. You will be able to understand the benefits of writing concurrent code in contrast to sequential code. Through this chapter, you will understand how to concurrently spawn functions such as void functions, functions that return values, as well as anonymous functions. You will also learn how to share data between the main thread and the tasks that are spawned to run concurrently.

Technical requirements

The full source code for this chapter is available at `https://github.com/PacktPublishing/Getting-Started-with-V-Programming/tree/main/Chapter10`.

It is recommended that you run the code examples in each of the sections in a fresh console or file with a `.v` extension to avoid clashes among variable names across examples.

Introducing concurrency

Concurrency means running tasks concurrently. While this might seem like a very abstract definition, let's consider the following real-world example. You wake up in the morning of winter, and you need hot water to bathe. You can only bathe when the water is hot enough. However, you have other morning chores to finish off while the water gets hot. So, you turn on the water heater and then, let's say, you brush your teeth for some time while the water heater indicates the water is hot. Then, you switch off the water heater, enjoy a hot shower, and get ready for the day.

The advantage of concurrency is that you can do multiple things simultaneously that don't have to follow a specific order. So, in this scenario, you don't have to remain idle waiting for the water to get hot; you can finish brushing your teeth in parallel. So, the order the tasks are completed in is not very important.

The term *parallel* I used previously is being used in a general talking sense here. But in the programming world, concurrency and parallelism are two different concepts. I'll explain parallelism in more detail in the *Understanding parallelism* section.

Let's say you have finished brushing your teeth and the heater is still heating the water and hasn't indicated that the hot water is ready yet. During this time, you can get a pair of clothes ready that you want to wear for the day. Sometimes, you may find yourself brushing your teeth and finding a nice pair of clothes from your wardrobe at the same time. So, these tasks do not need to be done sequentially.

Also, notice that with concurrent tasks, the outcome of one task may not necessarily affect the other. The tasks of heating the water and brushing your teeth are done simultaneously or concurrently. It is also evident that these tasks do not depend on each other, but you, the main actor, are dependent on these tasks being completed so that you can finish your daily morning routine.

In the world of computer programming, concurrency is I/O-bound. In correlation to the previous explanation, this means you (the main program) will provide input or act on a task (switch on the heater). The task runs on a different thread (starts heating the water) or runs externally via a third-party API (uses a heater and electricity to heat the water). The task takes its own time to process your input request and returns the result to you (the hot water status of the heater in the form of a light indicator).

Some of the most common examples of I/O-bound operations where we can apply concurrency are as follows:

- Obtaining a response from a third-party API
- Sending data to a third-party API
- Reading data from or writing data to a disk
- Downloading files from a web server or uploading files to it

Now that we have got a firm understanding of the concept of concurrency, we will proceed to the next section, where we will understand parallelism with some real-life scenarios.

Understanding parallelism

Although the words concurrency and parallelism are used interchangeably in the general sense, they differ slightly when it comes to the world of computers. Both of them are used to speed up things. However, concurrency focuses on multiple independent tasks to be finished in the least possible time. In contrast to concurrency, **parallelism** focuses on splitting one single task into multiple resources to speed up finishing a particular job. The concept of parallelism is huge, and it could take a full chapter to explain it. For this chapter, we will keep things simple and concise in this section and try to understand a use case of parallelism by looking at a simple but intuitive real-world example.

Consider that you have a tank with a capacity of 1,000 liters where you store water to use for your farmland. You have an electrical motor pump that pulls water up from the ground and fills the tank at a rate of 10 liters per minute. To fill the empty tank using a single motor pump, it would take 100 minutes, or 1 hour 40 minutes.

In summer, you need to have at least 4,000 liters of water to maintain your farm. So, you buy three more tanks of a similar capacity and have a connecting pipe that fills all four tanks with water using your electrical motor pump. Previously, it used to take 1 hour 40 minutes for one tank. But with four tanks in place with only one electrical motor pump, you need to wait 6 hours 40 minutes to ensure all the tanks become full; only then can you go home.

Considering this is a waste of time and it is not efficient to let the electrical motor run for much longer periods, you plan to buy three similar electrical motor pumps.

Now, you have each electrical motor pump connected to fill only one tank, so each of the motor pumps fills one tank in parallel. You turn on all four motor pumps, which finish filling all four tanks in 1 hour 40 minutes. You feel happy and go home from your farm early.

It is worth noting that the task of filling each tank can be split across multiple motor pumps instead of having one motor pump fill all four tanks. So, the tasks that are fit for parallel processing must be suitable enough to be split across processes and ensure the result is not affected.

Also, the task that's performed by each of the motor pumps accomplishes one common major task, which is filling all four tanks. This means that the final task is dependent on the parallel tasks and the way they perform. If one of the motor pumps has a slower or faster rate of filling water per minute, it affects the overall time it takes to finish filling all four tanks, which is the end goal in this scenario.

In simple terms, this example is an analogy to the world of computing in a way that each electrical motor pump can be assumed as the core of a quad-core processor chip. The task of making the four empty tanks full can be correlated to any task that can be split into chunks to run in parallel, ensuring that the collective progress of parallel tasks eventually leads to the main task being completed.

This example stands out as a case of functional parallelism. In some cases where data parallelism is involved, the outcome of the tasks that are performed by parallel jobs needs to be clubbed in a particular order so that the task is considered a success.

An example of this is exporting data from a report to generate a PDF file. In this process, each of the parallel jobs picks up a chunk of data to be laid out in pages. The final process is clubbing all the individual chunks of pages rendered by every parallel job in a particular order to make it into a single PDF. If one of the parallel jobs fails, the PDF that's generated is deemed to contain missing data or a missing list of pages. So, in data parallelism, all the parallel jobs must finish doing their part successfully, which eventually leads to the task that was split to run in parallel to be completed.

Having understood the concepts of concurrency and parallelism, let's learn about the basic terminologies that will be used in the rest of this chapter.

Learning the basic terminology

Before we begin understanding how to implement concurrency in V, we will start by learning a few basic terms that we commonly use when working with concurrency:

- **Program**: A program is a set of instructions in the form of functions and statements that help us achieve a particular job.
- **Process**: A program with one or more functions and statements, when it starts running, is associated with the process. A process can have one or more sub-processes, each of them running on a different thread.
- **Thread**: A thread allows one or more tasks to run in sequential order.
- **Task**: A task is a unit of work that runs on a thread. It can be represented as a function in V.

Now that we understand these basic terminologies, let's get started with the concepts of concurrency that will help us implement concurrent programs in V.

Getting started with concurrency

Before we deep dive into the programming world of concurrency, we ought to know a couple of basics about time, a standard library in V, and the thread type. In this section, I will provide a very brief introduction to the time module and the thread type. Understanding these concepts will be helpful as we continue this chapter.

Understanding the time module

V ships along with it a classy suite of handy libraries and time is among them. I will be using the time module to mimic long-running activities in functions that run concurrently. To use the time module, you need to import it, as follows:

```
import time
```

The time module in V has a vast number of functionalities, including telling the current time on the system using the time.now() expression. If we are just interested in the hours, minutes, and seconds part of the time at the time of execution, you can write the corresponding expression as time.now().hhmmss(). These are a few functions among a vast set of functionalities available in the time module.

In the following sections, we will be focusing on the sleep and new_stopwatch functions. We will be using these functionalities in this chapter when writing concurrent code in V.

sleep

The sleep function, as the name suggests, halts the execution of the program for the specified duration provided to it as an argument. The sleep function of the time module accepts only one input argument of the time.Duration type in nanoseconds, microseconds, milliseconds, seconds, minutes, and hours. All these units are of the time. Duration type, which has an underlying data type of i64.

For example, if you want to hold the program execution for half a second, all you need to do is write the following statement:

```
import time
```

```
time.sleep(0.5 * time.second)
```

Alternatively, you can write time.sleep(500 * time.millisecond) since 1,000 milliseconds is equal to 1 second.

stopwatch

The time module also has a stopwatch feature. The new_stopwatch() method is used to start the stopwatch. At any point during the program, you can check the time that's elapsed from the moment you started the stopwatch using the following syntax:

```
sw.elapsed().nanoseconds()
```

In the aforementioned syntax, the sw variable holds the instance of initiation of the stopwatch using time.new_stopwatch(). The duration of time that's elapsed is in nanoseconds, which is of the i64 type. You can have the elapsed time in other units instead of calling nanoseconds(), such as microseconds() and milliseconds(), which return the i64 values of the time that's elapsed. Alternatively, the seconds(), minutes(), and hours() methods return f64 values.

This feature is handy for measuring the time that's elapsed while running a set of instructions. For example, the following code demonstrates the time elapsed from the moment the program starts until it finishes printing the value of the i variable for each iteration:

```
module main

import time

fn main() {
    sw := time.new_stopwatch()

    for i in 1 .. 5 {
        println('$i')
    }
    println('Total time took to finish:
            $sw.elapsed().seconds() seconds')
}
```

The following is the output:

```
1
2
3
4
Total time took to finish: 0.0141559 seconds
```

The preceding code demonstrates the usage of the `new_stopwatch()` method, which prints the time elapsed after printing four numbers in the range to the console. The time this took to finish on my system was `0.0141559` seconds. It might differ from one system to another.

This basic information about the time module is enough for us to get started with this chapter. In the next section, we will understand the `thread` type in detail.

Understanding the thread type

The handle that's obtained when you spawn any function using the `go` keyword is of the `thread` type. With access to the `thread` type, you can `wait()` on the thread to finish executing its job.

Thread array

You can create an array of threads with the following syntax:

```
mut t1 := []thread OPTIONAL_TYPE{}
```

The preceding syntax shows you how to declare an array of threads. `OPTIONAL_TYPE` indicates the return type of the functions held by the handlers contained in the thread array. All the elements of the thread array must be handlers of a function of a similar return type. For example, if you are adding the elements to the thread array and each of the elements spawns a concurrent function with the `void` type, then the array definition will be as follows:

```
mut t1 := []thread{}
```

In the preceding code, the type of the `t1` variable is `[]thread`. To ensure all the tasks that are held by `t1` are executed completely, you can call a blocking function on the thread array with the `t1.wait()` expression. Calling the `wait()` function on `t1` will ensure that all the concurrent tasks held by `t1` are executed to completion. A detailed demonstration of `[]thread` is provided in the *Spawning multiple tasks to run concurrently* section of this chapter.

Alternatively, if you want to create a thread array that holds the concurrent tasks and all of them have a `string` return type, then the array definition will be as follows:

```
mut t2 := []thread string{}
```

In the preceding code, the t2 type is a []thread string. The call to the wait() function on t2 will ensure that all the concurrent tasks that spawn functions with string execute and return values in t2.

The following code shows how to access the values returned by the string functions that were spawned to run concurrently in their threads:

```
t2_res := t2.wait()
```

You will get the []string type for the t2_res variable. A detailed demonstration of a thread array of the []thread type is mentioned in the *Spawning functions with return values to run concurrently* and *Spawning anonymous functions that accept input arguments* sections of this chapter.

All you should know about wait()

The following are a few points to know about the wait() function with regards to the thread type in V:

- This function blocks the execution of the main process until the tasks that have been spawned to run concurrently in the other thread have finished executing.

- This function does not take any input arguments.

- This function is available on the handle of a single thread, as well as on the variable that was assigned with a thread array filled with handles to concurrent tasks.

- The return type of the wait() function is similar to that of the function that is being run concurrently.

- When calling the wait() function on the thread array, all the elements of the thread array must handle the functions with similar return types.

Having understood the basic concepts of the time module, the thread type, and the wait() function, we will start learning how to write and work with concurrent programming in V.

Implementing concurrency in V

Using V, you can write a program that runs functions concurrently using the go keyword. The go keyword is a built-in keyword in V. The go keyword is available anywhere in the program without any explicit `import` statements required. In the next section, we will understand the basic syntax of the go keyword.

The go keyword syntax

You can run any function concurrently using the go keyword, just by writing the go keyword followed by the name of the function, as shown here:

```
go FUNCTION_NAME_1(OPTIONAL_ARGUMENTS)
```

In the preceding syntax, which demonstrates the usage of the go keyword in V, all we can see is a simple function named FUNCTION_NAME_1 that is being run concurrently. You do not need to make any special syntactical changes to a function to run it concurrently.

With the approach mentioned in the preceding syntax, the active program spawns a new thread and lets the function run concurrently. If the active program is interested in knowing the completion status of the FUNCTION_NAME_1 function, then it can wait for the thread to finish executing FUNCTION_NAME_1. The syntax will be as follows:

```
h := go FUNCTION_NAME_1(OPTIONAL_ARGUMENTS)
h.wait()
```

In the preceding syntax, we can see that the result of FUNCTION_NAME_1(OPTIONAL_ARGUMENTS) gives us access to the thread that the FUNCTION_NAME_1 function is executing on. Here, the h variable will be of the `thread` type. The h variable in this syntax is often termed as a *handle* to the concurrent task running in another thread. We are then calling the `wait()` function on the handle. The `wait()` function blocks the execution of the main program until the concurrent task has finished executing.

The preceding syntax shows how to spawn functions to run in concurrent threads using the go keyword. It also shows the syntax for waiting on threads until they finish executing. Having learned this, let's understand how to spawn a void function so that it can run concurrently.

Spawning a void function to run concurrently

In this section, we will write a simple function that does not have any return type. The function just prints a message to the console. Then, we will spawn this function so that it runs in a concurrent thread using the go keyword, as follows:

```
module main

fn greet() {
    println('Hello from other side!')
}

fn main() {
    h := go greet()
    println(typeof(h).name) // thread
}
```

In the preceding code, the h variable provides access to handle the concurrent task. The h variable is of the thread type in the preceding code. The output of the preceding code could be any of the following outputs:

The following is the first output you may receive:

```
thread
```

The following is the second output you may receive:

```
thread
Hello from other side!
```

You will see either of these outputs, which appear to be inconsistent outcomes from the program. Notice that the greet() function is written to print a nice message, but the message is missing in the first output. Let's understand how we can get the message printed to the standard output with the help of the wait() function.

Waiting on a concurrent thread

In the previous example, we spawned the `greet()` function to run in a concurrent thread using the `go greet()` statement. But the process, which is the main application that spawned the function, doesn't care about the thread it spawned to run concurrently. And thus, the program in the preceding example exits out of the execution without actually waiting on the concurrent thread that it has spawned.

To make the main program wait for the concurrent thread to finish, it can wait on the handle that was obtained from the `go greet()` statement by calling the `wait()` function.

Let's update our example with a call to the `wait()` function, as follows:

```
module main

fn greet() {
    println('Hello from other side!')
}

fn main() {
    h := go greet()
    println(typeof(h).name)
    h.wait()
}
```

The following is the output:

```
thread
Hello from other side!
```

From the preceding code, we can see that the main process is waiting for the subprocess that it initiated to run in a concurrent thread using the `h.wait()` statement. Simply put, when the program starts, the execution's control enters the `main` function, and then it spawns the `greet()` function to run in a concurrent thread. The main program gains access to the concurrent task through the h handle variable.

The main process proceeds to execute other statements if there are any that it encounters during the execution flow. So, it jumps to the next line in the sequence of statements, where we are printing h. As the statement gets evaluated in the sequence, the main program prints the type of h to the console, and the execution control then flows to the `h.wait()` statement. This is where the main process, which has no other work to do, will wait for the h thread instance to finish executing the `greet()` function, which prints the message to the standard console.

Now that we understood how to run a void function concurrently using the go keyword, let's learn how to implement a real-life scenario programmatically.

Implementing a real-life concurrency scenario programmatically

It is equally important for you to not just understand the concept of concurrency but also experience it by writing concurrent code using basic real-life examples. In this section, we will mimic the example of concurrency that we explained at the beginning of this chapter programmatically using three tasks. These are the early morning routine tasks we mentioned; that is, heating the water, brushing your teeth, and choosing a pair of clothes from your wardrobe.

Since I believe that adding the realistic times it takes to perform each of these tasks is trivial, I'll provide some dummy values in terms of seconds to mimic these tasks. Hence, I chose to represent the time taken for each of these tasks in a matter of seconds just for brevity. This makes it easier for us to run the code faster and understand the results in a neat and organized manner. The following table shows the times I am mimicking for each of the three tasks we are going to spawn concurrently:

#	Task	Mimic time used in code (seconds)	Approximate time in real life (minutes)
1	hot_water	5 seconds	10 to 15 minutes
2	brush_teeth	3 seconds	3 to 5 minutes
3	select_clothes	3 seconds	3 to 5 minutes

Table 10.1 – Tasks with the mimic time used in code and the approximate time in real life

Now that we've set these times, let's start understanding the challenges of sequentially executing these tasks. Later, we will optimize the code to minimize the time it takes to run these tasks by implementing a concurrent program that spawns these three tasks concurrently.

Running multiple tasks in a sequence

In this section, we will understand the impact of executing long-running and time-consuming tasks sequentially. Consider the following code, which simply calls the `hot_water`, `brush_teeth`, and `select_clothes` tasks, which are represented programmatically in a sequential manner:

```
module main

import time

fn hot_water() {
    println('Started Switch on Water heater:
        $time.now().hhmmss()')
    time.sleep(5 * time.second)
    println('Water heater indicates hot water ready!:
        $time.now().hhmmss()')
}

fn brush_teeth() {
    println('Started brushing:  $time.now().hhmmss()')
    time.sleep(3 * time.second)
    println('End Brushing:  $time.now().hhmmss()')
}

fn select_clothes() {
    println('Started choosing pair of clothes :
$time.now().hhmmss()')
    time.sleep(3 * time.second)
    println('End choosing pair of
        clothes:  $time.now().hhmmss()')
}
```

```
fn main() {
    sw := time.new_stopwatch()
    hot_water()
    brush_teeth()
    select_clothes()
    println('Your pre bath morning chores took:
            $sw.elapsed().seconds() seconds')
}
```

The preceding code is performing sequential calls to the three void functions; that is, `hot_water()`, `brush_teeth()`, and `select_clothes()`. Void functions are functions that have no return values in their method signatures.

To mimic the time it takes each of these tasks to run, represented as void functions, we are calling `time.sleep` with the number of seconds specified in the table for the respective tasks. We are also printing the respective task's status messages to the console to indicate its start and completion times. This status message will help us understand the order they followed to start and finish each task.

We also have a stopwatch, represented by `sw` variable, that starts just before the tasks in the `main` function are executed sequentially. Finally, we are calculating the time that's elapsed in seconds after the three tasks have finished executing.

The output of the preceding code is as follows:

```
Started Switch on Water heater: 07:15:02
Water heater indicates hot water ready!: 07:15:07
Started brushing: 07:15:07
End Brushing: 07:15:10
Started choosing pair of clothes : 07:15:10
End choosing pair of clothes: 07:15:13
Your pre bath morning chores took: 11.0601946 seconds
```

When the program invoked these tasks, as shown in the preceding output, each of these tasks was executed sequentially. This means you only start brushing your teeth after the water heater indicates that the hot water is ready. Also, it took a little over 11 seconds to finish all three tasks:

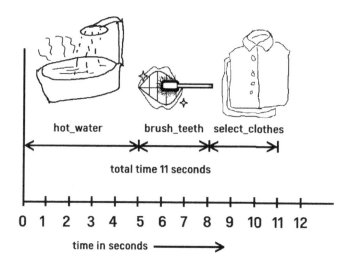

Figure 10.1 – Running multiple tasks in a sequence

Do you need to be idle while the water gets hot? In the real world, unless you are sleepy, you continue doing other chores such as brush_teeth or select_clothes, as demonstrated in the program, to finish off your morning routine.

In the world of programming, you can achieve this using concurrency. In the next section, we'll write some concurrent code in V to perform the aforementioned tasks quickly and efficiently.

Spawning multiple tasks to run concurrently

In the previous section, we understood that sequentially performing the morning tasks took approximately 11 seconds. There is a scope for these tasks to be accomplished faster as they are independent of each other. In this section, we will focus on concurrently running the tasks, and then we will understand the outcome and time taken to finish these tasks when they're run concurrently. Finally, we will analyze the advantage of running the tasks concurrently in contrast to running them sequentially.

In the following code, I'll be using the example of daily morning routines in terms of concurrent programming in V. To run the hot_water(), brush_teeth(), and select_clothes() functions concurrently, their function signatures or function bodies don't need to be changed. We will just be calling these functions using the go keyword. V offers the advantage of being able to run any function without any additional syntax to run concurrently.

As we are aware from the preceding section, these three tasks are void functions. All they do is print their starting and finishing statuses. These tasks also have time.sleep statements to mimic the time it took for each of these tasks to complete:

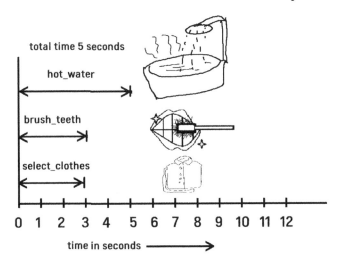

Figure 10.2 – Spawning multiple tasks to run concurrently

As we learned in the previous sections, we can create an array of concurrent processes using void functions. In this section, we will learn how to add concurrent tasks to a thread array. We will define a thread array, t, of the [] thread type and then add three concurrent tasks to it. After that, we will wait until all the tasks in the thread array finish executing.

The following code demonstrates spawning these three tasks concurrently:

```
module main

import time

fn hot_water() {
    println('Started Switch on Water heater:
        $time.now().hhmmss()')
```

```
        time.sleep(5 * time.second)
        println('Water heater indicates hot water ready! :
                $time.now().hhmmss()')
}


fn brush_teeth() {
    println('Started brushing:  $time.now().hhmmss()')
    time.sleep(3 * time.second)
    println('End Brushing:  $time.now().hhmmss()')
}


fn select_clothes() {
    println('Started choosing pair of
            clothes:  $time.now().hhmmss()')
    time.sleep(3 * time.second)
    println('End choosing pair of
            clothes:  $time.now().hhmmss()')
}


fn main() {
    mut t := []thread{}
    sw := time.new_stopwatch()
    t << go hot_water()
    t << go brush_teeth()
    t << go select_clothes()
    t.wait()
    println('Your pre bath morning chores took:
            $sw.elapsed().seconds() seconds')
}
```

In the preceding code, we have three tasks represented as void functions. We also have a stopwatch represented by the sw variable, which starts just before the tasks are executed. Finally, we are calculating the time that had elapsed in seconds after the three tasks finished executing.

We also created a mutable array, t, of the [] thread type. Then, we added the thread array with handles to concurrent tasks. We let each of these tasks execute on different threads other than the one that the main program is running on. We can see that all the functions – hot_water(), brush_teeth(), and select_clothes() – are void functions, so they fit in the thread array of the [] thread type.

After spawning the three tasks so that they run concurrently, the program is waiting for all of these tasks to finish executing. It does so by invoking the t.wait() statement. A call to the wait() function on the array of threads blocks the main program until all the concurrent tasks held in that array have been completed.

hot_water() is the most time-consuming task as it takes about 5 seconds to heat the water. So, you wake up in the morning and the first thing you do is switch on the water heater. Instead of wasting time by remaining idle until the water gets hot, you decide to brush_teeth(). Let's say that, on an average, you brush for about 3 seconds (mimicking time for brevity). As you can quickly walk and move while you brush, you go to your wardrobe and select_clothes() you want to wear for the day.

Here, we are assuming that it took 3 seconds to choose the pair of clothes and set them aside so that you can wear them once you're done with your hot shower/bath.

You can run the code in this example by copying it to a file and running it using the v run filename.v command from the command prompt. Running the code multiple times will give you different results.

Having represented the times for each of the tasks programmatically in the preceding code, the output will appear something similar to one of the following outputs.

The following is the first output you may get:

```
Started Switch on Water heater: 07:15:05
Started choosing pair of clothes:  07:15:05
Started brushing:  07:15:05
End choosing pair of clothes:  07:15:08
End Brushing:  07:15:08
Water heater indicates hot water ready! : 07:15:10
Your pre bath morning chores took: 5.0044861 seconds
```

The following is the second output you may get:

```
Started Switch on Water heater: 07:15:11
Started choosing pair of clothes:  07:15:11
Started brushing:  07:15:11
End Brushing:  07:15:14
End choosing pair of clothes:  07:15:14
Water heater indicates hot water ready! : 07:15:16
Your pre bath morning chores took: 5.0028225 seconds
```

You will see either Output 1 or Output 2 for each run. For each output, we can see that the three tasks begin at the same time, which shows that they are being run concurrently. The difference in these outputs is that the order that the brush_teeth() and select_clothes() tasks are completed in alters. This is because both of them have a task completion duration of 3 seconds. This means that no specified order is predetermined for the execution of these tasks.

In comparison to the sequential tasks, which took approximately 11 seconds to complete, with a concurrent programming approach, we finished running all three tasks in just 5 seconds.

From this example, we can see that the maximum time it took for the program to finish running all the concurrent tasks is approximately greater than or equal to the time it took the longest-running task, among the other concurrent tasks, to be spawned by the program. This is evident from both of the outputs, which took 5.0044861 and 5.0029784 seconds, respectively. This is approximately the same amount of time required to complete the task of heating the water.

The advantage of concurrently spawning time-consuming tasks is that you have faster runtimes. In the next section, we will compare the results of the sequential and concurrent program runtimes and understand the results.

Comparing sequential and concurrent program runtimes

As we noticed from the output of the sequential and concurrent code in the previous sections, the time the sequential code took to run was approximately 11 seconds. But the same set of tasks, when run concurrently using the go keyword and waiting for all of them to run concurrently, took just 5 seconds approximately.

The results of the sequential programming approach stress the need for speed and less wait time, which can be achieved through concurrent programming.

Looking at the example in the *Spawning multiple tasks to run concurrently* section, it is evident from the results that we finished three tasks twice as fast in comparison to the tasks when they're run sequentially. With the concurrent programming approach, were almost 2.2 times faster (11/5 = 2.2). Alternatively, when the three tasks were run concurrently, the speed of execution was 220% faster than when the tasks were run sequentially for the use case.

By comparing these results, we learned about several benefits, such as faster runtimes and less wait time. In the next section, we will look at the various approaches to implementing concurrent programming.

Learning different approaches to implement concurrent programs

Now that we have understood the benefits of concurrent programming over the sequential approach, it is beneficial for you to understand a couple of other ways to deal with spawning concurrent tasks in V. So far, the programming examples we've looked at have dealt with void functions. In the following sections, we will learn how to write concurrent code for anonymous functions and how to retrieve the results from the functions that have return values.

Spawning functions with return values to run concurrently

Till now, we have spawned tasks that do not return any value to the main thread to run concurrently. We accessed the handle to these concurrent tasks and waited for these tasks to finish. What if the concurrent task has a return value? In this section, we will alter the example of morning routines that we looked at in the preceding section, where we ran void functions concurrently.

Let's consider the following code:

```
module main

import time

fn hot_water() string {
    println('Started Switch on Water heater:
            $time.now().hhmmss()')
    time.sleep(5 * time.second)
```

```
        println('Water heater indicates hot water ready! :
                $time.now().hhmmss()')
        return 'Hot water ready!'
}


fn brush_teeth() string {
    println('Started brushing:  $time.now().hhmmss()')
    time.sleep(3 * time.second)
    println('End Brushing:  $time.now().hhmmss()')
    return 'Sparkling Teeth ready!'
}


fn select_clothes() string {
    println('Started choosing pair of
            clothes:  $time.now().hhmmss()')
    time.sleep(3 * time.second)
    println('End choosing pair of
            clothes:  $time.now().hhmmss()')
    return 'Pair of clothes ready!'
}


fn main() {
    mut t := []thread string{}
    sw := time.new_stopwatch()
    t << go hot_water()
    t << go brush_teeth()
    t << go select_clothes()
    res := t.wait()
    println('Your pre bath morning chores took:
            $sw.elapsed().seconds() seconds')
    println('*** Type Check ***')
    println('Type of thread array of strings t:
            ${typeof(t).name}')
```

```
    println('Type of res: ${typeof(res).name}')
    println('*** Values returned by concurrently executed
        tasks ***')
    println(res)
}
```

We can modify the tasks so that each of the tasks returns messages. The three tasks –
hot_water, brush_teeth, and select_clothes – will now have updated method
signatures, indicating their return values are of the string type. The values that were
returned by the handles that are part of the thread array were taken into a variable called
res. We are also printing the type of the t variable, which in this case is a thread array
of strings represented by the [] thread string type. This can be seen in the following
output. The res variable is a type of [] string as all three tasks have signatures
indicating the string return type.

The output of the preceding code will appear as follows:

```
Started Switch on Water heater: 07:15:40
Started choosing pair of clothes:  07:15:40
Started brushing:  07:15:40
End choosing pair of clothes:  07:15:43
End Brushing:  07:15:43
Water heater indicates hot water ready! : 07:15:45
Your pre bath morning chores took: 5.0048506 seconds
*** Type Check ***
Type of thread array of strings t: []thread string
Type of res: []string
*** Values returned by concurrently executed tasks ***
['Hot water ready!', 'Sparkling Teeth ready!', 'Pair of clothes
ready!']
```

Here, we can see that even though the order of execution for the concurrently spawned
tasks differs based on the time taken by each of them, the res array, which is of the []
string type, holds the values in the order that matches the order that we pushed the
handles to the thread array of strings, t.

Spawning anonymous functions to run concurrently

Anonymous functions are functions that can fit inside any other method, and they do not have a name. Their scope is limited to the containing method. We learned about these functions in the *Anonymous functions* section of *Chapter 7, Functions*. V facilitates spawning anonymous functions so that they run concurrently.

In the next subsection, we will learn how to spawn anonymous functions that do not accept any input arguments. Then, we will look at spawning anonymous functions that accept input arguments with code examples.

Spawning anonymous functions that have no input arguments

To spawn an anonymous function that has no input arguments, you need to define an anonymous function after the go keyword. As the anonymous functions just need to be spawned right after the definition, when used in combination with the go keyword, we need to invoke the call by calling empty, (), after the body of the anonymous function. The following syntax shows how to spawn anonymous functions:

```
module main

fn main() {
    t := go fn () string {
        return 'hi'
    }()
    x := t.wait()
    println(typeof(x).name) // string
    println(x) // hi
}
```

From the preceding code, we can see that we are spawning an anonymous function that returns a string message stating hi. Here, the anonymous functions that are spawned to run concurrently using the go keyword have empty () after the body. This empty () indicates the input arguments section of the function signature. In this scenario, the anonymous function does not accept any input arguments, so we close the function body with an empty ().

Spawning anonymous functions that accept input arguments

To spawn an anonymous function that accepts input arguments, you need to define an anonymous function after the go keyword. As the anonymous functions just need to be spawned right after the definition, when used in combination with the go keyword, we need to invoke the call by providing a list of arguments that match the type specified in the list of accepted input arguments for the anonymous function, in-between (and), after the body of the anonymous function.

The following syntax shows how to spawn anonymous functions:

```
module main

fn main() {
    mut t := []thread string{}
    for i in 1 .. 3 {
        t << go fn (i int, msg string) string {
            return 'iteration: $i, message: $msg'
        }(i, 'hello') // <- arguments must match list in
                      // the anonymous function definition
    }
    res := t.wait()
    println('Type of t: ${typeof(t).name}')
    println('Type of res: ${typeof(res).name}')
    println(res)
}
```

From the preceding code, we can see that we are spawning an anonymous function that returns a string. Here, the anonymous functions that are spawned to run concurrently using the go keyword have been provided with values of each iteration in the range 1..3 as the first argument; the same message, hello, of the string type is provided as the second argument. They are represented together in rounded brackets; that is, (i, 'hello').(i, 'hello') indicates the values that were passed as input arguments to the anonymous function. In this scenario, the anonymous function is defined with (i int, msg string), which are the input arguments, so we must close the function body with (i, 'hello'), which indicates invoking the anonymous function with values for the respective arguments.

The following is the output:

```
Type of t: []thread string
Type of res: []string
['iteration: 1, message: hello', 'iteration: 2, message:
hello']
```

From the preceding output, we can see that the type of the t variable is a []thread string. This means that waiting on t will result in an array of strings. So, in this case, the result of t.wait() is assigned to the res variable, which is of the []string type. In the final line of the output, we are printing the value of the res array, where each element is formatted as a string representation that contains an iteration number for a range of 1..3 and a string message, hello, that's returned by an anonymous function.

So far, we have only learned how to spawn functions so that they run concurrently. In the next section, we will learn how to share data between the main thread and concurrent tasks.

Sharing data between the main thread and concurrent tasks

You can share or exchange the data from the main thread with the tasks that have been spawned to run concurrently. V allows you to share data between the main thread and the tasks it spawns, but only using the variables that are of the struct, map, or array type. These variables need to be specified using the shared keyword in such cases. Variables marked using the shared keyword need to be accessed using rlock when they are being read or lock when we want to read/write/modify those variables.

Let's consider a scenario where a fundraiser is raising money for a noble cause. A donor or multiple donors, if they wish to contribute to the fund, can contribute some amount to a fund manager (who represents the main function in our code). When the donations reach the target set by the fund, the fund manager stops collecting money. Assuming that this happens concurrently until the amount that's received is greater than or equal to the target amount, afterward, the fund manager will stop collecting further funds.

Since data sharing can only happen using structs, maps, or array types, we will define a struct that represents a Fund, as follows:

```
struct Fund {
    name    string
    target f32
mut:
    total          f32
    num_donors int
}
```

The preceding code contains four fields. Two of them are name and target, where name represents the fund name and target represents the amount that must be achieved to fulfill the cause. name and target will be set by the fund manager (the main program). The other two fields are total and num_donors. The struct field total is used to represent the amount that's been accumulated in the fund via donations, while num_donors field is used to indicate the total number of donors that have contributed to this fund so far.

Now, let's define a method called collect for the Fund struct that accepts an input argument called amt, which represents the amount that's been collected from any generous donor, as follows:

```
fn (shared f Fund) collect(amt f32) {
    lock f { // read - write lock
        if f.total < f.target {
            f.num_donors += 1
            f.total += amt
            println('$f.num_donors \t before: ${f.total - amt}
\t funds received: $amt \t total: $f.total')
        }
    }
}
```

The collect method has a receiver argument, f, for the Fund struct that's marked using the shared keyword. We marked the receiver argument as shared because the collect method will be accessed concurrently by multiple threads. In such cases, it is essential to avoid collisions, so we should use rlock or lock to acquire the lock on the instance of f being accessed by a concurrent task. In the collect method, we are reading and updating the total and num_donors mutable fields, so it is essential to acquire a read-write lock using lock, as shown in the preceding code.

Now, let's move on and see what the fund manager (main function) will be doing to collect funds from concurrent sources. The first thing we must do is create a shared variable for `Fund` whose `name` is of the cause that the funds are being raised for, along with the `target` amount needed to fulfill the amount needed for the fund. This can be represented programmatically as follows:

```
shared fund := Fund{
    name: 'A noble cause'
    target: 1000.00
}
```

Here, we can see that `A noble cause` requires a minimum target amount of `1000.00` USD. Having defined the fund for a noble cause, let's say there is a minimum and maximum amount that the donors can donate in the range of `100` to `250` USD. This can be seen in the following code:

```
import rand

fn donation() f32 {
    return rand.f32_in_range(100.00, 250.00)
}
```

Notice the usage of the `f32_in_range(100.00,250.00)` function from the `rand` module. The `donation` function returns the random amount that represents the amount that was contributed by a generous donor in USD. The `f32_in_range` function, which is available in the `rand` module, returns a uniformly distributed 32-bit floating-point value that is greater than or equal to the starting value, but less than the ending value in the range specified.

Next, the fund manager keeps seeking donations and updating the total amount that's been collected by calling the `collect` method of the `Fund` struct, as follows:

```
for {
    rlock fund {
        if fund.total >= fund.target {
            break
        }
    }
    h := go donation()
    go fund.collect(h.wait())
}
```

From the preceding code snippet, the `fund.collect(amt)` process, which is used to collect donations, is spawned across various threads. At the same time, the fund manager (main program) has shared access to the `fund` data, so the fund manager keeps collecting donations until the total amount, `fund.total`, is greater than or equal to the target amount, `fund.target`.

Putting all the pieces of code we've looked at together, the full source code will appear as follows:

```v
module main

import rand

struct Fund {
    name    string
    target  f32
mut:
    total           f32
    num_donors int
}

fn (shared f Fund) collect(amt f32) {
    lock f { // read - write lock
        if f.total < f.target {
            f.num_donors += 1
            f.total += amt
            println('$f.num_donors \t before: ${f.total -
                amt} \t funds received: $amt \t total:
                $f.total')
        }
    }
}

fn donation() f32 {
    return rand.f32_in_range(100.00, 250.00)
}

fn main() {
```

```
shared fund := Fund{
    name: 'A noble cause'
    target: 1000.00
}

for {
    rlock fund {
        if fund.total >= fund.target {
            break
        }
    }
    h := go donation()
    go fund.collect(h.wait())
}

rlock fund { // acquire read lock
    println('$fund.num_donors donors donated for
        $fund.name')
    println('$fund.name raised total fund amount: \$
        $fund.total')
}
}
```

In the preceding code, we can see that the main thread, which we assumed to be the fund manager, created a fund as a shared object and collected donations before summarizing the fund details, after having acquired rlock (read lock on funds). The output of the preceding code is as follows:

```
1  before: 0          funds received: 144.0963  total: 144.0963
2  before: 144.0963   funds received: 105.0710  total: 249.1673
3  before: 249.1673   funds received: 113.9490  total: 363.1163
4  before: 363.1163   funds received: 131.2242  total: 494.3405
5  before: 494.3405   funds received: 107.1498  total: 601.4903
6  before: 601.4903   funds received: 208.2496  total: 809.7399
7  before: 809.7399   funds received: 126.8787  total: 936.6186
8  before: 936.6187   funds received: 103.0450  total: 1039.664
8 donors donated for A noble cause
A noble cause raised total fund amount: $ 1039.664
```

From the preceding output, we can see that the fund manager – in our case, the `main` method – has collected donations from 8 donors for `fund` initiated for `A noble cause`. The `total` fund amount raised with 8 donors was `$1039.664`. Soon after the `fund.total >= fund.target` condition was met, the fund manager stopped collecting further donations by breaking the infinite `for` loop.

Note that you might see a different number of donors and total fund amount as we used a random amount that was generated using the `rand.f32_in_range()` function.

Summary

In this chapter, we started by providing a brief introduction to concurrency and parallelism by explaining these concepts while looking at brief examples. We then understood the basic terminologies related to concurrent programming, such as *program*, *process*, *thread*, and *task*. We then understood the syntax that's used to write concurrent programs in V using the `go` keyword. We also understood the basic programming modules in V, such as the `time` module and the `thread` type.

Later, based on a real-life scenario that I explained to help you understand concurrency in the introduction to this chapter, we learned how to implement the sequential and concurrent versions of this scenario programmatically in V. We then compared both the sequential and concurrent programs and understood the benefits of concurrent programming over sequentially executing tasks. While explaining the scenario that we implemented programmatically, we also learned how to spawn multiple tasks using `[]` `thread`. This demonstration helped us learn how to ensure the main program waits on the `[]thread` handler until all the concurrent tasks have finished executing.

Then, we went ahead and saw some programmatic approaches when working with concurrency in V, including spawning functions with return values and obtaining return values of a function when we spawn to run concurrently using the `wait()` function. We also learned how to spawn anonymous functions so that they run concurrently and work with various scenarios, including spawning anonymous functions with and without input arguments. Finally, we learned how to share data between the main thread and concurrent tasks with the help of the `shared` keyword, which can only be used on objects of the `array`, `map`, or `struct` type.

Having gained the foundational knowledge of concurrent programming in V, in the next chapter, we will learn about channels.

11
Channels – An Advanced Concurrency Pattern

The term **channel** indicates a medium or a path that allows you to transfer information or data from one end to the other. In the context of concurrency, channels allow us to share data by establishing a communication channel between the concurrent tasks. These concurrent tasks are often termed **coroutines**, which share the data by communicating through the channels. Channels are advanced concurrency patterns in V that solve the problem of explicitly handling data synchronization techniques among coroutines.

We can communicate between the coroutines with the help of shared objects. In V, these can be structs, arrays, or maps. But the problem with this approach is that you need to take explicit care of concurrency synchronization techniques such as protecting the shared objects using locks such as the read-only `rlock` or the `read/write` lock to prevent data races, as we learned in the *Sharing data between the main thread and concurrent tasks* section of *Chapter 10, Concurrency*.

Channels in V can be compared to queues. Generally, a queue allows things or elements to pass through it in one direction. The first one to enter the queue is the first one to exit the queue. So, the values that are sent to the channel are accessed in a **First In First Out (FIFO)** manner.

In the world of programming, a queue is a data structure that allows the data to flow only in one direction. In V, the process of adding data to the channel is known as **push**, and the process to take the data out of the channel is termed **pop**.

In this chapter, we will begin by looking at the syntax for declaring channels and then understand different types of channels, such as buffered and unbuffered channels. We will then learn about the properties of channels. Finally, we will learn about various methods available on a channel.

The following topics will be covered in this chapter:

- Syntax to define a channel
- Channel operations
- Channel properties
- Channel methods
- Working with unbuffered channels
- Working with buffered channels
- Channel select

With this chapter, you will gain a thorough understanding of the blocking behavior of unbuffered channels. You will learn how to deal with such channels by dealing with code examples. You will also be able to work with buffered channels in detail. This chapter will also help you gain knowledge of the `select` statement and demonstrates how to implement channel operations as the conditional branches of a `select` statement. By the end of this chapter, you will be able to write seamless V programs using channels.

Technical requirements

The full source code for this chapter is available at `https://github.com/ PacktPublishing/Getting-Started-with-V-Programming/tree/main/ Chapter11`.

It is recommended that you run the code examples in each of the sections of this chapter in a fresh console or file with a `.v` extension. This will avoid clashes among variable names across examples.

Syntax to define a channel

In this section, we will look at the syntax for defining a channel. Channels are a built-in feature in V, and you are not required to import any package to use them. The chan keyword is used to define a channel in V. To define a channel, you can use the following syntax:

```
CHANNEL_VARIABLE := chan DATA_TYPE{OPTIONAL_CAPACITY: CAPACITY_
VALUE}
```

In this syntax, the channel variable will be of the chan DATA_TYPE. OPTIONAL_
CAPACITY type. This is a syntactical representation of the cap property that accepts an integer value. The cap property is available on a channel variable that represents the capacity of the values the channel could hold. The type could be any type, such as a primitive type, or it could be a struct, a map, or an array.

Having understood the basic syntax, we will learn about **unbuffered channels** and **buffered channels** in the following subsections.

Unbuffered channel

A channel defined without capacity is referred to as an unbuffered channel. An unbuffered channel has a capacity of 0 by default. The following code shows how to define an unbuffered channel. This channel accepts integer values that are pushed onto it:

```
uc := chan int{}
println(uc.cap) // 0
```

In the preceding code, the uc variable is of the chan int type. The capacity of the unbuffered channel, uc, is 0. The following code prints the type of uc to the console:

```
println(typeof(uc).name) // chan int
```

From the preceding code, we can see that the type of the unbuffered channel, uc, is chan int.

Buffered channel

Unlike unbuffered channels, a buffered channel is defined with a *non-zero* capacity, with its cap property assigned with an integer value. The following code shows how to define a buffered channel:

```
bc := chan string{cap: 2}
println(bc.cap)
println(typeof(bc).name)
```

The following is the output:

```
2

chan string
```

In the preceding code, we are defining a channel of the chan string type with a capacity of 2. This means that the channel can accommodate a maximum of two string values at a time. Now, let's learn how to perform various operations on a channel in V.

Channel operations

In this section, we will learn about the basic operations that we can perform on a channel. First, we will understand the *arrow operator*, which is identified by the < - symbol. This represents the flow of data into a channel in V. Then, we will learn about the two basic channel operations, which include pushing a value into the channel and popping the value out of the channel using the arrow operator.

Arrow operator <-

As we mentioned in the introduction to this chapter, a channel in V lets information flow in only one direction, and it is an analogy of a queue. As a rule of thumb, the data in a channel always flows from right to left in V.

The syntactic representation is also consistent in V, and the representation of the data flow is always identified from right to left. Even if we look at the sign of the arrow operator, < -, it too always points toward the left.

The direction of the arrow operator, < -, indicates that the values always enter the channel from the right and exit the channel to the left.

Push operation

In this section, we will understand the syntax that pushes data into a channel in V. Later, we will look at a simple example that demonstrates pushing an integer value into a buffered channel of integers.

Syntax to push data into a channel

The push operation in V happens from right to left. This means that with the *arrow operator*, <-, in place, the data value that needs to be pushed into the channel will be placed on the right and that the channel variable will be placed to the left of <-. The following is the syntax to push data into the channel:

```
ch := chan VALUE_TYPE {OPTIONAL_CAPACITY: CAPACITY_VALUE}
ch <- VALUE_TO_PUSH
```

The preceding syntax shows pushing data into the ch channel. Here, we can see that if you want to push a value into the channel, the value is placed to the right of the arrow operator and the channel variable is placed to the left of the arrow operator in V.

It is worth noting that the push operation on a channel, ch <- VALUE_TO_PUSH, is a void expression.

Pushing data into a channel

The following code shows defining and pushing data to a buffered channel of the chan int type with a capacity of 1:

```
ch := chan int{cap: 1}
ch <- 51
println(ch)
```

Place the preceding code in a file and run it using the v run filename.v command. You should see the following output:

```
chan int{cap: 1, closed: 0}
```

From the preceding output, we can see that we are calling the str() method on the channel variable. This method prints the channel's information, which includes the channel's type, values related to the channel's capacity, and closed status. We will discuss these properties in detail in the *Channel properties* section of this chapter.

In the case of unbuffered channels, the push operation, as specified in the `ch <-VALUE_TO_PUSH` syntax, is a blocking statement. For example, consider the code that we used to define and push a value into the buffered channel, but this time, we won't specify the capacity, as shown here:

```
ch := chan int{}
ch <- 51
println(ch)
```

Place the preceding code in a file and run it using the `v run filename.v` command. You should see that the console halts and doesn't show any output. This means that the program entered the blocked state as soon as it encountered the push operation; that is, `ch <- 51`. We will understand why using push operations on an unbuffered channel blocks the program's execution in more detail in the *Working with unbuffered channels* section of this chapter.

To stop the program and gain access to the control from the blocked execution of the preceding program, you need to force stop the execution. To do that, hit the *Ctrl + C* key combination on your keyboard, and you will be fine.

Pop operation

In this section, we will understand how to pop the data out of the channel in V. Later, we will look at a simple example that demonstrates popping an integer value out of the channel of integers after pushing an integer value into a buffered channel of integers.

Syntax to pop the data out of the channel

Similar to the push operation, the pop operation in V also happens from right to left since the data that is entered from the right during the push operation exits to the left.

This means that with the arrow operator, `<-`, in place, the channel variable will be placed to the right of the arrow operator. The data that pops out of the channel is captured in a variable that's placed to the left of the arrow operator. The following is the syntax for popping the data out of the channel:

```
ch := chan VALUE_TYPE{OPTIONAL_CAPACITY: CAPACITY_VALUE}
ch <- VALUE_TO_PUSH
x := <- ch
```

In the preceding syntax, we defined a channel, followed by a statement that pushes a value into the channel. In the last line, we can see an expression, that is, <- ch. This expression is the value being popped out of the channel, and if a variable such as x, in this case, is placed to the left, then the x variable will be assigned with the value that popped out of the channel.

Popping the data out of the channel

The following code shows popping the value out of the channel:

```
ch := chan int{cap: 1}
ch <- 51
println('channel after push: $ch.str()')

println('popping value out of the channel and storing it in
immutable variable x')
x := <-ch
println('value of x: $x')
println('channel after pop: $ch.str()')
```

Place the preceding code in a file with the .v extension and run it using the v run filename.v command. The output of the preceding program will be as follows:

```
channel after push: chan int{cap: 1, closed: 0}
popping value out of the channel and storing it in immutable
variable x
value of x: 51
channel after pop: chan int{cap: 1, closed: 0}
```

From the preceding output, we can see that the value, after popping the value from the channel, is assigned to the x variable, since printing the x variable shows a value of 51. So far, we have learned about various operations that we can perform on a channel using the arrow operator, <-. Next, we will learn about channel properties.

Channel properties

You can obtain information about a channel variable by accessing the properties it exposes. The properties of the channel include `len`, `cap`, and `closed`. These properties provide the following information about a channel at the time of accessing them:

- `cap` is an integer property that indicates the capacity of the channel. This is 0 for the unbuffered channel. In the case of a buffered channel, the `cap` property indicates the maximum number of values a channel can hold.

- `len` is an integer property that indicates the actual number of values that the channel holds at the time of accessing this property. At any given point in time, the `len` value can only be less than or equal to the `cap` property.

- `closed` is a Boolean property, and when its value is `true`, it indicates that the channel is closed. If a channel is not closed, the value of the `closed` property will be `false`.

Understanding channel properties using examples

In this section, we will understand the three properties of a channel that were stated in the previous section with a simple example. Consider the following buffered channel:

```
b := chan string{cap: 2}
b <- 'hello'
println('capacity: $b.cap')
println('length: $b.len')
println('closed: $b.closed')
```

In the preceding code, we created a buffered channel with the `cap` property set to 2. Then, we pushed the `hello` value into the buffered channel, b. Then, we are printing the three properties in each of the print statements, which results in the following output:

```
capacity: 2
length: 1
closed: false
```

Note that the capacity is 2, as we defined for the buffered channel. However, the length is 1 as we have only pushed one string value to channel b. The `closed` property prints a value of `false`, which means channel b is open.

Now that we have understood a channel's properties, let's look at the various methods that are available on the channel and learn how to work with them.

Channel methods

V exposes some public methods to control a channel's behavior. These methods include the following:

- `try_push()`
- `try_pop()`
- `close()`

Except for the `close()` method, the `try_push()` and `try_pop()` methods have a return value, which is a built-in enum type called `ChanState`. The `ChanState` enum has three enum values:

- `not_ready`
- `closed`
- `success`

Performing `try_push()` or `try_pop()` on a channel can return one of the three aforementioned states. In this section, we will learn how to work with the `try_push()` function with buffered and unbuffered channels and then we cover how to work with the `try_pop()` and `close()` methods.

Using try_push() on unbuffered channels

`try_push()` gracefully pushes data into the channel and returns the status in the form of an enum value from `ChanState`. The `try_push()` method accepts values of the type that the channel accepts. For an unbuffered channel, the `try_push()` operation returns a `.not_ready` value of `ChanState` enum, when there is no coroutine ready to pop a value out of the channel. To demonstrate this, consider the following code:

```
v := 'hi'
ch := chan string{} // unbuffered channel
res := ch.try_push(v)
println(res) // not_ready
```

The preceding code demonstrates the usage of the `try_push()` method on an unbuffered channel.

Caveats of using try_push on unbuffered channels

In the preceding code, we used the `try_push()` operation on an unbuffered channel, which immediately returned control to the program. Then, the execution control proceeded to the next line and printed a value of `res`. However, the push operation, which uses the arrow operator, `<-`, is blocking in nature, while with `try_push()`, you lose the blocking behavior for such an unbuffered channel. In such cases, the program continues executing the next sequence of statements, so if any data is pushed to this channel, it will be lost as we run past the execution flow. So, you must be cautious when you want to use `try_push()` as it stops the fun of working with channels that are shared across coroutines that are running concurrently, thereby leading to unexpected behavior. A more detailed explanation of the blocking behavior of unbuffered channels will be discussed in the *Working with unbuffered channels* section of this chapter.

Using try_push() on buffered channels

The following code demonstrates the usage of `try_push()` on a buffered channel of strings:

```
x := 'hello'
ch := chan string{cap: 2}
for {
    status := ch.try_push(x)
    if status == .success {
        println('Channel length: $ch.len')
    } else {
        println('channel status: $status')
        break
    }
}
```

In the preceding code, we defined a buffered channel, ch, of the `chan string` type with a capacity of 2. This means that when more than two string values are pushed to this channel without them popping any values, the status of the third `try_push()` method indicates `not_ready`, as shown here:

```
Channel length: 1
Channel length: 2
channel status: not_ready
```

Caveats of using try_push on buffered channels

The preceding output indicates that the `try_push()` operation succeeded until the channel's length equaled the channel capacity, which is 2 in this example. The moment the program tried to push the third value, the channel's status changed to `not_ready`. We end up having a race condition, such as a conditional `if` block to identify the result of the `try_push()` operation on channels. In such scenarios, dealing with different cases and making decisions based on the channel status will become complex. Although this seems to be clean and concise code, the usage of `try_push()` is not indicating that the channel is at its full capacity by throwing an exception.

try_pop()

`try_pop()` gracefully pops data out of the channel and returns the status in the form of an `enum` value from `ChanState`. The `try_pop()` method accepts mutable variables as input arguments whose type matches the type of value a channel accepts. The following code demonstrates the usage of `try_pop()` on a buffered channel of the `chan int` type:

```
ch := chan int{cap: 1}
mut x, mut y := 0, 0
ch <- 101
mut status := ch.try_pop(mut x)
println('try pop resulted in status: $status, Value of x: $x')
status = ch.try_pop(mut y)
println('try pop resulted in status: $status, Value of y: $y')
```

In the preceding code block, we created a buffered channel of the `chan int` type with a capacity of 1. Then, we defined two mutable variables, x and y, and initialized them with a value of 0. Then, we pushed the `101` integer value into the channel. In the very next line, we called `try_pop()` on the channel and then printed the status of the operation, along with the value that was popped, in the x variable. Now that the channel has popped out the only element that it had, performing `try_pop()` again yields no proper result. Hence, the value of y, which was 0, remained intact, as per the following output:

```
try pop resulted in status: success, Value of x: 101
try pop resulted in status: not_ready, Value of y: 0
```

Caveats of using try_pop on channels

From the preceding output, we can see that the value of y is still 0. There is no way to properly identify if the value of 0 that was assigned to y is an initial value or if it was assigned a value that popped out an incoming value from the channel. Although there are ways that you can figure this out by looking at the channel status or channel length, you might end up having multiple race conditions and might fail to add a few more conditions you were unaware of as the program requirements or functionality changes. So, the try_pop() method takes away the true essence of channels, which are meant to allow you to share data by establishing a communication channel between the coroutines.

Summarizing the usage of try_push() and try_pop()

Having understood the caveats of using the try_push() and try_pop() methods on channels in the preceding sections, you are discouraged from using these methods in production environments. You can evaluate these methods for developing and debugging purposes, though. To enjoy the true nature of channels, which allows you to share data by establishing communication channels between coroutines, it is recommended that you use the standard arrow operator, <-, which helps transfer data in and out of the channel. With this approach of using <-, any unhandled scenarios can lead to errors, and the data will be in sync among coroutines. In the case of unhandled exceptions, we have the flexibility to use an or{} blocks, as demonstrated in the following section, or we can choose to let the exceptions propagate.

close()

The close() method is used to close the incoming data being pushed into a channel. The close() method does not accept any input arguments. The close() method is a void method, so it does not return anything. It will set the channel's state to .closed.

When a channel is closed, this effectively means the following:

- You cannot push data into a closed channel.

- You are allowed to pop data out of the closed channel if there is data left to pop.

- Performing try_push() on the channel will result in a status of .closed.

The following code demonstrates the usage of the `close()` method on a buffered channel:

```
module main

fn main() {
    ch := chan int{cap: 2}
    // push using arrow operator: <-
    ch <- 123 // Push 1st element into the channel
    ch <- 222 // Push 2nd element into the channel
    println(<-ch) // pop using: <- First in is the first to
                  // out. So prints 123
    ch.close() // Close channel
    // try_push will result .closed
    new_val := 999
    status := ch.try_push(new_val)
    println('try_push on a closed channel resulted in
            status: $status')

    // We still have one more element to pop
    println(<-ch) // 222
}
```

From the preceding code, we can see that we are performing various operations on a buffered channel of the `chan int` type. We pushed two values and then popped a value out of the channel before closing it by calling the `ch.close()` statement.

After closing the channel, we performed `try_push()` and wrote the status to the console. Also, we are popping up the only value left in the channel in the final print statement. The output of all the operations shown here is self-explanatory:

```
123
try_push on a closed channel resulted in status: closed
222
```

Sometimes, you need to close the channel before you exit the routine. To close the channel in a deferred way, you can make use of the defer{} block, wherein you can close the channel, as shown here:

```
module main

fn main() {
    ch := chan int{cap: 2}
    defer {
        ch.close()
    } // Deferred execution to Close channel

    // push using arrow operator: <-
    ch <- 123 // Push 1st element into the channel
    ch <- 222 // Push 2nd element into the channel
    println(<-ch) // pop using: <- First in is the first to
                  // out. So prints 123



                  channel') }

    // try_push will result .closed
    new_val := 999
    status := ch.try_push(new_val)
    println('try_push on a closed channel resulted in
            status: $status')

    // We still have one more element to pop
    println(<-ch) // 222
}
```

Details of how the defer blocks work were covered in the *Functions allow you to defer the execution flow using defer blocks* section of *Chapter 7, Functions*.

Having understood the try_push(), try_pop(), and close() channel method, let's learn how to work with unbuffered channels.

Working with unbuffered channels

By default, channels are unbuffered in V unless you specify the capacity. In this section, we will learn how to work with unbuffered channels. The main aspect of working with unbuffered channels is that the push operations on them block code from executing, so long as no coroutine pops the value out of the unbuffered channel.

Understanding the blocking nature of unbuffered channels

In this section, we will learn why unbuffered channels are blocking in nature. Consider the following code, which demonstrates the blocking behavior of the unbuffered channel:

```
module main

fn main() {
    ch := chan int{}
    defer {
        ch.close()
    }
    ch <- 3
    x := <-ch
    println(x)
    println('End main')
}
```

In the preceding code, we have the main function, with the first line having the ch variable declared as an unbuffered channel.

In the next line, we defer on closing the channel. Then follows the ch <- 3 statement, where a value is pushed into the unbuffered channel, ch. This operation blocks the execution of the program until there is someone (probably a coroutine) who pops up the value.

Simply put, the unbuffered channels block the execution when a value is pushed on them. The execution gets blocked because the channel waits until the value gets popped out by another coroutine. This is equivalent to the .not_ready value of the ChanState enum, if we were performing try_push() on the channel, until there is a coroutine that actively pops the values out of the channel.

Although the preceding code has an expression of x <- ch, it comes after the ch <- 3 blocking statement. So, the execution halts at the ch <- 3 statement forever unless some other coroutine pops this value from the channel.

Placing the preceding code in a file with a .v extension and running it using the v run filename.v command will halt the execution and you will not see any output printed to the console. To kill the program from the command-line terminal, you need to hit the *Ctrl + C* key combination.

So, this demands a concurrent routine that has access to the channel and pops up the value as soon as the value is pushed into the channel.

Dealing with the blocking behavior of unbuffered channels

To prevent the program from blocking the code's execution, we need to add a coroutine that pops the value as soon as a value is pushed onto the unbuffered channel. Let's modify the preceding code so that it has a receiver coroutine that accepts a channel as an input argument, as shown here:

```
module main

fn receiver(ch chan int) {
    println('Received value from the channel ${<-ch}')
}

fn main() {
    ch := chan int{}
    defer {
        ch.close()
    }
    go receiver(ch)
    ch <- 3
    println('End main')
}
```

The receiver function accepts a channel as the input argument. It then pops the value from the ch channel and prints it to the console output whenever an integer is pushed into the unbuffered channel, ch.

Looking at the `main` function in the preceding code, we are declaring an unbuffered channel of the `chan int` type that accepts integer values to be pushed into it. In the very next line, we are spawning a coroutine that accepts `ch` as an input argument.

With the coroutine spawned to run concurrently, it will wait until a value is pushed into the channel. Only then will it print and exit out of the routine. Back in the `main` function, the execution flows to the next line, which is pushing a value of 3 into `ch`.

We are aware from the code example earlier that performing the push operation on an unbuffered channel blocks execution. But the preceding code has already spawned a coroutine named `receiver`, directly before the `ch <- 3` expression. The `receiver` function prints a message to the console, along with the message stating where we are popping the value from the channel, using the `${<-ch}` expression, which is written as part of the `print` statement.

With this explanation, we will get either of the following outputs.

The following is the first output:

```
End main
Received value from the channel 3
```

The following is the second output:

```
End main
```

If you run the program multiple times, you will see changes in either of the outputs shown. In output 1, the program took more time to exit, so it had to print the message from the `receiver` function after printing `End main`. However, the expectation is to have the message from the `receiver` function be printed first, followed by `End main`. Are you wondering why the coroutine failed to print the message to the output console in output 2? This is because the calling thread is not waiting for the coroutine to finish executing. And as we know, for this program to show the output as expected, we will need to wait until the coroutine finishes executing its work completely. So, in the `main` function, we will wait for the handle that is being obtained from the spawned `receiver` coroutine, as follows:

```
module main

fn receiver(ch chan int) {
    println('Received value from the channel ${<-ch}')
}
```

```
fn main() {
    ch := chan int{}
    defer {
        ch.close()
    }
    t := go receiver(ch)
    ch <- 3
    t.wait()
    println('End main')
}
```

Now that we are waiting for the coroutine to finish executing the code, the output of the preceding code will be as follows:

```
Received value in the channel 3
End main
```

In the preceding code, we are only pushing data to the channel once. The receiver is designed to receive the first data item that is pushed onto the unbuffered channel of the `chan int` type.

Synchronizing data between coroutines that communicate via an unbuffered channel

What happens when there is a coroutine that keeps sending values? Do you think the receiver is designed to be in sync with the sender and how it sends data to the channel? Let's consider the following code, where we are modifying the preceding code and introducing a coroutine named `sender` that shares data through the communication channel to `receiver`:

```
module main

const (
    count = 4
)

fn sender(ch chan int) {
    for i in 0 .. count {
        ch <- i // since the push operation is a void
```

```
            // expression, this cannot be placed in a println
            println('Sent $i into the channel')
    }
}


fn receiver(ch chan int) {
    println('Received value from the channel ${<-ch}')
}


fn main() {
    ch := chan int{}
    defer {
        ch.close()
    }
    t := go receiver(ch)
    go sender(ch)
    t.wait()
    println('End main')
}
```

In the preceding code, we moved the logic that pushes data into the ch <- 3 channel to the sender coroutine. This coroutine, instead of pushing a value of 3, iterates over a range of numbers, 0..4, so for each iteration, it is expected to push the respective values, that is, 0, 1, 2, and 3. Having said that, the receiver is still the same function that just prints the value, which is pushed onto the channel. This code will print the following output, which sometimes misses to print "Sent 1 into the channel"which is not what we want to see:

```
Sent 0 into the channel
Received value from the channel 0
End main
```

From the preceding output, we are expecting to see all the send and receives for the range of values; that is, 0, 1, 2, and 3. This is because after the value is received by the receiver coroutine, it returns control to the main program. This is because the receiver is designed to receive only one value from the channel. So, after the sender pushes 0 to the channel, the receiver pops it. For the next iteration, the sender then pushes 1 and blocks the execution, hoping that there are some other coroutines ready to pop 1 out of it.

So, to achieve synchronization, the `receiver` coroutine can either pop the channel in an infinite loop, which is kind of overkill and not recommended. The other plausible way to achieve perfect synchronization is by having awareness about how many data values are being pushed into the channel. In this case, the `sender` coroutine is iterating over the range of `0..count` and `count` being defined as constant, which is enough for the `receiver` coroutine to iterate 4 times. The following code demonstrates a proper synchronization mechanism that lets coroutines share data by communicating through the unbuffered channel that's been established between them:

```
module main

const (
    count = 4
)

fn sender(ch chan int) {
    for i in 0 .. count {
        ch <- i // since the push operation is a void
            // expression, this cannot be placed in a println
        println('Sent $i into the channel')
    }
}

fn receiver(ch chan int) {
    for _ in 0 .. count {
        println('Received value from the channel ${<-ch}')
    }
}

fn main() {
    ch := chan int{}
    defer {
        ch.close()
    }
    t := go receiver(ch)
    go sender(ch)
    t.wait()
```

```
    println('End main')
}
```

In the preceding code, this time, the data synchronization happens smoothly between the coroutines without the program's execution being blocked. This is evident in the output, where the sender and receiver coroutines share data, as expected:

```
Received value in the channel 0
Sent 0 into the channel
Received value from the channel 1
Sent 1 into the channel
Received value from the channel 2
Sent 2 into the channel
Received value from the channel 3
Sent 3 into the channel
End main
```

So far, we have learned how to work with unbuffered channels and learned how to deal with their blocking behavior. Now, we will learn how to work with buffered channels.

Working with buffered channels

Earlier in this chapter, we learned that buffered channels would have the cap property defined with a non-zero integer value. In this section, we will learn how to work with buffered channels and how to share data by establishing communication among coroutines.

Understanding the behavior of a buffered channel

Unlike unbuffered channels, buffered channels are non-blocking channels, and they have a non-zero capacity specified in their declaration. The following code demonstrates a simple example of a buffered channel:

```
module main

fn main() {
    ch := chan int{cap: 1}
    defer {
        ch.close()
    }
```

```
    ch <- 3
    x := <-ch
    println(x)
    println('End main')
}
```

In the preceding code, we are creating a buffered channel of the chan int type with a capacity of 1. All we need to do here is push and pop of the data from the channel. If you look back at the *Working with unbuffered channels* section, the first code example in that section was similar to what is shown in the preceding code block. The only exception is that the ch channel in this code block is specified with a capacity of {cap: 1}.

We can also see that, in the case of buffered channels, the push is non-blocking until the buffer is full, and the program doesn't halt its execution. Here, we can see that the execution control proceeds to the next lines and thus prints the value to the output console, as shown here:

```
3
End main
```

Establishing buffered communication channel between coroutines

Now, let's learn how to implement a simple program that allows coroutines to share data through a buffered channel. Consider the following code, which establishes a buffered communication channel between the coroutines:

```
module main

fn sender(ch chan int) {
    val := 3
    println('Sending value: $val in the channel')
    ch <- val
    println('sent value: $val in the channel')
}

fn receiver(ch chan int) {
    println('Received value from the channel ${<-ch}')
}
```

```
fn main() {
    ch := chan int{cap: 1}
    defer {
        ch.close()
    }
    t := go receiver(ch)
    go sender(ch)

    t.wait()
    println('End main')
}
```

In the preceding code, a channel of the chan int type is created by the main function and is being passed as an input argument to the sender and receiver functions. sender pushes a value of 3 into the channel and receiver pops the data out of the channel. Also, notice that the main function spawns the function sender to run concurrently. As we are interested in printing the value that is popped out of the channel, we are assigning a handler of the go receiver coroutine to a variable, t, and we are waiting for the coroutine until it finishes executing by calling the t.wait() statement. The output of the preceding code will be as follows:

```
Sending value: 3 in the channel
sent value: 3 in the channel
Received value from the channel 3
End main
```

Synchronizing data between coroutines that communicate through a buffered channel

In the preceding code, we saw that a buffered channel with a capacity of 1 worked successfully when a pop operation occurred in a coroutine for a corresponding push in another coroutine. Consider the following code. Here, we have a buffered channel, ch, with a capacity of 2. The sender coroutine keeps sending messages as it iterates through the range of 0..count, with count being a constant value of 4:

```
module main

const (
    count = 4
```

```
    )

fn sender(ch chan int) {
    for i in 0 .. count {
        ch <- i
        println('sent value: $i in the channel')
    }
}

fn receiver(ch chan int) {
    println('Received value from the channel ${<-ch}')
}

fn main() {
    ch := chan int{cap: 2}
    defer {
        ch.close()
    }
    t := go receiver(ch)
    go sender(ch)

    t.wait()
    println('End main')
}
```

Let's look at the output of the preceding code and try to analyze the problem:

```
sent value: 0 in the channel
sent value: 1 in the channel
Received value from the channel 0
sent value: 2 in the channel
End main
```

Here, we can see that there are two problems with the code that produced the preceding output:

- The first problem is that `receiver` was only able to print 0, even though the capacity of the buffered channel is 2.

- The second problem is that `sender` stopped after pushing a value of 2 into the buffered channel.

The cause for the first problem is that `sender` is pushing the data to the buffered channel 4 times, whereas `receiver` is popping the data out of the channel only once.

The cause for the second problem is that `sender` stopped after pushing 0, 1, and 2 into the buffered channel. What happened behind the scenes was that the moment 0 was pushed, the `receiver` function popped 0 out of the channel, so the length of the channel became zero again. Since `receiver` has exhausted performing its only routine, which is printing the value by popping it out of the channel, the execution control flows back to the calling thread.

But the `sender` coroutine continues to push the next set of values in the range, such as 1 and 2. After pushing 1 and 2, the buffered channel maxes out the capacity since it is defined with a capacity of 2. So, from the preceding output, we can see that 0, 1, and 2 are sent but only the 0 value is received from the channel.

To address these two problems, we need to modify the code so that the `receiver` coroutine will be popping the data from the channel so that it matches the number of times `sender` is pushing the data into the channel. So, the `receiver` coroutine must be modified as follows:

```
module main

const (
    count = 4
)

fn sender(ch chan int) {
    for i in 0 .. count {
        ch <- i
        println('sent value: $i in the channel')
    }
}
```

```
fn receiver(ch chan int) {
    for _ in 0 .. count {
        println('Received value from the channel ${<-ch}')
    }
}


fn main() {
    ch := chan int{cap: 2}
    defer {
        ch.close()
    }
    t := go receiver(ch)
    go sender(ch)

    t.wait()
    println('End main')
}
```

The preceding code is now in sync with the number of push operations and pop operations, so the output will look as follows:

```
sent value: 0 in the channel
sent value: 1 in the channel
Received value from the channel 0
sent value: 2 in the channel
Received value from the channel 1
sent value: 3 in the channel
Received value from the channel 2
Received value from the channel 3
End main
```

Channel select

V has a `select` statement, which you can use to wait on multiple channels and their operations. A select statement can have multiple branches and cases, all of which can be used to represent channel push or pop operations. It can also have a timeout case, which we can define to exit out of `select` if none of the channel operation cases get triggered.

The `select` statement is syntactically similar to a `match` block, except that the cases of a `select` do not have to be of channels that accept similar data types. But for `match`, as explained in *Chapter 6, Conditionals and Iterative Statements*, all the conditional branches need to be of similar data types.

The following are a few points to keep note of when working with `select` statements:

- The `select` statement randomly picks the cases that are ready to be executed.
- The `select` statement blocks other cases until the active case finishes and exits out of the case.
- The cases of `select` statements can be of any channel operation, such as `push` or `pop`.
- For a given `select` statement, the cases can have buffered and unbuffered channels of any type.
- The `select` statement can be used as a Boolean expression and returns `true` if the channels are open and `false` when all the channels are closed.

Let's understand the usage of the `select` statement when working with channels. For the sake of this demonstration, I am creating two functions, as follows:

```
fn process1(ch chan int) {
    for i in 1 .. 6 {
        sq := i * i
        println('process1: value being pushed on ch1: $sq')
        ch <- sq
    }
}

fn process2(ch chan string) {
    msg := 'hello from process 2'
    println('process2: value being pushed on ch2: $msg')
    ch <- msg
}
```

From the preceding code, we can see that the `process1` function accepts an input argument of the `chan int` type. It iterates over a range of `1 .. 6` and pushes the square of the value into the channel using the `ch<-sq` statement. Similarly, the `process2` function accepts an input argument of the `chan string` type. It also pushes some `msg` into the channel that is being passed to the function.

Now, we will write the `main` function so that it spawns these two functions to run concurrently. Since these two functions need input channel arguments, we will define them in the `main` function, as follows:

```
fn main() {
    ch1 := chan int{cap: 5} // buffered channel
    ch2 := chan string{} // unbuffered channel
    defer {
        ch1.close()
        ch2.close()
    }
    go process1(ch1)
    go process2(ch2)
}
```

Continuing from the preceding code, after spawning the `process1` and `process2` coroutines so that they run concurrently, we will add the `select` statement, which has cases, as shown in the following code:

```
select {
    a := <-ch1 {
        println('main: value popped from ch1: $a')
    }
    b := <-ch2 {
        println('main: value popped from ch2: $b')
    }
}
```

The preceding code just shows the `select` statement, which becomes part of the `main` function we have implemented so far.

If we place the code that we have implemented so far in a .v file and run it using the v run filename.v command, we will see the following output:

```
process1: value being pushed on ch1: 1
process2: value being pushed on ch2: hello from process 2
process1: value being pushed on ch1: 4
process1: value being pushed on ch1: 9
main: value popped from ch1: 1
process1: value being pushed on ch1: 16
```

From the preceding output, we can see that process1 is pushing the values. But the a := <-ch1 case in the select statement gets executed only once. We can also see that there is no sign of the code block executing in the b := <-ch2 case.

To keep track of the data flowing across the ch1 and ch2 channels, we need to make the two cases we specified in the select statement work, which we can do by wrapping the select statement we have implemented so far in an infinite for loop. After the for loop, we must write a print statement with a message of done, which we expect to run after the infinite for loop. At this point, the main function will look like this:

```
fn main() {
    ch1 := chan int{cap: 5} // buffered channel
    ch2 := chan string{} // unbuffered channel
    defer {
        ch1.close()
        ch2.close()
    }
    go process1(ch1)
    go process2(ch2)
    for {
        select {
            a := <-ch1 {
                println('main: value popped from ch1: $a')
            }
            b := <-ch2 {
                println('main: value popped from ch2: $b')
            }
        }
    }
}
```

```
        println('done')
}
```

After executing the program with the aforementioned changes, it will look as follows:

```
process2: value being pushed on ch2: hello from process 2
process1: value being pushed on ch1: 1
main: value popped from ch2: hello from process 2
process1: value being pushed on ch1: 4
main: value popped from ch1: 1
process1: value being pushed on ch1: 9
main: value popped from ch1: 4
process1: value being pushed on ch1: 16
process1: value being pushed on ch1: 25
main: value popped from ch1: 9
main: value popped from ch1: 16
main: value popped from ch1: 25
```

From the preceding output, we can see that even though all the cases of the select statement have finished executing their respective code blocks, there is no further execution of the program. This is because it gets blocked and keeps executing in an infinite for loop, waiting for any of the operations specified in the conditional branches of the select statement to succeed. Hence, we will never reach the statement that prints done to the console output.

As we mentioned earlier, we can specify a condition in the select statement that executes every 2 seconds. Let's modify select so that the new case keeps executing for every 2 seconds of inactivity:

```
    mut sec := 0
    for {
        select {
            a := <-ch1 {
                sec = 0
                println('main: value popped from ch1: $a')
            }
            b := <-ch2 {
                sec = 0
                println('main: value popped from ch2: $b')
```

```
            }
        2 * time.second {
            // this case executes for every 2 seconds of
inactivity by any other channels in this select statement
            sec = sec + 2
            println('main: more than ${sec}s passed without
a channel being ready')
            if sec >= 6 {
                println('exiting out of select after $sec
seconds of inactivity amongst channels')
                break
            }
        }
    }
}
```

From the preceding code, we can see that we added a case called 2 * time.second, in addition to other channel operation cases. This case executes every 2 seconds if there is no activity among other channels that belong to the select statement. So, we can leverage this case and try to exit out of the infinite for loop based on some predefined timeout, such as 6 seconds. To achieve this, we created a mutable variable called sec that keeps increasing by 2 every time this case gets executed by a select statement. Whenever the value of sec becomes greater than or equal to 6, we can choose to break the infinite for loop and exit out of it. As we are using time.second, you must ensure to add the import time statement to the code file you are working on.

The output at this point will appear as follows:

```
process1: value being pushed on ch1: 1
process2: value being pushed on ch2: hello from process 2
process1: value being pushed on ch1: 4
main: value popped from ch1: 1
process1: value being pushed on ch1: 9
process1: value being pushed on ch1: 16
process1: value being pushed on ch1: 25
main: value popped from ch2: hello from process 2
main: value popped from ch1: 4
main: value popped from ch1: 9
main: value popped from ch1: 16
```

```
main: value popped from ch1: 25
main: more than 2s passed without a channel being ready
main: more than 4s passed without a channel being ready
main: more than 6s passed without a channel being ready
exiting out of select after 6 seconds of inactivity amongst
channels
done
```

But what if one of the processes takes too long to respond? Let's say that `process1` takes 3 seconds to push a value into the channel from now on, as shown here:

```
import time


fn process1(ch chan int) {
    for i in 1 .. 6 {
        sq := i * i
        time.sleep(3 * time.second)
        println('process1: value being pushed on ch1: $sq')
        ch <- sq
    }
}
```

The output in such a case will appear as follows:

```
process2: value being pushed on ch2: hello from process 2
main: value popped from ch2: hello from process 2
main: more than 2s passed without a channel being ready
process1: value being pushed on ch1: 1
main: value popped from ch1: 1
main: more than 4s passed without a channel being ready
process1: value being pushed on ch1: 4
main: value popped from ch1: 4
main: more than 6s passed without a channel being ready
exiting out of select after 6 seconds of inactivity amongst
channels
done
```

Here, we can see that we are not resetting the timeout counter variable, `sec`, whenever there is any activity in one of the cases of the `select` statement. So, we will reset `sec` to 0 only in two cases of the `select` statement that perform channel operations. At this point, the full source code will look as follows:

```
module main

import time

fn process1(ch chan int) {
    for i in 1 .. 6 {
        sq := i * i
        time.sleep(3 * time.second)
        println('process1: value being pushed on ch1: $sq')
        ch <- sq
    }
}

fn process2(ch chan string) {
    msg := 'hello from process 2'
    println('process2: value being pushed on ch2: $msg')
    ch <- msg
}

fn main() {
    ch1 := chan int{cap: 5} // buffered channel
    ch2 := chan string{} // unbuffered channel
    defer {
        ch1.close()
        ch2.close()
    }
    go process1(ch1)
    go process2(ch2)
    mut sec := 0
    for {
```

```
    select {
        a := <-ch1 {
            sec = 0
            println('main: value popped from ch1: $a')
        }
        b := <-ch2 {
            sec = 0
            println('main: value popped from ch2: $b')
        }
        2 * time.second {
            /* this case executes for every 2 seconds of
inactivity by any other channels in this select statement*/
            sec = sec + 2
            println('main: more than ${sec}s passed
                    without a channel being ready')
            if sec >= 6 {
                println('exiting out of select after
                        $sec seconds of inactivity
                        amongst channels')
                break
            }
        }
    }
    println('done')
}
```

The output of the preceding code will be as follows:

```
process2: value being pushed on ch2: hello from process 2
main: value popped from ch2: hello from process 2
main: more than 2s passed without a channel being ready
process1: value being pushed on ch1: 1
main: value popped from ch1: 1
main: more than 2s passed without a channel being ready
process1: value being pushed on ch1: 4
main: value popped from ch1: 4
main: more than 2s passed without a channel being ready
process1: value being pushed on ch1: 9
main: value popped from ch1: 9
main: more than 2s passed without a channel being ready
process1: value being pushed on ch1: 16
main: value popped from ch1: 16
main: more than 2s passed without a channel being ready
process1: value being pushed on ch1: 25
main: value popped from ch1: 25
main: more than 2s passed without a channel being ready
main: more than 4s passed without a channel being ready
main: more than 6s passed without a channel being ready
exiting out of select after 6 seconds of inactivity amongst
channels
done
```

From the preceding output, we can see that the timeout counter gets initiated after every 2 seconds of inactivity, but after 3 seconds, it gets reset to 0 for every third second. This reset is triggered by the `a := <-ch1` case as it gets invoked for every 3 seconds until `process1` finishes pushing the range of values; that is, `1 .. 6`. Once all the values have been pushed into `ch1`, due to inactivity by any other channel operations contained in the `select` statement as cases, the `sec` counter keeps incrementing until it reaches 6 seconds. Finally, it exits the infinite `for` loop and prints `done` to the console.

Summary

In this chapter, we learned how to share data by communicating between the channels. We started by looking at the syntax for defining unbuffered and buffered channels. Later, we learned how to perform push and pop operations on the channel using the `<-` arrow operator. We then learned about the various properties that are available on channel variables. We also learned how to use the `try_push()`, `try_pop()` and `close()` channel methods.

Later, we learned how to work with unbuffered channels by writing a code example in V, and we also understood the blocking nature of unbuffered channels and how to deal with them. We then covered how to synchronize data between the coroutines of an unbuffered channel. Similarly, we learned how to work with buffered channels and their behavior by looking at code examples.

Finally, we looked at how to work with the `select` statement and wrote channel operations that became part of the conditional branches of the `select` statement. Having learned these concepts, you will now be able to write robust concurrent programs in V with the help of channels.

In the next chapter, we will learn about how to add tests to the V code.

12
Testing

Writing tests is an essential part of developing maintainable software applications. Tests ensure that a certain function that is implemented as part of the software works as expected in various scenarios. Proofing the software applications with tests ensures that the application works as expected. So, if there are any changes made to the core logic in the future or if you are extending the functionality, the existing tests scenarios will help you identify how the new changes affect the existing behavior.

In this chapter, we will cover the following topics:

- Introduction to tests in V
- Understanding `testsuite` functions
- AAA pattern of writing tests
- Writing tests for functions with optional return types
- Approaches to writing and running tests

By the end of this chapter, you will know how to write tests for simple programs written in V and for programs that have modules. You will know different approaches to running tests and the benefit of using the `stats` argument to run tests in V.

Technical requirements

The full source code of this chapter is available at `https://github.com/ PacktPublishing/Getting-Started-with-V-Programming/tree/main/ Chapter12`.

Introduction to tests in V

Writing tests in V is straightforward. In this section, we will explore three simple concepts that will get you started with writing tests in V. They are as follows:

- Use the `assert` keyword to compare the actual and expected outcome.
- A file containing tests must end with the `_test.v` extension.
- Each test is a function and must start with the prefix `test_`.

In the next subsection, we will learn the syntax of the `assert` keyword and its usage in V.

The assert keyword

In V, you can use the `assert` keyword to compare the outcome of a function you are writing tests for with the expected outcome. Following is the syntax that shows how to use the `assert` keyword in V followed by a Boolean expression:

```
assert boolean_expression
```

In the preceding syntax, we can see that the `assert` keyword is followed by an expression whose output must always evaluate to a Boolean result. If the Boolean result is `true` then the assertion succeeds, otherwise, it will fail. We generally use **relational operators** such as `<`, `>`, `!=`, `==`, `<=`, or `>=`, or an expression such as `.contains()` on `string` data type that provides a Boolean result. We learned a great deal about relational operators in *Chapter 4, Primitive Data Types*.

An `assert` expression can also be used in normal functions. When the expression placed next to the `assert` keyword evaluates to `true`, the program continues its execution. If the expression evaluates to `false`, the program will stop and the error is reported to the `stderr`. Consider the following code, which demonstrates the usage of `assert` in normal functions:

```
module main

fn main() {
    println('1st assert')
```

```
    msg := 'hello there!'
    assert msg.contains('hello') // true
    println('2nd assert')
    assert 'apple' == 'orange' // stops execution
    println('done')
}
```

Now, if we run this file using the `v run filename.v` command, the output of the preceding code will be as follows:

```
1st assert
2nd assert
s.v:8: FAIL: fn main.main: assert 'apple' == 'orange'
   left value: 'apple' = apple
  right value: 'orange' = orange
V panic: Assertion failed...
v hash: ddc62ab
C:/Users/pavan/AppData/Local/Temp/v/s.1904660688325513120.
tmp.c:5830: at _v_panic: Backtrace
C:/Users/pavan/AppData/Local/Temp/v/s.1904660688325513120.
tmp.c:10467: by main__main
C:/Users/pavan/AppData/Local/Temp/v/s.1904660688325513120.
tmp.c:10825: by wmain
00448e10 : by ???
00448f73 : by ???
7ff86bb87974 : by ???
```

In the preceding output (you might see a somewhat different error message depending on your operating system), we notice that the program executes and prints statements until it encounters the second `assert` followed by the expression `'apple'=='orange'`. As this expression evaluates to `false`, the program stops and prints the error, and hence we don't see the string value `done` printed to the output.

We also see that when the `assert` failed, it had to print the `left value` and `right value`. Using the information contained in the *left* and *right* values, you can understand why the tests failed. This happens when the `assert` has an expression that uses a relational operator.

As we have seen, we run the file with the `main` function using `v run filename.v`. In the next sections, we will see how to write an actual test in a test file and learn how to run tests.

Writing a simple test

As stated previously, to write tests, the name of the file must end with `_test.v`. We will now create a file named `demo_test.v` and add a simple test to it.

From Command Prompt, navigate to the directory where you want to create a simple test file and run the following command:

```
mkdir v_test_demo
cd v_test_demo
echo '' > demo_test.v
```

Although you can have normal functions inside a test file, it is essential to have at least one test function in a test file, without which the V compiler will throw errors, as follows:

```
demo_test.v:1:1: error: a _test.v file should have *at least*
one 'test_' function
Details: The name of a test function in V, should start with
'test_'.
The test function should take 0 parameters, and no return type.
Example:
fn test_xyz(){ assert 2 + 2 == 4 }
```

Before we start writing our first test function, which just compares integer values using some relational operators, let's take a look at a few properties of test functions:

- A test function must start with `test_`.

- A test function should not accept any input arguments.

- A test function should always be a void function. This means it cannot have a return type, or it can be marked to return an optional type.

Having understood the basic properties of test functions, we will now write the first test in the test file we just created. From the editor of your choice, open the `demo_test.v` file and add the following code so that the `demo_test.v` file appears as follows:

```
fn test_first() {
    assert 2 != 2
}
```

From the preceding code, we see that the `demo_test.v` file has a single test function, `test_first()`. As we have learned, the test name starts with `test_`. You can try renaming this function so that it doesn't start with `test_`; V won't consider that function a test.

Alright, we have a test file with a `test_first` test function that just asserts the outcome of a relational operation, `!=`, performed between integers with both the right and left value specified as 2. Based on the expression 2 `!=` 2, we expect our test to fail. But we are yet to learn how to run tests contained in a test file. So, let's proceed and see how to run the tests in the next subsection.

Running tests

Generally, we use the `v run filename.v` command to run the logic contained in a V file. But for files containing tests, you just use `v filename_test.v`. So, in this case, we will run the following command to execute tests present in `demo_test.v`:

```
v demo_test.v
```

The preceding command will run all the tests inside `demo_tests.v`. As we have only one test in the `demo_test.v` file, it will just run the `test_first` test. As the `assert` fails and evaluates to `false`, the output after running the test file will be as follows:

```
demo_test.v:2: ✗ fn test_first
    > assert 2 != 2
        Left value: 2
       Right value: 2
```

So, our test failed for the expression that said 2 `!=` 2. In the preceding output, we notice that the `stderr` shows the line `demo_test.v:2: ✗ fn test_first`, which indicates the test has failed. Also, it is pointing, using the `>` symbol, to the line where the test failed to assert. The next lines also show values held by the expression along with labels `Left value` and `Right value`.

Since this test is failing, let's make this test pass by changing the Boolean expression so that it evaluates to `true`, as follows:

```
fn test_first() {
    assert 2 == 2
}
```

From the preceding code, we notice that the 2 == 2 expression, which follows the `assert` keyword, will evaluate to `true`. So, we again run the tests using the following command after saving the changes to the `demo_test.v` file:

```
v demo_test.v
```

The output of the preceding command will not print anything to the standard output.

Having understood the concept of `assert` and also how to name a test file and test function, we will proceed with exploring **testsuite functions** in V.

Understanding testsuite functions

V facilitates writing pre- and post-test execution routines in the form of `testsuite` functions, namely `testsuite_begin` and `testsuite_end`, respectively:

- `testsuite_begin`: This function will be helpful when you are planning to set up certain resources, such as data or environment variables, or create files if any are needed by the tests that are part of the test file.

- `testsuite_end`: Alternatively, the `testsuite_end` function can be used to clean up the resources introduced by `testsuite_begin`. The `testsuite_end` function can be used to clean data and environment variables, or delete files if any are created during the test run.

Also, these `testsuite` functions neither accept input arguments nor specify a return type. These functions execute only once, but not for every test that is present in a test file. When you start running tests, the test runner will look for the presence of `testsuite_begin` and executes this function first. Similarly, if there is a `testsuite_end` function, it will be executed at the very end.

Demonstrating the usage of testsuite functions

In this section, we will look at the usage of `testsuite` functions with some example code. Consider the following code, which demonstrates the usage of `testsuite` functions:

```
import os

fn testsuite_begin() {
    os.setenv('foo', 'bar', true)
    println('About to start executing all tests')
```

```
}

fn test_env_foo_has_value_bar() {
    println('Executing test')

    // arrange
    inp := 'foo'
    expected := 'bar'

    // act
    actual := os.getenv(inp)

    // assert
    assert actual == expected
}

fn testsuite_end() {
    os.unsetenv('foo')
    println('Finished executing all tests')
}
```

In the preceding code, we notice that the testsuite_begin function is setting an environment variable with the name foo and the value bar using the call to the os.setenv function. Alternatively, the testsuite_end function is removing the foo environment variable by making a call to the os.unsetenv function. In addition to setting and unsetting operations with these testsuite functions, for the sake of demonstration, I have added a print statement with a message that will show you the order of execution of these testsuite functions.

Also, there is a test function, test_env_foo_has_value_bar, that tries to assert the *actual value* of the foo environment variable with the *expected value,* bar.

To run the preceding code block, place it in a file named testsuite_demo_test.v and run the following command:

```
v testsuite_demo_test.v
```

The output of the preceding command will be as follows:

```
About to start executing all tests
Executing test
Finished executing all tests
```

From the preceding output, we can see that the test passed. We also observe from the order of the `print` messages that the `testsuite_begin` function was executed first and then the other tests were executed, followed by the `testsuite_end` function executed at the very end.

One thing to notice in the `test_env_foo_has_value_bar` test is that it is written in the **AAA pattern**. In the next section, we will briefly explain this pattern.

The AAA pattern of writing tests

The AAA pattern of writing tests refers to the initials of the words **arrange**, **act**, and **assert**. This pattern provides a clean approach to organizing the instructions that become part of a test case. Following this pattern also enhances the readability of the test cases. The following points give a brief explanation of all three phases of the AAA pattern that help you write clean, organized, and readable tests:

- **Arrange**: This is the first of all the phases. In this phase, you *arrange* the inputs needed for the function that you are about to *act* on. You can also arrange and set expectations such as expected output assigned to the variables that you can use in the *assert* phase.

- **Act**: Having made arrangements for the test, we then *act* on the function we want to test. This could be done by invoking a call to the function under test. If any input arguments are needed by the function, we can pass them on to the function under test based on the arrangements made in the *arrange* phase.

- **Assert**: We finally *assert* whether the results obtained from the *act* phase are matching the expectations set in the *arrange* phase.

Writing tests for functions with optional return types

We have learned that test functions must not specify a return type. But we have also learned that test function properties can be marked with the symbol ? when the test logic deals with functions with optional return types. To demonstrate this, consider the following greet function:

```
fn greet(name string) ?string {
    if name != '' {
        return 'Hello $name!'
    }
    return error('name not provided')
}
```

The greet function returns a ?string type. This means greet will return a string value only when a non-empty name is provided to it as an input argument. If the name is an empty string, it will return an error with the message name not provided. The following code shows the test case when the name parameter is provided with a non-empty string:

```
fn test_greet_given_a_name() {
    exp := 'Hello Pavan!'
    assert greet('Pavan') or { err.msg } == exp
}
```

In the preceding code, we will not see any failure of assert because it satisfies the expression using the relational operator, ==, that the left value and right value are being compared with. Logically speaking, the left value of the expression greet('Pavan') or { err.msg } will evaluate to Hello Pavan!, which is the same as the expected value.

But consider a scenario when the function is provided with an empty string. There are two approaches to write tests for such a scenario. The first approach is to let the function under test (greet in this case) propagate the error, thus leading to the failure of the test. So, to implement this, let's create a test function named test_greet_propagates_error as follows:

```
fn test_greet_propagates_error() ? {
    greet('') ?
}
```

Notice that the preceding test function is marked with a ? return type as we are just calling the function under test, `greet`, with an empty string value in place of the `name` argument. This test is expected to fail, and it is obvious from the output as follows:

```
demo_test.v:14: X fn test_greet_propagates_error failed
propagation with error: name not provided
   14 |                    greet('') ?
```

If you want to clean up your test and capture the exact error message that is being returned by the function `greet`, we can write a test as follows:

```
fn test_greet_when_empty() {
    exp := 'name not provided'
    assert greet('') or { err.msg } == exp
}
```

In the preceding code, we are not marking the test function with a ? return type. Instead, we are asserting that the error message returned by the `greet` function with an empty string value will be the same as the expected value held by the `exp` variable.

Following is the full working code after combining all the code we have learned so far in this section:

```
fn greet(name string) ?string {
    if name != '' {
        return 'Hello $name!'
    }
    return error('name not provided')
}

fn test_greet_given_a_name() {
    exp := 'Hello Pavan!'
    assert greet('Pavan') or { err.msg } == exp
}

fn test_greet_propagates_error() ? {
    greet('') ?
}

fn test_greet_when_empty() {
```

```
    exp := 'name not provided'
    assert greet('') or { err.msg } == exp
}
```

We can place the preceding code in a test file, let's say `optional_demo_test.v`, and run all three tests using the `v optional_demo_test.v` command. Executing the tests with the aforementioned command will result in the following output, where we see that only the test named `test_greet_propagates_error` fails:

```
demo_test.v:14: X fn test_greet_propagates_error failed
propagation with error: name not provided
   14 |              greet('') ?
```

In the next section, we will learn approaches to writing tests for a simple project and also for a project with modules. We will also learn different ways to run tests for these project types.

Approaches to writing and running tests

In this section, we will see how to structure tests for a simple program written in V. We will also see how to add tests to a program with modules. This section will also cover how to run tests in different ways, such as in a single `_test.v` file, inside a module, and running all the tests of a project. In addition, we will also see the advantage of the `stats` argument and the information produced in the test output when we use this argument.

Writing tests for a simple program

Let's begin by writing tests for a simple greeting application written in V. In this scenario, we will have only one module, which will be the main module. The main module will have a file named `greet.v` with a private function, `greet`, and the `main` function, which prints the response returned by the `greet` function:

```
module main

fn greet(name string) string {
    return 'Hello $name!'
}

fn main() {
    msg := greet('Bob')
```

```
    println(msg)
}
```

Now we will add a `_test.v` file called `greet_test.v` in the directory that `greet.v` is located. We then add the tests, as shown:

```
module main

fn test_greet() {
    // Arrange
    name := 'Bob'
    exp_msg := 'Hello Bob!'

    // Act
    act_msg := greet(name)

    // Assert
    assert act_msg == exp_msg
    assert act_msg.contains(name)
}
```

The preceding code has a test named `test_greet` that asserts the value returned by the `greet` function, which is not marked as public as there is no `pub` keyword. Since the `greet_test.v` file is defining `module main`, which is the same as `greet.v`, all the functions, regardless of whether they are public or non-public, will be accessible for the tests contained in `greet_test.v`. Also, in our `test_greet` test, we are acting on this `greet` function, which accepts strings. After making a call to that function with the known `name` parameter, we expect that function to return a message by prefixing `Hello` to the name, like `Hello Bob!`.

In this scenario, the structure of files contained in this simple project will appear as follows:

```
+---01_simple_test
|       greet.v
|       greet_test.v
```

Running tests contained in _test.v file

To run the tests contained in `greet_test.v` we need to change the current working directory to `01_simple_test` from Command Prompt and run the `v greet_test.v` command.

The output of the preceding command will produce detailed output when there is an error. The detailed error output will include information such as the name of the test and information to help identify why the test failed. But in our case, the test will pass, and hence we will not see any errors reported to the console.

V does not allow writing tests for the `main` function of the main module. If we try to add a test or call it in any of the tests, then you will see a message saying `error: the main function cannot be called in the program`.

Writing tests for a project with modules

We will now see how to write tests for a project with modules. For the sake of demonstration, we will have a simple project named `modulebasics`, as discussed in the *Accessing members of module* section of *Chapter 9, Modules*. The following is the directory structure before we proceed to add any tests for this project:

```
02_modulebasics
|    .gitignore
|    modulebasics.v
|    README.md
|    v.mod
|
\---mod1
            file1.v
```

As mentioned earlier, we are referring to the code from *Chapter 9, Modules*, and to ease things up to be suitable enough for this topic, we will make slight changes. The first change is made to the `hello()` function of `mod1` contained in `file1.v` to return a string instead of just printing a message to the console. This will facilitate writing a test and assert on the return value. So, the `hello` function will appear as follows:

```
// file: mod1/file1.v
module mod1
```

```
pub fn hello() string {
    return 'Hello from mod1!'
}
```

The second change is made to the main function to print the return value from the mod1.hello function to the console. So, the main function in modulebasics.v will be updated as follows:

```
// file: modulebasics.v
module main

import mod1

fn main() {
    res := mod1.hello()
    println(res)
}
```

Now we will add tests for the hello function of mod1. The first thing to do is to add the tests within the mod1 module inside the mod1 directory. So, we will create a file called mod1_test.v inside the mod1 directory with the following test implemented in the AAA pattern:

```
// file: mod1/mod1_test.v
module mod1

fn test_hello() {
    // arrange
    exp := 'Hello from mod1!'

    // act
    act := hello()

    // assert
    assert act == exp
}
```

The preceding code shows a simple test that asserts the actual and expected values after acting on the `hello` function. Since `mod1_test.v` is defining `module mod1` and is located in the same directory, `mod1`, the tests contained in `mod1_test.v` can access all the public and non-public functions of the `mod1` module.

Running tests contained in a module

As we learned in the previous sections, to run tests in a `_test.v` file, we need to just run the `v mod1_test.v` command. But to run this command, you must ensure that your working directory is the same as the location of `mod1_test.v`. Alternatively, you can also run tests by providing the relative path to the `_test.v` file.

To avoid this confusion, V allows you to specify a module name when running the command using `v test MODULE_NAME`. So, from the root directory of our `modulebasics` project, run the following command to execute tests that are only present in `mod1`:

```
v test mod1
```

The output of the preceding command will be as follows:

```
---- Testing... ------------------------------------------------
--------------------------------
  OK      2597.143 ms C:/Learn-V-Programming/Chapter12/02_
modulebasics/mod1/mod1_test.v
  --------------------------------------------------------------
--------------------------------
```

Writing tests for members of a sub-module from the main module

Now we will proceed further and add tests at the project level, where we access the functions contained inside the module. To achieve this, we will add a file called `main_test.v` at the root of the `modulebasics` project. We then add a test to act on the `hello` function of the `mod1` module:

```
// file: main_test.v

module main

import mod1
```

```
fn test_hello() {
    // arrange
    exp := 'Hello from mod1!'

    // act
    act := mod1.hello()

    // assert
    assert act == exp
    assert mod1.hello().contains('Hello')
}
```

In the preceding code, as we can see, this test file is at the root of our project, where we are defining `module main`. To access the `hello` function, which is marked as `pub` inside `file1.v` of `mod1`, we need to `import mod1` in our `main_test.v` file. So, the test can now act on the `hello` function using the call `mod1.hello()`.

At this stage, the directory structure of our `modulebasics` project will be updated and appears as follows:

```
02_modulebasics
|    .gitignore
|    main_test.v
|    modulebasics.v
|    README.md
|    v.mod
|
\---mod1
        file1.v
        mod1_test.v
```

Running all the tests contained in a project

Let's run all the tests from the `main_test.v` and `mod1_test.v` files. From Command Prompt, set the working directory to the root of this project. Next, we will run all the tests that are present in our `modulebasics` project using the following command:

```
v test .
```

The preceding command will look for the presence of files that end with `_test.v` recursively in all the directories and will execute tests that start with `test_`. We will see the following output:

```
---- Testing... ------------------------------------------------
------------------------------------------------
  OK      [1/2]    2801.779 ms C:/Learn-V-Programming/Chapter12/02_
modulebasics/main_test.v
  OK      [2/2]    2816.950 ms C:/Learn-V-Programming/Chapter12/02_
modulebasics/mod1/mod1_test.v
  ------------------------------------------------------
  ------------------------------------------------
```

In the next section, we will see how to run tests with the `stats` flag enabled.

Running tests with stats

V allows you to run tests that generate a detailed output of the test execution results. You can enable it by passing the `-stats` argument, which is demonstrated in this section. With the `stats` argument, you will get details such as the time taken to compile the code, with the compilation speed in units of vlines/sec for each test run. In addition to this information, you will also see the time taken by each test and the number of asserts for each test.

To enable capturing stats for our `modulebasics` project, navigate to the root directory from Command Prompt and run the following command:

```
v -stats test .
```

The output of the preceding command will be as follows:

```
---- Testing... ---------------------------------------------
-------------------------------------------------------------
-------------------------------------------------------------
-----------
-------------------------------------------------------------
-------------------------------------------------------------
-------------------------------------------------------------
-----------
-------------------------------------------------------------
-------------------------------------------------------------
-------------------------------------------------------------
-----------
```

```
          V  source  code  size:        19308
lines,       519623 bytes
generated  target  code  size:        17395 lines,        588891
bytes
compilation took: 2126.836 ms, compilation speed: 9078 vlines/s
          V  source  code  size:        19319
lines,       519726 bytes
generated  target  code  size:        17401 lines,        588992
bytes
compilation took: 2223.528 ms, compilation speed: 8688 vlines/s
running tests in: C:Learn-V-ProgrammingChapter12_
modulebasicsmod1mod1_test.v
       OK         0.041 ms      1 assert  | mod1.test_hello()
    Summary for running V tests in "C:Learn-V-
ProgrammingChapter12_modulebasicsmod1mod1_test.v": 1 passed, 1
total. Runtime: 5 ms.


running tests in: C:Learn-V-ProgrammingChapter12_
modulebasicsmain_test.v
       OK         0.016 ms      1 assert  | main.test_hello()
    Summary for running V tests in "C:Learn-V-
ProgrammingChapter12_modulebasicsmain_test.v": 1 passed, 1
total. Runtime: 2 ms.


-------------------------------------------------------------
-------------------------------------------------------------
-------------------------------------------------------------
-----------
```

It is evident from the preceding output that when the stats flag is used while running tests, the output shows the details of the execution of tests.

Summary

In this chapter, we learned how to write tests in V. We saw the syntax and usage of the `assert` keyword and learned how to write a simple test and run it. We then learned about the `testsuite_begin` and `testsuite_end` functions and learned how to use those functions in performing pre- and post-test activities, respectively. This chapter also covered the popular AAA pattern of writing tests. We also learned how to write tests for functions with optional return types.

In the latter parts of this chapter, we saw various approaches to writing and running tests that span from a simple program to a program with modules. We also learned different approaches to running tests contained in a single file, tests that belong to a module, and also, all tests contained in a project. Finally, we saw how to see the detailed output generated by the test runner using the `stats` argument. Having learned how to write and run tests in V, you will now be able to write applications in V that are covered with tests.

In the next chapter we will learn how to work with built-in libraries in V namely JSON and ORM.

13
Introduction to JSON and ORM

In this chapter, we will learn how to work with the built-in libraries in V, namely json and orm. When building web services such as RESTful APIs, it is essential to understand the content type that you are exchanging with the clients or other RESTful APIs. **JavaScript Object Notation (JSON)** has become the go-to format for modern applications to exchange data. In this chapter, we will briefly introduce JSON and how to work with it in V.

When building data-driven applications, **Object Relational Mappers (ORMs)** become a crucial part of establishing communication between the world of objects and the world of relational databases. Through this chapter, we will introduce the built-in library known as orm, which ships along with the V installer.

We will be covering the following topics:

- Getting started with JSON
- Learning ORM

By the end of this chapter, you will have learned about the built-in json and orm V libraries. Understanding these libraries will help you write data-driven web APIs or microservices that exchange data in JSON format.

Technical requirements

Knowledge of SQL is preferred but not mandatory. The full source code for this chapter is available at `https://github.com/PacktPublishing/Getting-Started-with-V-Programming/tree/main/Chapter13`.

Getting started with JSON

JSON is the most used format to communicate data among applications, such as HTTP APIs or web applications. The other formats of data include XML, CSV, TSV, and text files, to mention a few.

For the sake of demonstration, consider the following `Note` struct:

```
struct Note {
    id      int
    message string
    status  bool
}
```

We can represent this `Note` struct in JSON format as follows:

```
{
    "id": 1,
    "message": "Plan a holiday",
    "status": false
}
```

The representation of a JSON object in the preceding code is easy to read and understand:

- A JSON object typically starts with { (an opening curly bracket) and ends with } (a closing curly bracket).

- A JSON object has various properties represented as key-value pairs separated by a : (colon).

- The key will always be enclosed in " (double quotes).

- The value can be of any data type, such as a string, integer, float, Boolean, array, or any other JSON object.

An array of JSON objects is separated by a comma, and all these objects are wrapped inside [and]. For example, we can represent multiple Note objects as a JSON array as follows:

```
[
    {
        "id": 1,
        "message": "Plan a holiday",
        "status": false
    },
    {
        "id": 2,
        "message": "Get groceries",
        "status": false
    }
]
```

A file with a JSON object, as shown in the preceding example, ends with a .json extension. These files are called JSON files.

V has a third-party library named json to *encode* and *decode* JSON. To work with JSON data, we need to import the json library in the code where we either encode or decode JSON. In the following sections, we will look at how to decode and encode JSON in V.

Decoding a JSON object

JSON decoding is the process of converting JSON data into an object in V.

The decode function accepts two arguments. The first argument is the type that the JSON needs to be decoded into. The second argument is the JSON data represented as a string.

The decode function has an optional return type. Thus, if improper input is provided, we can handle the errors using the or {} block. In the case of successful decoding, it returns an object whose type is equivalent to the first argument provided as an input argument to the decode function. The following example shows decoding a JSON object:

```
import json

fn main() {
    n := json.decode(Note, '{"id":1,"message":"Plan a
```

```
        holiday","status":false}') or {
        panic('invalid json data')
    }
    println(typeof(n).name) // Note
    println(n)
}
```

For brevity, the Note struct is not specified in the preceding code. We can see that to decode a JSON string, we must use the import json statement, and that we are invoking the decode function with the two input arguments. In this example, we want to decode the JSON string into the Note type. We can also see that the decode function is followed by an or block and that we are handling the scenario in case of improper JSON data.

The output of the preceding code will be as follows:

```
Note
Note{
    id: 1
    message: 'Plan a holiday'
    status: false
}
```

If the JSON string is malformed, as shown in the following code, we will see an error message printed to the console:

```
n := json.decode(Note, '{"id":1,"message":"Plan a
holiday","status":false') or {
    panic('invalid json data')
}
```

The preceding code is missing a } at the end of the JSON string. Hence, in this case, the program will panic with the message invalid json data.

Next, we will learn how to encode an object in V into JSON data.

Encoding an object into JSON data

Encoding an object into JSON refers to the process of converting an object in V into a JSON string. The `encode` function accepts an input argument and returns a string that represents JSON data.

The following code demonstrates the use of the `encode` method:

```
import json

fn main() {
    m := Note{
        id: 2
        message: 'Get groceries'
        status: false
    }

    j := json.encode(m)
    println(j)
}
```

In the preceding code, we are encoding the `Note` struct and printing the output to the console, which will appear as follows:

```
{"id":2,"message":"Get groceries","status":false}
```

Having understood the concepts of JSON decoding and encoding in V, we will start learning about the built-in ORM module in V.

Learning ORM

The ORM module is used to communicate with relational databases (such as **Postgres**, **MySQL**, **SQLite**, **MSSQL**, and **Oracle**). The communication to the database happens from the programming languages (such as **V**, **Python**, or **C#**, to mention a few) using the objects that are created to reflect the database table schema.

At the time of writing this book, V's standard library (`vlib`) ships with a built-in ORM that supports Postgres, MySQL, and SQLite. It has planned support for the other two popular relational databases, namely MSSQL and Oracle.

Generally, each database defines a standard way to interact and query against the data and this is often referred to as **Structured Query Language (SQL)**. Each of these databases has its version of SQL that we refer to as dialects. Each database has a different dialect that specifies how to communicate with the database to perform queries.

However, by using V's ORM, you don't need to learn about, write, or manage different SQL dialects for different relational databases. There is only one syntax for all SQL dialects and it is written using the API provided by the ORM built into V. Thus, we are free to switch between the databases without having to rewrite the queries in V.

To summarize, the built-in ORM in V has the following benefits:

- There is just one syntax for all SQL dialects, which makes migrating between databases much easier.

- All the queries to interact with the database are written using V's syntax.

- All the queries are automatically sanitized to prevent SQL injection.

- The queries are easier to read and understand.

- The results obtained from a query are automatically converted into objects in V.

Now, let's learn how to build a struct in V that reflects a table in a relational database. For the sake of demonstration, I will be connecting to a SQLite database, which is recommended for quick development and design purposes.

> **Note**
>
> Since V's ORM, at the time of writing this book, is still in its alpha stage, we will see more progress in the `orm` library in the future. What you are learning here is mostly expected to improve, but the concepts detailed will remain the same.

Understanding ORM attributes

There are certain attributes that you can use to decorate a struct and its fields so that it resembles the schema of a table in a relational database. Attributes must be enclosed in square brackets, [and] . These attributes are tabulated as follows:

Attribute	Decorator	Purpose
`[table: 'TABLE_NAME']`	Struct	`TABLE_NAME` can be any descriptive name that the table is being designed for. If this attribute is not specified, the name of the struct will be considered a table name.
`[primary]`	Field	Sets the field as a primary key.
`[sql: 'COLUMN_NAME']`	Field	Sets the name of the column in the table.
`[sql: COLUMN_TYPE]`	Field	Sets the type of the column in the table. The most common types are `int`, `string`, `bool`, and a special type called `serial` that's used to indicate auto increment. The `serial` type is typically used along with primary keys.
`[unique]`	Field	Sets the field to have a unique value in a list of rows.
`[unique: 'GROUP_NAME']`	Field	`GROUP_NAME` can be any group name. It adds the field to a unique group with the name provided.
`[nonull]`	Field	Must provide a value or a default zeroed value based on the type that will be assigned.

Table 13.1 - ORM attributes

While writing queries against the table using V's ORM, the syntax in V's SQL syntax must refer to the name of the struct, even though it is decorated with the `[table: 'TABLE_NAME']` attribute. The same applies to the field of a struct, regardless of whether it is decorated with a different column name using the `[sql: 'COLUMN_NAME']` attribute.

Creating a struct for ORM

Having learned about the attributes in V's ORM, we will now create a simple struct that resembles a mapping to a table in a relational database.

Consider the following `Note` struct, which we want to relate to a `Notes` table in the database:

```
[table: 'Notes']
struct Note {
    id      int     [primary; sql: serial]
```

```
    message string [sql: 'detail'; unique]
    status  bool    [nonull]
}
```

In the preceding code, we can see that the `table` attribute has specified the table name as `Notes`. But when we want to perform data manipulation on the `Notes` table, we will be referring to the name of the `Note` struct instead of the name of the table in the database.

You can also see that the `id` field is specified with two attributes, `primary` and `sql: serial`, separated by a `;`. The `message` field is marked as `unique`. Also, we want to have a different name for the `message` field, such as `detail`, as the corresponding column name in the database. Hence, we specified `sql: 'detail'` as an additional attribute on the `message` field. The `status` field is decorated with a `nonull` attribute to indicate whether the note is complete or not.

We will now understand how to establish a connection and perform **Data Definition Language** (**DDL**) operations such as creating and dropping a table from a database using V's ORM.

Working with the ORM library

Although ORM is a built-in library in V, we are just using its API to connect to the database. To work with the ORM library, we must follow these steps:

1. Install SQLite as a third-party library in V's installation directory.

2. Set up a new project to work on ORM using the SQLite library.

3. Establish a connection to the database.

We'll look at these steps in detail in the following subsections.

Installing SQLite as a third-party library in V's installation directory

To establish communication with a database, we will install SQLite as a third-party library in V's installation directory.

For that, go to `https://sqlite.org/download.html` and download the source code for SQLite. Once downloaded, you will see the archive. Extract the archive and place the files in the V installation, under the `~\v\thirdparty\sqlite` directory. Here is what this looks like on the Windows 10 OS:

```
C:\V\THIRDPARTY\SQLITE
    shell.c
```

```
sqlite3.c
sqlite3.h
sqlite3ext.h
```

If you are on an Ubuntu OS, you need to run the following commands as final steps to complete the SQLite installation:

```
sudo apt-get install libssl-dev
sudo apt-get install libsqlite3-dev
```

Now that we have installed SQLite as a third-party library in V's installation directory, in the next section, we will create a project to learn about ORM using SQLite.

Setting up a new project to work on ORM using the SQLite library

To set up a new project let us follow these steps:

1. Let's create a new project named `orm_demo` using the following command in the command prompt:

    ```
    v new orm_demo
    cd orm_demo
    ```

2. Once you run the `v new orm_demo` command, you will be prompted to provide a description, version, and license information, which are optional. Then, you can hit *Enter*.

    Our `orm_demo` project will look as follows:

    ```
    C:\ORM_DEMO
          .gitignore
          orm_demo.v
          v.mod
    ```

3. Now, set your current directory to the location of the new project we just created. We will modify the project gradually as we progress through the topics in this section related to ORM. So, if you want to see the output of every change, you can run the project from the command prompt using the following command:

    ```
    v run .
    ```

As it is a new project, you will see an output of `Hello World!` or something similar to what is present in the print statement of the main function of your app. Now, let's proceed and learn how to connect to the database using the SQLite third-party library that we just installed.

Establishing a connection to the database

To connect to the database, we need to import the `sqlite` library and then use the `connect` method, which will become available after the `sqlite` import.

Now, let's start editing the `orm_demo.v` file. Replace the contents of the `orm_demo.v` file so that it appears as follows:

```v
module main

import sqlite

[table: 'Notes']
struct Note {
    id      int    [primary; sql: serial]
    message string [sql: 'detail'; unique]
    status  bool   [nonull]
}

fn main() {
    db := sqlite.connect('NotesDB.db') or { panic(err) }
}
```

As we have installed SQLite as a third-party library, we will import it to establish a connection to the SQLite database. Hence, in the preceding code, we can see the `import sqlite` statement. After the import, we assign the `sqlite` database connection instance to the `db` variable inside the `main` function.

We will now learn about performing various database operations using V's ORM.

Briefly understanding database operations using V's ORM

In this section, we will learn about various database operations. These operations include DDL operations such as create and drop tables. We will also learn how to perform **Data Manipulation Operations (DML)** operations such as insert, select, update, and delete using V's ORM.

Note that the aforementioned DDL and DML do not make up the complete list. For brevity, we will just focus on the limited set of DDL and DML operations that will help us build a microservice.

Performing DDL operations using V's ORM

In this section, we will learn how to perform the basic and most common DDL operations, called create and drop, using V's ORM.

Creating a table

As we have already defined what our Notes table should look like in the form of a Note struct using V, we will modify the main function to create the table using the following code:

```
fn main() {
    db := sqlite.connect('NotesDB.db') or { panic(err) }
    db.exec('drop table if exists Notes')
    sql db {
        create table Note
    }
}
```

From the preceding code, we are ensuring that we drop the Notes table if it already exists using the plain SQL syntax provided as a string argument to the exec function of the db connection. This indicates that you can directly run SQL queries using the db.exec command. After this command, we are performing a table creation operation using V syntax. The create table Note operation will generate the following equivalent SQL syntax:

```
CREATE TABLE IF NOT EXISTS `Notes` (`id` INTEGER, `detail`
TEXT, `status` INTEGER NOT NULL, PRIMARY KEY(`id`),
UNIQUE(`detail`));
```

Next, we will learn how to perform the drop table operation.

Dropping a table

In the preceding code, we saw how to drop the table directly by invoking a SQL-based command using db.exec. Alternatively, you can drop a table using V's ORM syntax, as follows:

```
sql db {
    drop table Note
}
```

Now, let's learn how to perform DML operations.

Performing DML operations using V's ORM

In this section, we will learn how to perform basic DML operations on the Notes table. The ORM statements in V that we are going to learn about can be placed after the create table statement of the main function in the sequence that we are about to learn. To reduce repeated code, we will just focus on the DML statements of ORM in the following sections.

Inserting record(s)

To perform the insert operation, we will build a couple of objects of the Note struct type, as follows:

```
n1 := Note{
    message: 'Get some milk'
    status: false
}

n2 := Note{
    message: 'Get groceries'
    status: false
}
```

From the preceding code, we can see that the n1 and n2 objects are of the Note type. We will now perform the insert operation using V's ORM syntax, as follows:

```
sql db {
    insert OBJECT_VAR into STRUCT_NAME
}
```

From the preceding syntax, the term OBJECT_VAR refers to an object of the STRUCT_NAME type. The term STRUCT_NAME will be the name of the Note struct. As we have two note objects, n1 and n2, we will perform the insert operation on these two objects, as follows:

```
sql db {
    insert n1 into Note
    insert n2 into Note
}
```

The corresponding SQL code that's generated by V's ORM for the insert operation on the Notes table will be as follows:

```
INSERT INTO `Notes` (`detail`, `status`) VALUES (?1, ?2);
```

> **Note**
> The SQL statements in the preceding code will not be printed anywhere in the console, but they are generated internally by V's ORM. I have mentioned them for ease of understanding.

To obtain the primary key identity of a record that the ORM has performed any DML operation on, we can access it by calling the last_id() function, as shown here:

```
println(db.last_id())
```

This function returns the value in the format orm.Primitive(<VALUE>). The last_id() function, which can be accessed on the database connection, is of the Primitive type, and VALUE can be accessed by casting it to the respective primitive data type, including the time.Time type.

As the id primary key in Note is of the integer type, we can cast it to the int type, as follows:

```
println(db.last_id() as int)
```

The preceding print statement will cast `last_id()` to the `int` data type.

Selecting records

Now that we have successfully inserted the records into the database, we will query the database and verify the records using a `select` statement. The following syntax shows how to write a `select` query using V's ORM:

```
ROWS_VAR := sql db {
    select from STRUCT_NAME
}
```

In the preceding syntax, the `select` operation returns an array corresponding to the type of the struct. We will perform the `select` operation on our `Notes` table using V's ORM, as follows:

```
all_notes := sql db {
    select from Note
}
```

The SQL statement generated by V's ORM as a part of the preceding code will look as follows:

```
SELECT `id`, `detail`, `status` FROM `Notes` ORDER BY `id` ASC;
```

From the preceding SQL statement, we can see that the `select` statement implicitly specifies all the columns of a table. We can also see that a default ascending sort order is applied to the primary key, which is `id` in our case.

Now, let's print the `all_notes` variable and its type using the following code:

```
println(all_notes)
println('Type of all_notes is : ${typeof(all_notes).name}')
```

The output of the preceding code will be as follows:

```
[Note{
    id: 1
    message: 'Get some milk'
    status: false
}, Note{
    id: 2
```

```
    message: 'Get groceries'
    status: false
}]
Type of all_notes is : []Note
```

Here, we can see that the result of the `select` statement when using ORM is of the `[]` `Note` type. Now, let's learn how to sort the results using the `order by` clause.

Selecting using the order by clause

In the preceding code, we learned that, by default, V's ORM sorts the results in ascending order of `id`, which is the primary key column of the `Notes` table. If we want the results to be sorted on the `id` column in descending order, we must write the following code:

```
notes_sorted := sql db {
    select from Note order by id desc
}
```

The SQL statement generated by V's ORM as a part of the preceding query will look as follows:

```
SELECT `id`, `detail`, `status` FROM `Notes` ORDER BY `id`
DESC;
```

Here, the SQL generated by the ORM sorts the notes in descending order of `id`. If we print `notes_sorted`, we will see the following output:

```
[Note{
    id: 2
    message: 'Get groceries'
    status: false
}, Note{
    id: 1
    message: 'Get some milk'
    status: false
}]
```

From the preceding output, we can see that the results were sorted in the descending order of the `id` column of the `Notes` table.

Selecting using the limit clause

The limit clause specifies the number of records to be returned as a result of the query's execution. You can use the limit along with the `order by` or `where` clauses. We will learn about the `where` clause in the next section. Suppose you want to retrieve the last record that's been inserted into the `Notes` table. For this, we can use the following code:

```
notes_limited := sql db {
    select from Note order by id desc limit 1
}
```

In the preceding code, we are limiting our `select` statement to return just one record. This is evident from `limit 1`, which becomes part of the entire `select` statement.

The SQL statement generated by V's ORM as a part of the preceding query will look as follows:

```
SELECT `id`, `detail`, `status` FROM `Notes` ORDER BY `id` DESC
LIMIT ?1;
```

Here, we can see that the SQL generated by ORM sorts the notes in descending order of `id` and limits the results to just `1`.

Now, let's print the value and type of `notes_limited` using the following code:

```
println(notes_limited)
println('Type returned by select when limit is
1: ${typeof(notes_limited).name}')
```

The output of the preceding code will be as follows:

```
Note{
    id: 2
    message: 'Get groceries'
    status: false
}
Type returned by select when limit is 1:  Note
```

From the preceding output, we can see that the `select` statement returned just one record as expected. We can also see that having a limit clause with a limit value of `1` automatically results in a value that is of the `Note` type, unlike in other select statements in which we get `[]Note`.

Selecting using a where clause

A `where` clause is used to filter the number of records based on a conditional statement. We will use the `select` statement, along with the `where` clause, followed by a conditional statement. These conditions are used to filter records that match certain column values. The following code shows filtering a selection of rows based on `id` using the `>` relational operator:

```
notes_latest := sql db {
    select from Note where id > 1
}
```

The SQL statement that's generated by V's ORM as a part of the preceding query will look as follows:

```
SELECT `id`, `detail`, `status` FROM `Notes` WHERE `id` > ?1
ORDER BY `id` ASC;
```

Here, the SQL generated by the ORM filters the records based on the `id > 1` condition. If we print `notes_latest`, we will see the following output:

```
[Note{
    id: 2
    message: 'Get groceries'
    status: false
}]
```

The following are a few points to note about the `where` clause in V's ORM:

- The `where` clause can be used with `select`, `update`, or `delete`.
- The conditional statement of a `where` clause uses relational operators, which evaluates to a Boolean result.
- You can club multiple conditions using logical operators; that is, `&&` or `||`.
- You can club a `where` clause with either or both of the `order by` and `limit` clauses. In such cases, the `where` clause comes first in the statement, followed by `order by` and then `limit`.

Updating record(s)

To update any record in the Notes table, we can use an update query. Using V's ORM, the following code updates status to true for the Notes table whose id is 2:

```
sql db {
    update Note set status = true where id == 2
}
```

The SQL statement generated by V's ORM as a part of the preceding query will look as follows:

```
UPDATE `Notes` SET `status` = ?1 WHERE `id` = ?2;
```

To view the updated record, we can query as follows:

```
notes_updated := sql db {
    select from Note where id == 2
}
println(notes_updated)
```

The preceding code will generate the following output, where we can see a status of Note with an id of 2 set to true:

```
Note{
    id: 2
    message: 'Get groceries'
    status: true
}
```

From the preceding output, in addition to the status field being updated to true, V's ORM automatically returns the single record instead of [] Note as there is only one record that matches the id == 2 condition held by the where clause.

Deleting record(s)

The delete operation removes the record from the database. To delete a record based on a condition, we can use the where clause. The following code shows how to delete a record whose id is 2:

```
sql db {
    delete from Note where id == 2
}
```

The SQL statement generated by V's ORM as a part of the preceding query will look as follows:

```
DELETE FROM `Notes` WHERE `id` = ?1;
```

Now, let's look at the records that are left in the table by running the ORM `select` query, as shown here:

```
notes_leftover := sql db {
    select from Note
}
println(notes_leftover)
```

The output of the preceding code will be as follows:

```
[Note{
    id: 1
    message: 'Get some milk'
    status: false
}]
```

After performing the `delete` operation on a `Note` whose `status` is marked as `true`, we are left with only one `Note`, as shown in the preceding output.

Summary

In this chapter, we briefly introduced JSON and ORM. We then learned how to work with the `json` and `orm` libraries, which are available in V, in detail. In the earlier sections of this chapter, we learned how to perform JSON encoding and decoding using `json`, a third-party library that ships along with V.

In the later sections of this chapter, we focused on the built-in `orm` library. We learned how to work with the `orm` library and set up requirements such as manually installing the third-party `sqlite` library to work with the SQLite database. We then saw how to perform DDL and DML operations with the help of the `orm` library in V.

This chapter served as a foundation for you to write data-driven web APIs using the `orm` and `json` libraries. The knowledge of ORM that you've gained in this chapter will help you access and interact with a database. Also, the knowledge of working with JSON data formats in V will help you exchange data between various kinds of web-based APIs or services.

In the next chapter, we will learn how to build a microservice using the `vweb`, `orm`, `json`, and `sqlite` libraries.

14
Building a Microservice

In this chapter, we will learn how to build a simple microservice in V using a RESTful approach. To achieve this, we will be using the built-in vweb and orm libraries. Additionally, we will leverage the power of **SQLite** by installing it as a third-party library. With the help of the SQLite library, we will establish a database connection and interact with the database using that connection. We will also use the JSON data format as a form of communication.

In this chapter, we will cover the following topics:

- Introducing vweb
- Creating a project and organizing files
- Setting up the vweb web server
- Setting up the utility functions and constants for the microservice
- Implementing RESTful endpoints
- Implementing an endpoint to create a note using HTTP verb POST
- Implementing an endpoint to retrieve a note by id using HTTP verb GET
- Implementing an endpoint to retrieve all notes using HTTP verb GET

- Implementing an endpoint to update a note using HTTP verb `PUT`

- Implementing an endpoint to delete a note using HTTP verb `DELETE`

- Querying REST endpoints using Postman

By the end of this chapter, you will have a good understanding of how to implement RESTful microservices using V's built-in `vweb` library. Additionally, you will understand how to run microservices and perform queries on the endpoints of a microservice using Postman.

Technical requirements

- Install SQLite, as demonstrated in the *Installing SQLite as a third-party library in V's installation directory* section of *Chapter 13, Introduction to JSON and ORM*.

- Download and install **Postman** to interact with the microservice's RESTful endpoints.

The full source code for this chapter is available at `https://github.com/PacktPublishing/Getting-Started-with-V-Programming/tree/main/Chapter14`.

Introducing vweb

In the previous chapter, we learned about the `orm` and `json` libraries. Now, we will use the `vweb` library to build a microservice that performs **Create**, **Read**, **Update**, and **Delete** (**CRUD**) operations on a simple database table. The `vweb` library is a built-in library that ships along with V. It is a simple yet powerful web server with built-in routing, parameter handling, and comes with a templating engine. At the time of writing, `vweb` is an alpha-level software. Therefore, some of the features might not be complete. However, with `vweb` in its current state, nothing is stopping us from building a microservice using the RESTful approach.

The `vweb` library has the following features:

- It has a very fast performance, which is similar to that of C, on the web.

- It is easier to deploy an application built with `vweb` since it is just one binary file including all templates. There is no need to install dependencies.

- The templates are precompiled, so all errors are visible at compile time rather than at runtime.

We will build the notes microservice by performing the following simple steps:

1. Create a new project named `notes_api` and organize the files to make the code readable.

2. Set up the configuration of the web server using `vweb`.

3. Set up common constants and custom responses in the util file.

4. Implement RESTful endpoints for the `notes_api` microservice.

For our notes microservice to be up and running, we will be making use of `vweb` as a web server that exposes these endpoints running as a web application. So, let's build a microservice by creating a new project.

Creating a project and organizing files

We can implement a microservice by placing the entire code inside a single file. However, that does not offer readability. So, instead, we will break down the code into logically related blocks and place them within relevant files. This will give us the advantage of quickly identifying the place of logic while troubleshooting any issues in the code. Well-organized code also enhances code readability.

To begin implementing the `notes_api` microservice, we will create a project. Then, we will add a few files to make the code organized and readable.

Run the following command to create a new project named `notes_api`:

```
v new notes_api
```

Once you have run the `v new notes_api` command, you will be prompted to provide a description, the version number, and license information, which are optional. Then, you can hit *Enter*.

Rename the `notes_api.v` file to `main.v`. Add two new files within the project, namely, `util.v` and `note.v`. Our new `notes_api` project will now have the following folder structure:

```
c:/notes_api
    .gitignore
    main.v
    note.v
    util.v
    v.mod
```

In each of these files, we will organize our code for the microservice as follows:

- `main.v`: This is the logic to set up the web server using `vweb`.
- `util.v`: This is the utility file that holds project-specific constants, structs, and struct methods.
- `note.v`: This file will have REST endpoints which perform CRUD operations on the `Note` table.

Now, we will go ahead and write the logic to set up the `vweb` server.

Setting up the vweb web server

We will set up the web server in the `main.v` file by performing the following steps:

1. To begin, import the `vweb` and `sqlite` modules, as shown in the following code:

```
// file: main.v
module main


import vweb
import sqlite
```

2. Next, we will create a struct, named `App`, which appears as follows:

```
// file: main.v
struct App {
    vweb.Context
mut:
    db sqlite.DB
}
```

The preceding code shows the `App` struct, which holds `vweb.Context` along with fields such as the `port` field on which our app will be running and a mutable `db` field of the `sqlite.DB` type.

3. Next, we will modify the `main` function, which will appear as follows:

```
// file: main.v
fn main() {
    db := sqlite.connect('notes.db') or { panic(err) }
    db.exec('drop table if exists Notes')
```

```
    sql db {
        create table Note
    }
    http_port := 8000
    app := &App{
        db: db
    }
    vweb.run(app, http_port)
}
```

From the preceding code, we can observe that the `main` function does the following:

- It establishes a connection to the SQLite database.

- It drops the `Notes` table if it already exists in the database. This is an optional step if you want to work on a clean instance of the `Notes` table.

- It creates a table based on the attributes set on the `Note` struct, which we will be creating in the later sections of this chapter.

- It sets the HTTP port to `8000`. If this port is not available, you can choose to run the microservice on a freely available port.

- It populates the struct fields of the `App` struct with the `db` connection.

- Finally, it invokes the `run` method of the `vweb` web server, which takes two input arguments: `app` and `http_port`.

Setting up utility functions and constants for the microservice

In this section, we will add all of the common functions and constants, if any, to the `util.v` file. Let's say that we want our microservice to provide a custom JSON response that includes a status code and a descriptive message, whenever a request originates, to do the following:

- Retrieve record(s) that don't exist.

- Create or update a record with malformed JSON payloads in the request body.

- Create or update a `note` with a message that is not unique.

- Update a record that doesn't exist.

To achieve this, in the `util.v` file, we will add a struct, named `CustomResponse`, that has a `status` field to represent a status code and a `message` field that provides descriptive details about the state of action being performed by the microservice endpoint, as follows:

```
// file: util.v
module main


import json


struct CustomResponse {
    status   int
    message string
}


fn (c CustomResponse) to_json() string {
    return json.encode(c)
}
```

From the preceding code, in addition to the struct, we can observe a method for the `CustomResponse` struct, namely, `to_json`. This function returns a string after encoding an instance of the `CustomResponse` object into JSON format. Additionally, pay attention to the `json.encode` method, which was only possible since we imported the `json` library.

Now we will add a few constants to the `util.v` file, as follows:

```
// file: util.v
const (
    invalid_json    = 'Invalid JSON Payload'
    note_not_found = 'Note not found'
    unique_message = 'Please provide a unique message for
                     Note'
)
```

Since we will be showing a common message when a request tries to create a `note` or update an existing one, we will use the `unique_message` constant. Similarly, we have added the most commonly used responses in the list of constants, as demonstrated in the preceding code. Alternatively, you can keep constants in a separate file named `constants.v` in the main module if the list of constants grows in size.

Next, we will discuss how to write endpoints that perform CRUD operations through RESTful APIs.

Implementing RESTful endpoints

So far, we have set up the web server using `vweb` in the `main.v` file. Also, we wrote some commonly used code in `util.v`. Now, we will create RESTful endpoints. The endpoints of the microservice we are going to implement will extend the `App` struct such that each endpoint will be a method of the `App` struct. Additionally, each endpoint we are going to implement returns the response of the `vweb.Result` type.

In the following section, we will make a list of all the endpoints we are going to implement inside a file named `notes.v`.

The list of RESTful endpoints in our microservice

The microservice we are going to implement will have RESTful endpoints that perform CRUD operations on a database table. The following table shows the endpoints with their corresponding HTTP verb and URL and a description of what the endpoint does along with the request payload, if applicable:

HTTP verb	Resource	Description
POST	/notes	This creates a `Note`.
GET	/notes/:id	This gets a single `Note` by id.
GET	/notes	This gets a list of `Notes`.
PUT	/notes/:id	This updates a `Note` by id.
DELETE	/notes/:id	This deletes a `Note` by id.

Table 14.1 – A list of RESTful endpoints in our microservice

Next, we will define a struct that will represent a table in the database.

Defining the Note struct

We will begin by importing the required `vweb` and `json` libraries. Also, we will define a struct named `Note` in V code, which serves as an object that maps to the `Notes` database table in the relational database world, as follows:

```
// file: note.v
module main
```

```
import json
import vweb


[table: 'Notes']
struct Note {
    id      int     [primary; sql: serial]
    message string [sql: 'detail'; unique]
    status  bool    [nonull]
}


fn (n Note) to_json() string {
    return json.encode(n)
}
```

From the preceding code, in addition to the imports and struct, note that there is a to_json method for the Note struct, which returns a string after encoding an instance of the Note object into JSON format. Also, observe that the struct fields are decorated with orm attributes, as discussed in the previous chapter.

With the **object-relational mapper (ORM)** in place, now we can move on to write the first endpoint to create a Note struct.

Implementing an endpoint to create a note using HTTP verb POST

To create a record of Note in the database, we will implement the endpoint that meets specific requirements. Let's make a list of the requirements for our create endpoint to gain an understanding of what the request and response should look like.

The request is expected to meet the following criteria:

- The HTTP method will be POST.
- The HTTP route will be /notes/.
- The request body will have a payload representing Note in JSON format.

The response is expected to meet the following criteria:

- When a malformed JSON is present in the request payload, or when a message is not unique, we expect the following to occur:

  - The response body will have a `CustomResponse` struct encoded into JSON format whose `message` and `status` field are set accordingly.

  - The status code will show `400, Bad Request`.

- If the proper JSON payload of `Note` is present in the request body, respond with the following:

  - Insert the `Note` record into the database using the built-in `orm`-based syntax.

  - The response body should have a newly created JSON-encoded `Note`.

  - The status code should show `201, Created`.

  - The `Content-Location` response header should be set to indicate an alternate location (such as `/notes/:id`) to find the JSON data present in the response body.

  - The `Content-Type` response header should be set to `application/json`.

With this information, we will go on to define the route to create the `Note` operation.

Defining the route to create a note

Now, we will now create a struct method for `App` using the name `create`. The `create` method will have a return type of `vweb.Result`. Additionally, we will decorate the method with the attributes indicating the route and HTTP verb separated by `;`.

The route we are using, from which the `create` endpoint is accessible, is `/notes`, and the HTTP verb is `post`, as follows:

```
['/notes'; post]
fn (mut app App) create() vweb.Result {

}
```

Now we will keep adding the code, step by step, to the `create` method using an incremental approach.

Processing requests and handling custom responses for the create endpoint

When a malformed JSON is present in the request payload, or when a message is not unique, we expect the following to occur:

- The response body will have a `CustomResponse` struct encoded into JSON with a reasonable message.

- The status code will show `400, Bad Request`.

The following code implements the preceding points and should be added to `create()`:

```
n := json.decode(Note, app.req.data) or {
    app.set_status(400, 'Bad Request')
    er := CustomResponse{400, invalid_json}
    return app.json(er.to_json())
}
// before we save, we must ensure the note's message
// is unique
notes_found := sql app.db {
    select from Note where message == n.message
}
if notes_found.len > 0 {
    app.set_status(400, 'Bad Request')
    er := CustomResponse{400, unique_message}
    return app.json(er.to_json())
}
```

Inserting a record using the ORM query

If the proper JSON payload of `Note` is present in the request body, we insert `Note` into the database using the built-in `orm`-based syntax. Additionally, we retrieve the `id` field of the `Note` object that has just been created, as follows:

```
// save to db
sql app.db {
    insert n into Note
}
```

```
// retrieve the last id from the db to build full
// Note object
new_id := app.db.last_id() as int
```

Building a response body for the create endpoint

Now, we will build the response body for the `create` endpoint based on the following criteria:

- The response body will have a newly created JSON-encoded `Note`.

- The status code will show `201, Created`.

- The `Content-Location` response header is set to indicate an alternate location (such as `/notes/:id`) to find the JSON data present in the response body.

- The `Content-Type` response header is set to `application/json`.

The code that corresponds to the specifications mentioned in the preceding list appears as follows:

```
// build new note object including the new_id and send
// it as JSON response
note_created := Note{new_id, n.message, n.status}
app.set_status(201, 'created')
app.add_header('Content-Location', '/notes/$new_id')
return app.json(note_created.to_json())
```

Here, the `Content-Type` response header will be set to `application/json`, as we are returning the JSON response using `app.json` with an encoded `Note` that has just been created in the database.

Constructing the bits and pieces we have just learned so far, the create `Note` endpoint will appear as follows:

```
['/notes'; post]
fn (mut app App) create() vweb.Result {
    n := json.decode(Note, app.req.data) or {
        app.set_status(400, 'Bad Request')
        er := CustomResponse{400, invalid_json}
        return app.json(er.to_json())
    }
```

```
// before we save, we must ensure the note's message
// is unique
notes_found := sql app.db {
    select from Note where message == n.message
}
if notes_found.len > 0 {
    app.set_status(400, 'Bad Request')
    er := CustomResponse{400, unique_message}
    return app.json(er.to_json())
}

// save to db
sql app.db {
    insert n into Note
}

// retrieve the last id from the db to build full
// Note object
new_id := app.db.last_id() as int

// build new note object including the new_id and send
// it as JSON response
note_created := Note{new_id, n.message, n.status}
app.set_status(201, 'created')
app.add_header('Content-Location', '/notes/$new_id')
return app.json(note_created.to_json())
}
```

Next, we will learn how to write an endpoint that retrieves a Note when provided with the id argument.

Implementing an endpoint to retrieve a note by id using HTTP verb GET

To retrieve a record of `Note`, we will implement an endpoint that meets specific requirements. Let's make a list of these requirements to understand what the request and response should look like for our endpoint that returns a `Note` when an `id` argument is provided.

The request is expected to meet the following criteria:

- The HTTP method will be `GET`.
- The HTTP route will be `/notes/:id`.
- The resource URL will have the `id` argument of the `Note` we are trying to retrieve.

The response is expected to meet the following criteria:

- Select `Note` from the database using the built-in `orm`-based syntax whose `id` is the same as the `id` argument present in the resource URL.
- When the `id` argument that is present in the resource URL does not match any of the records in the database, the following will occur:

  - The response body will have a `CustomResponse` struct encoded into JSON with a reasonable message.
  - The status code will show `404, Not Found`.

- When we have a record that matches the `id` argument that is present in the resource URL, the following will occur:

  - The found `Note` will be encoded into JSON format.
  - The status code will show `200, Ok`.
  - The response body will have a JSON-encoded `Note`.
  - The `Content-Type` response header will be set to `application/json`.

With this information, we will go on to define a route to retrieve a `Note` given its `id`.

Defining a route to retrieve a note by id

Now, we will create a struct method for App using the name read. The read method will have a return type of vweb.Result. Additionally, we will decorate the method with the attributes indicating the route and the HTTP verb separated by ;.

The route we are using, from which the read endpoint is accessible, is /notes/:id, and the HTTP verb is get, as shown here:

```
['/notes/:id'; get]
fn (mut app App) read(id int) vweb.Result {
}
```

From the preceding code, we can observe that the read method accepts an id input argument that matches the id argument provided in the resource URL.

Now, we will keep adding the code, step by step, to the read method using an incremental approach.

Selecting a record given its id using the ORM query

Select Note from the database using the built-in orm-based syntax whose id is the same as the id argument that is present in the resource URL:

```
n := sql app.db {
    select from Note where id == id
}
```

Handling a custom response for the read a note endpoint

When the id argument that is present in the resource URL does not match any of the records in the database, then it should have the following:

- The response body should have a CustomResponse struct encoded into JSON with a reasonable message.

- The status code will show 404, Not Found.

The following code implements the preceding points:

```
// check if note exists
if n.id != id {
```

```
        app.set_status(404, 'Not Found')
        er := CustomResponse{400, note_not_found}
        return app.json(er.to_json())
    }
```

Next, we will build the response body for the `read` endpoint.

Building a response body for the read endpoint

When we have a record that matches the `id` argument that is present in the resource URL, we will ensure that the endpoint has the following:

- The found `Note` will be encoded in JSON format.
- The status code will show `200, Ok`.
- The response body will have a JSON-encoded `Note`.
- The `Content-Type` response header will be set to `application/json`.

The following code reflects the specifications mentioned in the preceding list:

```
    // found note, return it
    ret := json.encode(n)
    app.set_status(200, 'OK')
    return app.json(ret)
```

Here, the `Content-Type` response header will be set to `application/json`. This is because we are returning a JSON response using `app.json` with an encoded `Note` that has just been created inside the database.

Constructing the bits and pieces we have just learned so far, the `read` note endpoint will appear as follows:

```
['/notes/:id'; get]
fn (mut app App) read(id int) vweb.Result {
    n := sql app.db {
        select from Note where id == id
    }

    // check if note exists
    if n.id != id {
        app.set_status(404, 'Not Found')
```

```
        er := CustomResponse{400, note_not_found}
        return app.json(er.to_json())
    }


    // found note, return it
    ret := json.encode(n)
    app.set_status(200, 'OK')
    return app.json(ret)
}
```

Next, we will learn how to write an endpoint that retrieves all notes.

Implementing an endpoint to retrieve all notes using HTTP verb GET

To retrieve all notes, we will implement an endpoint that meets specific requirements. Let's make a list of these requirements to gain an understanding of what the request and response should look like.

The request is expected to meet the following criteria:

- The HTTP method will be GET.
- The HTTP route will be /notes/.

The response is expected to meet the following criteria:

- Select all of the notes from the database using the built-in orm-based syntax.
- Encode the notes retrieved from the database into JSON format, which results in a JSON array.
- The status code will show 200, Ok.
- The response body will have a JSON array of encoded Note collection.
- The Content-Type response header will be set to application/json.

With this information, we will go on to define a route to retrieve all notes.

Defining a route to retrieve all notes

Now, we will create a struct method for App using the name `read_all`. The `read_all` method will have a return type of `vweb.Result`.

Additionally, we will decorate the method with the attributes indicating the route and HTTP verb separated by `;`.

The route we are using, from which the `read_all` endpoint is accessible, is `/notes`, and the HTTP verb is `get`, as shown here:

```
['/notes'; get]
fn (mut app App) read_all() vweb.Result {
}
```

Now, we will keep adding the code, step by step, to the `read_all` method using an incremental approach.

Selecting all the records from a table using the ORM query

Select all the notes from the database using the built-in `orm`-based syntax, as follows:

```
    n := sql app.db {
        select from Note
    }
```

Now, we will build the response body for the read all notes endpoint.

Building a response body for the read all notes endpoint

When we have a list of all notes read from the database, we will implement the following steps:

- Encode the notes retrieved from the database into JSON format, which results in a JSON array.

- The status code should show `200, Ok`.

- The response body should have a JSON array of an encoded `Note` collection.

- The `Content-Type` response header should be set to `application/json`.

The code for the preceding steps will appear as follows:

```
    ret := json.encode(n)
    app.set_status(200, 'OK')
    return app.json(ret)
```

Here, the Content-Type response header will be set to application/json. This is because we are returning a JSON response using app.json with an encoded array of Note objects.

Constructing the bits and pieces we have just learned so far, the read all notes endpoint will appear as follows:

```
['/notes'; get]
fn (mut app App) read_all() vweb.Result {
    n := sql app.db {
        select from Note
    }


    ret := json.encode(n)
    app.set_status(200, 'OK')
    return app.json(ret)
}
```

Next, we will learn how to write an endpoint that updates a Note when provided with id.

Implementing an endpoint to update a note using HTTP verb PUT

To update Note, we will implement the endpoint that meets specific requirements. Let's make a list of these requirements for our update endpoint to gain an understanding of what the request and response should look like.

The request is expected to meet the following criteria:

- The HTTP method will be PUT.
- The HTTP route will be /notes/:id.
- The request body will have a payload representing a Note in JSON format.

The response is expected to meet the following criteria:

- When a malformed JSON is present in the request payload, the following will occur:

  - The response body will have a `CustomResponse` struct encoded into JSON with a reasonable message.

  - The status code will show `400, Bad Request`.

- If the proper JSON payload of the `Note` is present in the request body, do the following:

  - Check whether the `Note` to be updated exists in the database using the built-in `orm`-based syntax.

- When a `Note` is not found, the following should occur:

  - The response body should have `CustomResponse` encoded into JSON with a reasonable message.

  - The status code should show `404, Not Found`.

- When `Note` is found, do the following:

  - Check that the `message` field of the `Note` being updated is unique using the built-in `orm`-based syntax.

  - When the `message` field provided to update the `Note` is not unique, the following should occur:

    - The response body will have a `CustomResponse` struct encoded into JSON with a reasonable message.

    - The status code will show `400, Bad Request`.

  - When the `message` field is unique and the `id` of the `Note` to be updated is found, the following should occur:

    - The `Note` is updated based on the JSON payload present in the request body where the `Note id` matches the `id` present in the resource URL.

    - The response body will have an updated JSON-encoded `Note`.

    - The status code will show `200, Ok`.

    - The `Content-Type` response header will be set to `application/json`.

With this information, we can go ahead and define a route for the update
`Note` operation.

Defining a route to update a note by id

Now, we will create a struct method for `App` using the name `update`. The `update`
method will have a return type of `vweb.Result`.

Additionally, we will decorate the method with the attributes indicating the route
and HTTP verb separated by `;`.

The route we are using, from which the `update` endpoint is accessible, is `/notes/:id`,
and the HTTP verb is `put`, as shown here:

```
['/notes/:id'; put]
fn (mut app App) update(id int) vweb.Result {

}
```

From the preceding code, the `update` method accepts an `id` input argument that
matches the `id` argument provided in the resource URL.

Now we will keep adding the code, step by step, to the `update` method using an
incremental approach.

Processing requests and handling custom responses for the update endpoint

When a malformed JSON is present in the request payload, we will build a response such
that the following will occur:

- The response body has `CustomResponse` encoded into JSON with
  a reasonable message.

- The status code will show `400, Bad Request`.

The following code reflects the preceding specifications to process the request in the case
of malformed JSON:

```
    // malformed json
n := json.decode(Note, app.req.data) or {
    app.set_status(400, 'Bad Request')
    er := CustomResponse{400, invalid_json}
    return app.json(er.to_json())
}
```

Next, we will implement logic when we have a properly formatted JSON.

Verifying a record exits given its id using the ORM query

Check whether the Note to be updated exists in the database using the built-in orm-based syntax. When a Note is not found, build the response such that the following will occur:

- The response body has CustomResponse encoded into JSON with a reasonable message.

- The status code will show 404, Not Found.

Based on the preceding conditions, the response code for a record that doesn't exist based on the provided id will appear as follows:

```
    // check if note to be updated exists
    note_to_update := sql app.db {
        select from Note where id == id
    }


    if note_to_update.id != id {
        app.set_status(404, 'Not Found')
        er := CustomResponse{404, note_not_found}
        return app.json(er.to_json())
    }
```

Next, we will implement the logic to verify the uniqueness of the message field of Note.

Verifying the uniqueness of the message field of note

When we have found Note based on the provided id, we need to check whether the message field of the Note being updated is unique using the built-in orm-based syntax, as follows:

```
    // before update, we must ensure the note's message is
// unique
    // id != id for idempotency
    // message == n.message for unique check
    res := sql app.db {
```

```
        select from Note where message == n.message && id != id
    }
```

When the message provided to update `Note` is not unique, build the response such that the following will occur:

- The response body has `CustomResponse` encoded into JSON with a reasonable message.

- The status code will show `400, Bad Request`.

When the message of `Note` is not unique, the response code for the preceding points will appear as follows:

```
if res.len > 0 {
    app.set_status(400, 'Bad Request')
    er := CustomResponse{400, unique_message}
    return app.json(er.to_json())
}
```

Next, we will go on to update the record when the message is proved to be unique.

Updating the record using the ORM query

When the `Note` to be updated is found and the message is unique, you can update the `Note` based on the JSON payload present in the request body where the `Note id` matches the `id` present in the resource URL, as follows:

```
// update the note
sql app.db {
    update Note set message = n.message, status =
        n.status where id == id
}
```

Now, let's proceed to build the response for the `update` endpoint.

Building a response for the update endpoint

Now we will build the updated Note sending the id and request body as the response, ensuring the following:

- The response body will have an updated JSON-encoded Note.

- The status code will show 200, Ok.

- The Content-Type response header will be set to application/json.

The corresponding code will appear as follows:

```
updated_note := Note{id, n.message, n.status}
ret := json.encode(updated_note)
app.set_status(200, 'OK')
return app.json(ret)
```

Constructing the bits and pieces we have just learned so far, the update Note endpoint will appear as follows:

```
['/notes/:id'; put]
fn (mut app App) update(id int) vweb.Result {
    // malformed json
    n := json.decode(Note, app.req.data) or {
        app.set_status(400, 'Bad Request')
        er := CustomResponse{400, invalid_json}
        return app.json(er.to_json())
    }


    // check if note to be updated exists

    note_to_update := sql app.db {
        select from Note where id == id
    }

    if note_to_update.id != id {
        app.set_status(404, 'Not Found')
        er := CustomResponse{404, note_not_found}
        return app.json(er.to_json())
```

```
    }

    // before update, we must ensure the note's message is
    // unique
    // id != id for idempotency
    // message == n.message for unique check
    res := sql app.db {
        select from Note where message == n.message &&
          id != id
    }

    if res.len > 0 {
        app.set_status(400, 'Bad Request')
        er := CustomResponse{400, unique_message}
        return app.json(er.to_json())
    }

    // update the note
    sql app.db {
        update Note set message = n.message, status =
          n.status where id == id
    }

    // build the updated note using the :id and request
    // body
    // instead of making one more db call
    updated_note := Note{id, n.message, n.status}

    ret := json.encode(updated_note)
    app.set_status(200, 'OK')
    return app.json(ret)
}
```

Now, we will learn how to write an endpoint that deletes a Note when provided with id.

Implementing an endpoint to delete a note using the HTTP verb DELETE

To delete Note, we will implement the endpoint that meets specific requirements. Let's make a list of these requirements to gain an understanding of what the request and response should look like.

The request is expected to meet the following criteria:

- The HTTP method will be DELETE.
- The HTTP route will be /notes/:id.
- The resource URL will have the id of the Note that we are trying to delete.

The response is expected to meet the following criteria:

- Delete the Note from the database using the built-in orm-based syntax whose id is the same as the id argument that is present in the resource URL.
- After processing the delete request, the following will occur:

  - The status code will show 204, No Content.
  - The response body will be empty.
  - The Content-Type response header will be set to application/json.

With this information, we will go ahead and define the route to delete Note.

Defining the route to delete a note by id

Now, we will create a struct method for App using the name delete. The delete method will have a return type of vweb.Result. Additionally, we will decorate the method with the attributes indicating the route and HTTP verb separated by ;.

The route we are using, from which the delete endpoint is accessible, is /notes/:id, and the HTTP verb is delete, as shown here:

```
['/notes/:id'; delete]
fn (mut app App) delete(id int) vweb.Result {

}
```

From the preceding code, the delete method accepts an id input argument that matches the id argument provided in the resource URL.

Now, we will keep adding the code, step by step, to the `delete` method using an incremental approach.

Deleting a record given its id using the ORM query

The following code deletes `Note` from the database using the built-in `orm`-based syntax whose `id` is the same as the `id` argument that is present in the resource URL:

```
sql app.db {
    delete from Note where id == id
}
```

The delete operation is idempotent, which means that deleting a record based on its id will always give some result, and it will be the same as deleting a record that doesn't exist or a record that has already been deleted. In all of these cases, the resulting state will be the same when you perform the delete operation.

Next, we will discuss how to build the response for the delete endpoint.

Building a response for the delete endpoint

After processing the delete request, we will build a response such that it meets the following criteria:

- The status code will show `204, No Content`.
- The response body will be empty.
- The `Content-Type` response header will be set to `text/plain`.

The code that matches the preceding criteria is as follows:

```
app.set_status(204, 'No Content')
return app.ok('')
```

Here, the `Content-Type` response header will be set to `text/plain`. This is because we are returning the plain text form of an empty response using `app.ok`.

Constructing the bits and pieces we have just learned so far, the `delete` endpoint will appear as follows:

```
['/notes/:id'; delete]
fn (mut app App) delete(id int) vweb.Result {
    sql app.db {
```

```
        delete from Note where id == id
    }
    app.set_status(204, 'No Content')
    return app.ok('')
}
```

Next, we will learn how to run the microservice that we have built so far.

Running the microservice

As we have implemented all the endpoints that perform CRUD operations on a table in the database, now we will start interacting with this microservice.

To interact with the microservice, such as performing CRUD operations, from Command Prompt, set the working directory to the root of the `notes_api` project and run the following command:

```
v run .
```

Running the preceding command will result in two new files being created in our project, namely, `notes_api.exe` if you are on Windows OS. Alternatively, if you are on a *nix OS, such as Ubuntu, you will observe a file named `notes_api` without a file extension. Additionally, `notes.db`, which is an SQLite database, is created if it doesn't already exist.

The output of the command will appear as follows:

```
[Vweb] Running app on http://localhost:8000
```

From the preceding output, we can observe that the URL from where the microservice can be accessed is `http://localhost:8000`. As we have configured the vweb web server to run on port `8000`, the same port reflects in the URL. The localhost indicates that the microservice we learned to develop in V using vweb is running locally on the host PC.

In the next section, we will learn how to query the microservice.

Querying REST endpoints using Postman

In this section, we will take a look at how to use **Postman**. This is free software that is used to interact with web-based APIs. You can download it from the *Download Postman* section at `https://www.postman.com/downloads/` on the official **Postman** website.

Once you have downloaded the free version of **Postman** for your OS, launch the **Postman** software to send requests to the microservice we have implemented using vweb.

Next, we will learn how to perform CRUD operations on the endpoints of the microservice that we created in this chapter using Postman.

Using Postman to create a note with the POST HTTP verb

In this section, we will perform the POST operation on the create note endpoint. In the earlier sections of this chapter, we defined the behavior of the create Note endpoint, which will respond differently based on different payloads. We will evaluate them in more detail in the following sections.

The 201 Ok status after successfully creating a note

Now, we will evaluate the behavior of a create endpoint such that the API responds with 201 Created:

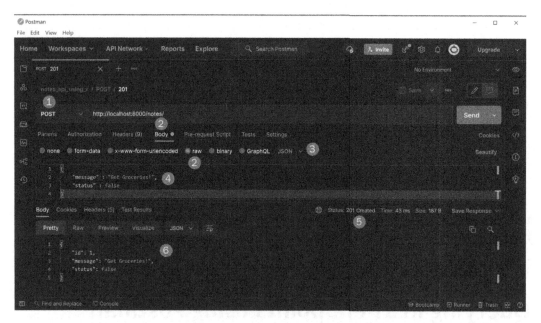

Figure 14.1 – Creating a note using HTTP verb POST using Postman

The following is a list of the operations that we will be performing to create a `Note`:

1. In the Postman application, select the HTTP verb from the drop-down list of **POST** and enter the `http://localhost:8000/notes/` URL into the textbox next to it.

2. Now select the **Body** tab and check the **raw** radio button.

3. Then, select **JSON** from the drop-down list to set the content type of the request.

4. In the textbox, enter the following JSON payload and click on the **Send** button:

```
{
    "message" : "Get Groceries!",
    "status" : false
}
```

You should see the response body, as shown in the preceding screenshot. `Note` that the response body has `Note` in JSON format, along with the `id` created in the database:

```
{
    "id": 1,
    "message": "Get Groceries!",
    "status": false
}
```

5. Now, select the **Headers (5)** tab, as indicated in the preceding screenshot. You will be able to view the response headers that appear:

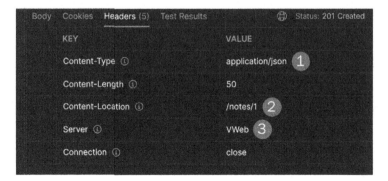

Figure 14.2 – The response headers for creating a Note using HTTP Post verb

Now, we will attempt to gain an understanding of the response headers for the successful create Note operation:

- From the preceding screenshot, we can observe that Content-Type is application/json. This is because we are returning the response in JSON format.

- The other significant Content-Location response header is set to /notes/1. This indicates the alternate way in which to access the JSON data present in the response body.

- By default, the Server response header is set to VWeb, and we are interacting with the microservice that is built and running on the web server implemented using vweb.

- The other Content-Length response header indicates the length of the JSON response, and Connection set to close indicates that either the client or the server would like to close the connection.

To get hands-on with Postman, I recommend that you try posting another Note with the following JSON payload:

```
{
    "message" : "Check the status of the college
                    application",
    "status" : false
}
```

Performing the preceding steps to create a Note with the preceding JSON payload will result in the following output:

```
{
    "id": 2,
    "message": "Check the status of the college application",
    "status": false
}
```

The 400 Bad Request status when a message is not unique

Now, we will try to create another Note whose message is the same as the Note we just created with id 1. So, we will set the HTTP verb as **POST** with the JSON payload the same as the message field of the Note that already exists in the database, as shown in the following screenshot:

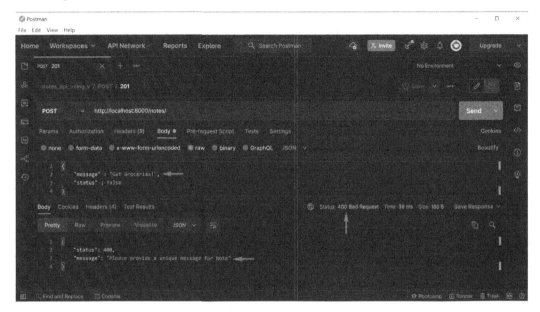

Figure 14.3 – Creating a note using HTTP verb POST using Postman when the message is not unique

We can observe that after sending the message that is not unique, we view the following response body with the status set to 400 Bad Request:

```
{
    "status": 400,
    "message": "Please provide a unique message for Note"
}
```

We will proceed further to view how to retrieve a Note given its id.

The 400 Bad Request status when the request body has malformed JSON

Using Postman, we will send a POST HTTP verb to create a Note with an invalid JSON format in the payload, as shown in the following screenshot:

Figure 14.4 – Creating a note using HTTP verb POST using Postman in the case
of an improper JSON format in the request payload

Notice that the request body has a JSON payload that has an extra comma at the end of the status field. Now, if we click on the **Send** button, we will view the following response along with the status field that indicates 400 Bad Request:

```
{
    "status": 400,
    "message": "Invalid JSON Payload"
}
```

Additionally, let's take a look at the response headers in the case of 400 Bad Request.

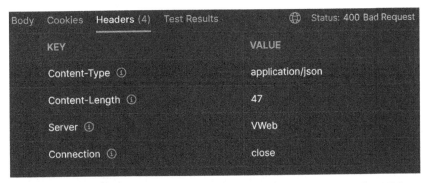

Figure 14.5 – The response headers to create a note using HTTP verb POST

From the preceding screenshot, it is evident that we will not have Content-Location. This is because the POST operation fails to create a Note in the database due to a malformed JSON payload.

Using Postman to retrieve a note by id with the GET HTTP verb

In this section, we will perform the GET operation on the read Note endpoint using an id. In the earlier sections of this chapter, we defined the behavior of the read Note API, which will respond differently based on different conditions. We will evaluate them in more detail in the following sections.

The 404 Not Found status when a note with the given id does not exist

Using **Postman**, we will query using the GET HTTP verb to retrieve a Note whose id doesn't currently exist in the database, as shown in the following screenshot:

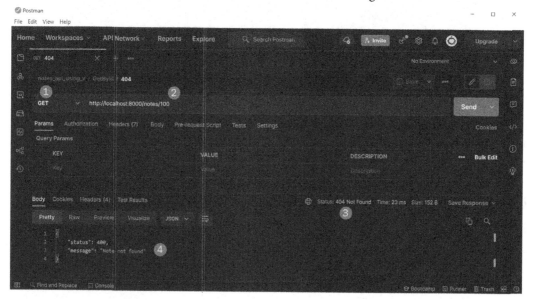

Figure 14.6 – Retrieving a note using HTTP verb GET whose id doesn't exist using Postman

To retrieve Note given its id, we need to perform the following steps, as shown in the preceding screenshot:

1. Set the HTTP verb to **GET**.

2. Set the URL to http://localhost:8000/notes/id/. Replace the id with the id of the Note you are looking for. For this section, as we are trying to view the 404 Not Found status, replace id with 100 or any number that doesn't already exist in the database. To view the response, click on the **Send** button.

3. Notice that the response has a status set to 404 Not Found, as it's obvious that the Note with the id set to 100 doesn't exist yet.

4. Additionally, Note that the response body will have a detailed message along with status, as follows:

```
{
    "status": 404,
    "message": "Note not found"
}
```

The 200 Ok status when a note is retrieved successfully by providing its id

Using **Postman**, we will query the endpoint that gets a Note given its id using the GET HTTP verb, as shown in the following screenshot:

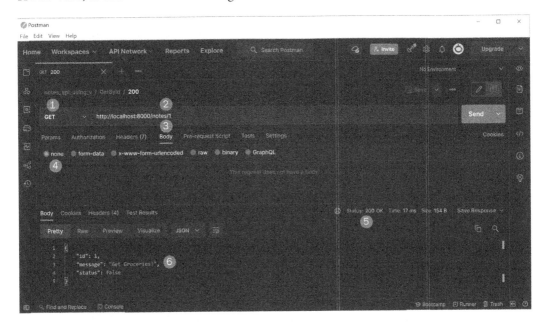

Figure 14.7 – Retrieve a note using HTTP verb GET by id using Postman

To retrieve a Note given an id, perform the following steps in the **Postman** application:

1. Set the HTTP verb to **GET**.

2. Set the URL to http://localhost:8000/notes/1.

3. Navigate to the **Body** tab.

4. Check the **none** radio button and click on the **Send** button.

    Notice that the response status is set to 200 OK.

    Additionally, note that the response body will have the Note that matches the id you set in *Step 2*.

5.   Now click on the **Headers** tab, and you will view the following response headers:

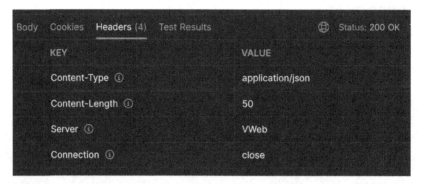

Figure 14.8 – The response headers to retrieve a note given its id using HTTP verb GET

As the response body is of JSON format, we can see that `Content-Type` is set to `application/json`.

Now, we will learn how to send a request to retrieve all the notes using **Postman**.

Using Postman to retrieve a collection of notes with the GET HTTP verb

In this section, we will perform the `GET` operation to read all notes. In the earlier sections of this chapter, we defined the behavior of the API that reads all notes and shows them in the response body. In the following section, we will learn how to query this endpoint using Postman.

The 200 Ok status when retrieving all notes

Using Postman, we will query the endpoint that gets all notes using the `GET` HTTP verb, as shown in the following screenshot:

Figure 14.9 – Retrieving all notes using HTTP verb GET using Postman

To retrieve all notes, perform the following steps in the **Postman** application:

1. Set the HTTP verb to **GET**.

2. Set the URL to `http://localhost:8000/notes/`.

3. Navigate to the **Body** tab.

4. Check the **none** radio button and click on the **Send** button.

5. Notice that the response status is set to `200 OK`.

   We can observe that the response body will have all the notes that we have created so far. Additionally, we can see that the response is wrapped inside [and] with each `Note` in its JSON format separated by `,`. This indicates that the response is in a JSON array format.

6. Now click on the **Headers** tab, and you will observe the following response headers:

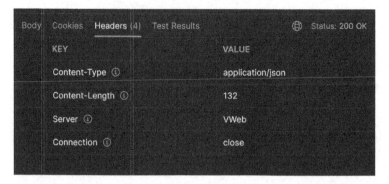

Figure 14.10 – The response headers after retrieving all of the notes using HTTP verb GET

As the response body is of JSON format, we can see that `Content-Type` is set to `application/json`. Now, we will learn how to send a request to update a `Note` using Postman.

Using Postman to update a note with the PUT HTTP verb

In this section, we will perform the `PUT` operation on the update `Note` endpoint. In the earlier sections of this chapter, we defined the behavior of the update `Note` endpoint, which will respond differently based on different payloads. We will evaluate those, in more detail, in the following sections.

The 404 status while updating a note given its id does not exist

Using **Postman**, let's try to send an update request to a `Note` whose id doesn't currently exist in the database using the `PUT` HTTP verb, as shown in the following screenshot:

Figure 14.11 – Updating retrieve a note using HTTP verb PUT whose id doesn't exist using Postman

To update a `Note` given its `id`, we need to perform the following steps in the Postman application, as shown in the preceding screenshot:

1. Set the HTTP verb to **PUT**.

2. Set the URL to `http://localhost:8000/notes/id/`. Replace `id` with the ID of the `Note` you want to update. For this section, as we are trying to view the `404 Not Found` status, replace `id` with `100` or any number that doesn't exist in the database.

3. Now select the **Body** tab, and check the **raw** radio button.

4. Select **JSON** from the drop-down list to set the content type of the request.

5. In the textbox, enter the following JSON payload and click on the **Send** button:

```
{
    "message" : "Get Biscuits!",
    "status" : true
}
```

6. Notice that the response has its status set to `404 Not Found`, as it's obvious that the `Note` with its `id` set to `100` doesn't exist yet.

7.   Additionally, notice that the response body will have a detailed `message` field and a `status` field, as follows:

```
{
    "status": 404,
    "message": "Note not found"
}
```

Now, we will move on and send an update request with a `Note` having a message that is not unique.

The 400 Bad Request status when a message is not unique

Using Postman, let's try to send an update request to a `Note` using the `PUT` HTTP verb. As a part of this request, we will update a `Note` in the database with a message that is not unique, as shown in the following screenshot:

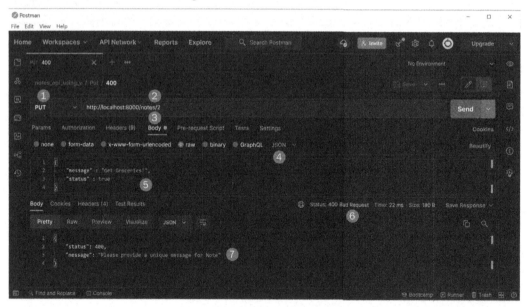

Figure 14.12 – Updating a note using HTTP verb PUT using Postman with a message that is not unique

To update a `Note` given its `id`, we need to perform the following steps in the Postman application, as shown in the preceding screenshot:

1. Set the HTTP Verb to **PUT**.

2. Set the URL to `http://localhost:8000/notes/id/`. Replace `id` with the id of the `Note` you want to update. For this section, as we are trying to view the `400 Bad Request` status, replace `id` with `2`.

3. Now select the **Body** tab, and check the **raw** radio button.

4. Then, select **JSON** from the drop-down list to set the content type of the request.

5. In the textbox, enter the following JSON payload with the message set to `Get Groceries!`. Notice that there is already a `Note` with an id `1` in the database whose message is `Get Groceries!`. As per the `Notes` table we defined, we want the message to be unique. So, we will proceed and click on the **Send** button with the JSON payload that has a non-unique message, as follows:

```
{
    "message" : "Get Groceries!",
    "status" : true
}
```

Notice the response has its status set to `400 Bad Request`, as it's obvious that the `Note` with the message in the payload is not unique. Additionally, note that the response body will have a detailed `message` field and a `status` field, as follows:

```
{
    "status": 400,
    "message": "Please provide a unique message for Note"
}
```

The 200 Ok status when a note is successfully updated

Using Postman, let's try to send an update request to a Note using the PUT HTTP verb, as shown in the following screenshot:

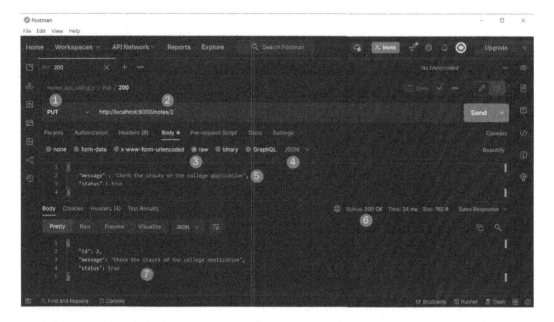

Figure 14.13 – Updating a note using HTTP verb PUT using Postman

To update a Note given its id, we need to perform the following steps in the Postman application, as shown in the preceding screenshot:

1. Set the HTTP verb to **PUT**.

2. Set the URL to http://localhost:8000/notes/id/. Replace the id with the id of the Note you want to update. For this section, as we are trying to view the 200 OK status, replace id with 2 or any number that already exists in the database.

3. Now select the **Body** tab, and check the **raw** radio button.

4. Then, select **JSON** from the drop-down list to set the content type of the request.

5. In the textbox, enter the JSON to update the `Note`. Here, we are trying to update the `status` field of the notes from `false` to `true`. Click on the **Send** button to update a `Note` with the payload that appears, as follows:

```
{
    "message" : "Check the status of the college
                 application",
    "status" : true
}
```

Notice the response has its status set to `200 OK`. Additionally, `Note` that the response body will have an updated `Note` whose `status` field is set to `true`, as follows:

```
{
    "id": 2,
    "message": "Check the status of the college
                 application",
    "status": true
}
```

Now, we will learn how to delete a `Note` using Postman.

Using Postman to delete a note with the DELETE HTTP verb

In this section, we will perform a `DELETE` operation that removes a `Note` from the database.

The 204 No Content status when a note is deleted

As we defined the delete Note API to respond with 204 No Content, we will be evaluating that behavior in the **Postman** application, as follows:

Figure 14.14 – Deleting a note by id using HTTP verb DELETE using Postman

To delete a Note given its id, which, in this case, is 1, perform the following steps in the Postman application:

1. Set the HTTP verb to **DELETE**.

2. Set the URL to http://localhost:8000/notes/1.

3. Navigate to the **Body** tab.

4. Check the **none** radio button and click on the **Send** button.

    Notice the response's status is set to 204 No Content. Additionally, note that the response body is empty.

5. When we switch to the **Headers** tab, we will see the response headers, as shown in the following screenshot:

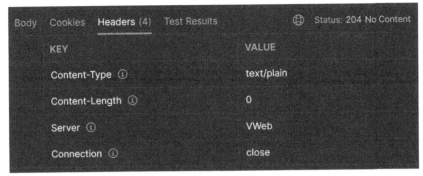

Figure 14.15 – The response headers after deleting a note using HTTP verb DELETE

As we are not sending any content because of the DELETE operation, we can see that Content-Type is set to text/plain.

Now, we have mastered how to run a microservice and perform queries on its endpoints using Postman.

Summary

In this chapter, we learned how to implement a RESTful microservice from the ground up. First, we created a new project and organized the code files. Then, we understood how to set up a vweb web server with SQLite as a database.

Following this, we implemented a Note struct that acted as a mapping between the object and relational database world. In the latter parts of this chapter, we implemented RESTful endpoints that performed CRUD operations on a Notes table. Additionally, we managed to define and implement the behavior associated with endpoints such as status codes, JSON payloads, and the JSON response format, to mention a few.

By the end of this chapter, we understood how to run the microservice implemented using a vweb web server. Additionally, we learned how to use **Postman**, which is a free software client that allows you to interact with web-based APIs. Then, we performed CRUD operations on the microservice we implemented.

This marks the end of this chapter as well as the end of the book. I am strongly hoping that the topics learned so far will definitely help you to get started for your next project using V programming.

`Packt.com`

Subscribe to our online digital library for full access to over 7,000 books and videos, as well as industry leading tools to help you plan your personal development and advance your career. For more information, please visit our website.

Why subscribe?

- Spend less time learning and more time coding with practical eBooks and Videos from over 4,000 industry professionals

- Improve your learning with Skill Plans built especially for you

- Get a free eBook or video every month

- Fully searchable for easy access to vital information

- Copy and paste, print, and bookmark content

Did you know that Packt offers eBook versions of every book published, with PDF and ePub files available? You can upgrade to the eBook version at `packt.com` and as a print book customer, you are entitled to a discount on the eBook copy. Get in touch with us at `customercare@packtpub.com` for more details.

At `www.packt.com`, you can also read a collection of free technical articles, sign up for a range of free newsletters, and receive exclusive discounts and offers on Packt books and eBooks.

Other Books You May Enjoy

If you enjoyed this book, you may be interested in these other books by Packt:

Learn Bosque Programming

Sebastian Kaczmarek, Joel Ibaceta

ISBN: 978-1-83921-197-3

- Find out what the Bosque project is
- Identify accidental complexity in code and how to overcome it with Bosque
- Understand the principles of the regularized programming paradigm
- Install and configure the Bosque environment
- Get hands-on experience using the Bosque language and its key features
- Recognize the advantages of explicit code intermediate representation design

Python for Geeks

Muhammad Asif

ISBN: 978-1-80107-011-9

- Understand how to design and manage complex Python projects
- Strategize test-driven development (TDD) in Python
- Explore multithreading and multiprogramming in Python
- Use Python for data processing with Apache Spark and Google Cloud Platform (GCP)
- Deploy serverless programs on public clouds such as GCP
- Use Python to build web applications and application programming interfaces
- Apply Python for network automation and serverless functions
- Get to grips with Python for data analysis and machine learning

Packt is searching for authors like you

If you're interested in becoming an author for Packt, please visit authors. packtpub.com and apply today. We have worked with thousands of developers and tech professionals, just like you, to help them share their insight with the global tech community. You can make a general application, apply for a specific hot topic that we are recruiting an author for, or submit your own idea.

Share Your Thoughts

Now you've finished *Getting Started with V Programming*, we'd love to hear your thoughts! Scan the QR code below to go straight to the Amazon review page for this book and share your feedback or leave a review on the site that you purchased it from.

https://packt.link/r/1-839-21343-4

Your review is important to us and the tech community and will help us make sure we're delivering excellent quality content.

Index

Made in the USA
Middletown, DE
30 August 2022

72632275R00230